To Charles E. Fry Jr. and Joan G. Fry

A PRAIRIE FAITH

LIBRARY OF RELIGIOUS BIOGRAPHY

Mark A. Noll, Kathryn Gin Lum, and Heath W. Carter, series editors

Long overlooked by historians, religion has emerged in recent years as a key factor in understanding the past. From politics to popular culture, from social struggles to the rhythms of family life, religion shapes every story. Religious biographies open a window to the sometimes surprising influence of religion on the lives of influential people and the worlds they inhabited.

The Library of Religious Biography is a series that brings to life important figures in United States history and beyond. Grounded in careful research, these volumes link the lives of their subjects to the broader cultural contexts and religious issues that surrounded them. The authors are respected historians and recognized authorities in the historical period in which their subject lived and worked.

Marked by careful scholarship yet free of academic jargon, the books in this series are well-written narratives meant to be read and enjoyed as well as studied.

Titles include:

*An Odd Cross to Bear: A Biography of **Ruth Bell Graham***
by Anne Blue Wills

*A Heart Lost in Wonder: The Life and Faith of **Gerard Manley Hopkins***
by Catharine Randall

***Abraham Lincoln**: Redeemer President*
by Allen C. Guelzo

*Strength for the Fight: The Life and Faith of **Jackie Robinson***
by Gary Scott Smith

*We Will Be Free: The Life and Faith of **Sojourner Truth***
by Nancy Koester

For a complete list of published volumes, see the back of this volume.

A PRAIRIE FAITH

The Religious Life of
Laura Ingalls Wilder

JOHN J. FRY

WILLIAM B. EERDMANS PUBLISHING COMPANY
GRAND RAPIDS, MICHIGAN

Wm. B. Eerdmans Publishing Co.
4035 Park East Court SE, Grand Rapids, Michigan 49546
www.eerdmans.com

Book design by Lydia Hall

Printed in the United States of America

30 29 28 27 26 25 24   1 2 3 4 5 6 7

ISBN 978-0-8028-7628-7

Library of Congress Cataloging-in-Publication Data

A catalog record for this book is available from the Library of Congress.

Contents

CONTENTS

NORTH DAKOTA

MINNESOTA

WISCONSIN

De Smet
•

Walnut Grove
•

Pepin
•

SOUTH DAKOTA

Spring Valley
•

Burr Oak
•

IOWA

NEBRASKA

ILLINOIS

KANSAS

MISSOURI

Independence
•

Mansfield
•

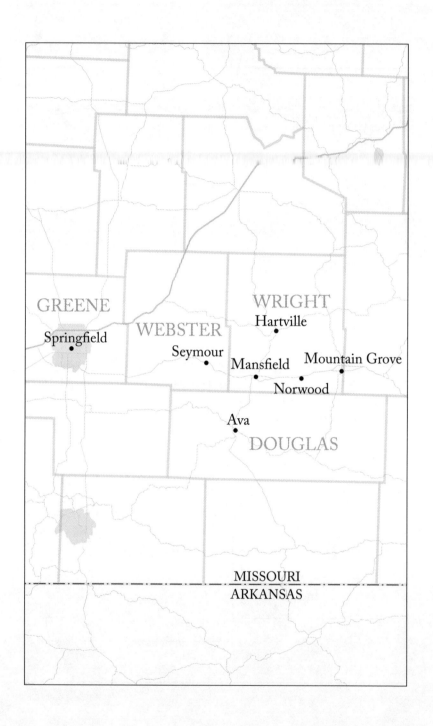

GREENE

WRIGHT

WEBSTER

Springfield

Hartville

Seymour

Mansfield

Mountain Grove

Norwood

Ava

DOUGLAS

MISSOURI
ARKANSAS

Foreword

A quick glance at Amazon.com suggests why the book before you answers a need. The site advertises dozens of editions of Laura Ingalls Wilder's seven Little House books, all ranking high in the categories "Children's Classics" and "Children's Historical Fiction" as well as several highly ranked video versions of the long-running television series based (very) loosely on the books, in addition to a number of biographies, literary studies, and appreciations of widely varying credibility about the author herself. As an additional indication of the enduring impact of Laura Ingalls Wilder on broader American culture, it is also possible to purchase Little House–themed dolls, dresses, coloring books, bumper stickers, pajamas, recipes, and canvas tote bags—and to take advantage of creative marketing sallies featuring items like a "Handmade Toddler Ingalls Bear Family & Cabin Play Set & Accessories."

If you are among the millions who have read or been read to out of the Little House books, and who have paid even partial attention, you know that religion was a secure part of the literary world Wilder created. The family sometimes attended church; on different occasions Laura expressed her unvarnished opinions about the ministers she knew; during evenings in their different homes Pa played hymns on his fiddle; author Wilder occasionally inserted quotations from the Bible. But what, John Fry is asking, did those references in the books amount to? Even more, what does thorough research into the author's life, especially before she began her literary career, reveal about Laura Ingalls Wilder's stance concerning churches, denominations, Christian theology, and religious belief in general?

John Fry's specialty as a historian is particularly relevant for answering these questions because he has written about the rural, usually weekly newspapers of an earlier Midwest. Why relevant? Well before she became famous for the Little House books, Wilder wrote scores of articles for one of those papers, the *Missouri Ruralist*. Fry has read those articles; he has visited the Wilder homesteads in Wisconsin, Kansas, Iowa, and South Dakota and the various depositories with Wilder manuscripts; he has read very widely in the popular as well as critical literature; and he has put together a thorough account of what the famous author believed and how that belief shaped her life.

The result is a book that details the varied church experiences of the young Laura Ingalls and then of Laura and her husband Almanzo Wilder, especially after they moved to Mansfield, Missouri, their home from 1894 until her death in 1957. Fans of the Little House books eager to enlist the author for "their team" may be disappointed with Fry's persuasive conclusion. The young Laura did indeed enjoy many church experiences, the Wilders were also faithful to the Methodist Church in Mansfield, and throughout her life she never scrupled to express her opinions on religious questions. But her basic stance, which Fry in the end calls "stoic," was neither explicitly evangelical nor liberal, neither modernist nor fundamentalist. In a carefully chosen phrase, Fry concludes that for Laura religion was "important but not central."

In following the evidence Fry assembles for that conclusion, readers will also benefit from the book's intelligent attention to many other pertinent issues. What was the relationship between the books' narratives and what can be documented from other sources about the Ingalls family? What did the Wilders' daughter, Rose, herself a published writer well before the first Little House book appeared and a constant correspondent with her mother, contribute to the final shape of the Little House books? (I found it revealing that Rose Wilder Lane, well known for her libertarian, post-Christian convictions, sometimes inserted religion-friendly words or incidents that Laura, the conventional churchgoer and Christian, had not included.) What can be learned from Wilder's contributions to the *Missouri Ruralist* about how she regarded religious matters against the challenges facing farmers and rural communities through years of great transition in American agriculture? And how does Fry's biography shed light on the critical controversies that have come to surround the Little House books concerning the Ingalls family's encounters with "savage" Native Americans and the books' occasional references to African Americans?

For readers most concerned about how completely the books' stories reflect actual events in the author's life, Fry's chronological approach is ideal. Most chapters begin with general information on the times, places, and events in Laura's life for the period covered in that chapter, followed by detailed examination of all possible evidence concerning her church involvements and expressions of opinions.

The pages at the beginning and end will be especially welcomed by those keen to learn more about the critical questions recently raised concerning Wilder and her books. The questions deal with ethnic prejudice, the veracity of the books, the role of Rose in the writing, the liberties taken by the television series, and the problem of judgments with contemporary standards applied to someone whose milieus were so different from what the United States has become. Fry's account in the personal afterword about his own long involvement with the books is also particularly appropriate when writing about an individual for whom so many others also feel a strong personal connection. The biography as a whole is an outstanding example of how detailed research can supplement, modify, or, in some cases, overthrow what everyone thought they knew about an author whose books are still much read and, by many, much loved.

Mark A. Noll

Acknowledgments

First and foremost, my thanks go to William "Bill" Anderson for his assistance and encouragement. When I first became interested in Wilder during the mid-1990s, Bill kindly answered my letters and emails. He has been answering my questions ever since. He also graciously read the entire manuscript and gave me invaluable guidance. As the living person who knows the most about the historical Laura Ingalls Wilder, Bill has been an incredible blessing.

John Miller's encouragement was also key. When he learned I was researching Wilder's faith, he was relentlessly optimistic about the project. It was an honor to be on a panel with him and Bill at the Midwestern History Conference in 2019, less than a year before he died suddenly of a heart attack. John is missed by all who were blessed by his questions, his insights, and his enthusiasm.

I have also been helped by the community of Wilder scholars and researchers, including, in alphabetical order, Barb Boustead, Caroline Fraser, Eddie Higgins, Pamela Smith Hill, Sandra Hume, Sanne Jakobsen, Nancy Tystad Koupal, Teresa Lynn, Connie Neumann, Melanie Stringer, Sarah Uthoff, Annette Whipple, and Christine Woodside. Thanks also to religion scholar Kathy Pulley at Missouri State for answering my questions about Christianity in the Ozarks. All errors are my fault, not theirs.

I am indebted to the staffs at the following archives, libraries, historic sites, and museums who answered questions, helped me access collections, and otherwise provided assistance: the Burton Historical Collection at the Detroit Public Library; Ellis Library at the University of Missouri;

the Herbert Hoover Presidential Library in West Branch, Iowa; the Independence Historical Museum in Independence, Kansas; the Ingalls Homestead and the Laura Ingalls Wilder Memorial Society in De Smet, South Dakota; the Laura Ingalls Wilder Home Association in Mansfield, Missouri; the Laura Ingalls Wilder Museum in Walnut Grove, Minnesota; the Laura Ingalls Wilder Museum and Birthplace in Pepin, Wisconsin, the Laura Ingalls Wilder Park and Museum in Burr Oak, Iowa, the Little House on the Prairie Museum in Montgomery County, Kansas; the Missouri United Methodist Archives at Central Methodist University in Fayette, Missouri; the Pomona Public Library in Pomona, California; and the State Historical Society of Missouri in both Columbia and Rolla. Thanks to the Herbert Hoover Presidential Foundation for a travel grant in 2016, which helped me start the entire project. Many thanks to the staff at Governors State University in University Park, Illinois, for allowing me to monopolize their microfilm reader for weeks.

Sincere thanks to all those at Eerdmans who enabled the book to be published: to David Bratt (now at BBH Literary) and Lisa Ann Cockrel for their care and guidance, to Heath Carter for proposing the project and for his support, to Laurel Draper for her leadership, and to Tom Raabe for his careful reading. Most of all, thanks to Mark Noll for providing encouragement and critique and for writing the foreword.

Trinity Christian College supported my work with summer grants, faculty development funding for travel, and a sabbatical during the spring of 2022. I thank Presidents Kurt Dykstra and Aaron Kuecker, the members of the Faculty Development Committee, and my colleagues who came to presentations I gave on campus. Thanks to Sarah Hoeksema for getting me so many interlibrary loans and to Kyle McCarrell for paying for them. Special thanks to my History Department colleagues David Brodnax, Kyle Dieleman, and particularly Bob Rice. Trinity's identity—a liberal arts college founded by Christians in the Reformed tradition of Protestantism but seeking to include faculty members from other traditions and actively reaching out to all kinds of students—has shaped my teaching, my writing, and my faith.

My faith has also been shaped by the leaders and members of Westminster Presbyterian Church (Orthodox Presbyterian), including Matt and Shana Anema, Tim and Lisa Karr, Rob and Melodie McKenzie,

Bob and Sarah Tarullo, and many others. I am deeply thankful for their interest, prayers, and encouragement.

My wife, Paula, has put up with me reading, thinking, and writing about another woman for more than twenty-five years. She also gave me important feedback on drafts. Her relationship with her mother and our daughter has provided ways into understanding the relationship between Laura and Rose, and I'm thankful that she shares everything with me. I could not have finished this book without her love and encouragement. I am also thankful for the love and support of my children, Deborah, Stephen, Benjamin, and Daniel.

I grew up on a farm in western Pennsylvania, about an hour north of Pittsburgh. Our family attended Calvary Orthodox Presbyterian Church in Harrisville. Sometime during the 1980s, my mother, Joan G. Fry, wrote a presentation for the mother-daughter dinner held each May at the church. It was titled "The Hers behind the Great Hymns," and it consisted of brief biographies of eleven women who wrote famous Christian songs. She did the research in books that our family owned, and she typed it on her Smith Corona electric typewriter. The presentation was well received, and she was asked to deliver it at a church dinner in a nearby town and again at several subsequent events in Harrisville. Mom was a self-taught writer. She was told by her father that girls didn't go to college, so she took the commercial classes, not the college preparatory ones, in high school. But she read a lot. She and my father, Charles E. Fry Jr., always encouraged my love for history and my desire to study it in college and graduate school. Although Mom passed away in February of 2020, this book is dedicated to her and Dad.

Introduction

"Between Him and God"

One day in the late fall of 1929, Laura Ingalls Wilder sat down in her rock house in the Ozark Mountains of Missouri and began to write a memoir. She was sixty-two years old. Laura used a pencil and inexpensive tablets of paper, filling their pages with stories from her youth. Some of the stories were told by her father, Charles Ingalls. Others she remembered herself. She wrote through the winter and early spring. The resulting manuscript began with her earliest memories and concluded with her marriage to Almanzo Wilder. She titled the memoir *Pioneer Girl* and gave the tablets to her daughter Rose Wilder Lane on May 7, 1930. Rose was a highly paid novelist who also had written for a variety of newspapers, magazines, and other publications. She edited and typed the manuscript, and that summer she sent it to her agent in New York City, hoping that the memoir would be accepted by a magazine for publication as a serial. Perhaps it could be published later as a book. Ultimately, no magazines or book publishers were interested.

Laura Ingalls Wilder had experienced a difficult life. While she was growing up in Wisconsin, Kansas, Minnesota, Iowa, and Dakota Territory, the Ingalls family had lived close to poverty. They moved ten times before Laura married. During the first five years of her marriage, she and Almanzo had buried a son, watched their house burn to the ground, and failed to obtain a farm under the provisions of the Homestead Act. Almanzo had suffered a stroke that left him with a limp and drained his strength. They ultimately built a new life in southwestern Missouri, hundreds of miles from both of their families. Their daughter traveled the world and became a successful writer, but she also rejected many of the values that Laura and Almanzo embodied. Almanzo was over seventy, Laura was over sixty, and their household finances were still not completely stable. The Great Depression loomed, and economic collapse reached toward the Wilders' small farm in the Ozarks. Rose revised and retyped *Pioneer Girl* two more times, but it still went unsold.

During the next two years, however, Laura and Rose launched a fictional retelling of Laura's childhood that eventually became seven novels for children and young adults, beginning with the publication of *Little House in the Big Woods* in 1932 and ending with *These Happy Golden Years* in 1943. An additional book was based on Almanzo's childhood. To create the Little House books, Laura and Rose rewrote many accounts from *Pioneer Girl*, sharpening details, combining characters, and providing story arcs for each book and for the series as a whole. The stories did not minimize the hardships faced by the Ingalls family, but they clearly depicted Laura's childhood as a happy one. Each of the books was a publishing success, and they ultimately provided ongoing income for Almanzo, Laura, and Rose until their deaths in 1949, 1957, and 1968, respectively.

The popularity of the Little House books during the twentieth century was staggering. In 2001, *Publishers Weekly* reported that over thirty-four million copies of the books had been sold. During the middle decades of the century, librarians and elementary school teachers embraced the books for teaching reading and social studies. They were excerpted for elementary-level reading textbooks and translated into dozens of languages. The books inspired *Little House on the Prairie*, a popular television series that ran from 1974 to 1983. The series prompted more to read the books and to become interested in the Ingalls and Wilder families. Historic sites founded in six different states enabled readers and television viewers to connect with the landscapes and artifacts from Laura's life.

During the twenty-first century, the books continue to be loved by a devoted core of fans and enjoyed by a broader audience. *Little House on the Prairie* has never gone off the air and is available via syndication and streaming. Disney created a six-episode miniseries inspired by the books in 2005, and several major movie studios considered making a feature film during the 2010s. Interest in Laura's life also remains strong. The last twenty years have seen the publication of a scholarly edition of the Little

House books by the Library of America, new biographies, a collection of her letters, and multiple memoirs of engagement with the books. When *Pioneer Girl* was published in an annotated edition in 2014, Amazon.com repeatedly could not keep it in stock. By early 2022, it had gone through fifteen printings, and there are over 190,000 copies in print. The most recent biography of Laura, *Prairie Fires: The American Dreams of Laura Ingalls Wilder* by Caroline Fraser, received the Pulitzer Prize for Biography in 2018. Two years later, the PBS documentary series *American Masters* dedicated an episode to Wilder. It quickly became the most-streamed biography in the history of the series. Every year, tens of thousands come from around the world to visit historical destinations in the multiple places where the Ingalls and Wilder families lived.

Not all readers of the Little House books endorse everything in them. Many have condemned the depiction of American Indians in the books, especially in *Little House on the Prairie*. Others take issue with the inclusion of a blackface minstrel show in *Little Town on the Prairie*. These concerns caused the Association for Library Service to Children, a division of the American Library Association, to rename the Laura Ingalls Wilder Award. The award had been created in 1954 to honor an author who had made significant contributions to children's literature; Wilder was its first recipient. In 2018, the award's name was changed to the Children's Literature Legacy Award. Opponents of the change argued that Wilder's portrayals of Indigenous Peoples were multifaceted, especially in comparison to popular ideas about American Indians during the early twentieth century. In this way, Wilder and her works became a subject for the cultural shouting matches of the early twenty-first century. Nevertheless, the Little House books continue to speak to large numbers of Americans, and to readers around the world.

Many readers are interested in how accurately the Little House books represent the historical Laura's life. They also seek information about characters' lives after the events described in the novels. Excellent historical work has been done since the 1970s to address these desires. I am indebted to books and articles by William Anderson, Caroline Fraser, Pamela Smith Hill, Teresa Lynn, and especially John Miller, and I enthusiastically endorse their biographies. Others have researched particular aspects of Wilder's life; some of that work has been published, and some has been presented at one of the LauraPalooza conferences, sponsored by the Laura Ingalls Wilder Legacy and Research Association and held six times between 2010 and 2022.

More than anything, readers want to know what Laura thought and what she was really like. Unfortunately, discovering this information is an incredibly challenging task: she wrote the Little House books, *Pioneer Girl*, dozens of articles and columns for the *Missouri Ruralist* (a biweekly farm newspaper), several travel diaries, and enough letters to fill one published volume. In general, however, few sources directly address her private life and inner thoughts. As Wilder scholar John Miller noted, "The greatest difficulty confronting a biographer of Laura Ingalls Wilder, interestingly enough, is the paucity of sources that speak directly to the questions of what kind of person she was and what kind of life she lived."[1] This is a dramatic contrast to her daughter Rose, who poured out her emotions in diaries, journals, and letters to friends.

This problem of lack of sources seems especially acute when it comes to Laura's religious beliefs. In *Pioneer Girl*, she described a childhood friend from Walnut Grove, Minnesota, and his penchant for talking publicly about his relationship with God: "Howard Ensign had joined the Congregational church after their revival and would testify at prayer meeting every Wednesday night. It someway offended my sense of privacy. It seemed to me that the things between one and God should be between him and God like loving ones [*sic*] mother. One didn't go around saying 'I love my mother, she has been so good to me.' One just loved her and did things that she liked one to do."[2] Wilder's reluctance to talk about "the things between one and God" is a primary reason that she did not often provide detailed evidence about her faith. As a result, Laura's Christianity has not received extended attention. For instance, the 2020 *American Masters* documentary is eighty minutes long and features interviews with twenty different people, but it does not mention Christianity beyond the use of the word "churches" two times by one interviewee and the showing of several images of churches in towns where the Ingalls and Wilder

1. John E. Miller, *Becoming Laura Ingalls Wilder: The Woman behind the Legend* (Columbia: University of Missouri Press, 1998), 11.

2. Laura Ingalls Wilder, *Pioneer Girl: The Annotated Autobiography*, ed. Pamela Smith Hill (Pierre: South Dakota State Historical Society, 2014), 136.

families lived. Some biographers have ignored her religious beliefs, others have taken them for granted, and still others have addressed them but not attempted to unpack their complexity. Even though evidence for Wilder's religious beliefs is scattered, this book will present as complete a description of her faith as possible.

Author Stephen Hines has engaged Laura's faith in two books. Hines edited multiple works that reprinted Laura's *Missouri Ruralist* columns in a variety of ways. *Saving Graces: The Inspirational Faith of Laura Ingalls Wilder* reproduces selections from forty-eight pieces from the *Ruralist*. The book gives a new title to each piece and adds a large-print Bible passage in the middle of each selection. The titles and Scripture verses connect the content of the selections to Christian virtues, topics, and themes. The book also reproduces ten of Wilder's best-loved hymns with music, and there is a brief introduction. Hines has also written *A Prairie Girl's Faith: The Spiritual Legacy of Laura Ingalls Wilder*, a collection of reflections and observations about Wilder's life, faith, and writings. He engages the many ways that the Little House books mention Christianity, especially descriptions of Sunday school, church worship services, and hymns sung by the Ingalls family. *Saving Graces* interprets Laura's faith mainly in terms of inspiration. In *A Prairie Girl's Faith*, Christianity is presented mainly as "Christian values" or the "values of hearth and home." It is taken for granted that the reader is a Christian and identifies with Laura's experience.[3]

John Miller's scholarly work about Wilder has paid more nuanced attention to the role of Christianity and faith in her life. Still, he describes her as "devout" and asserts that her "abiding religious faith" was an "indispensable part of her life."[4] I believe that Laura's relationship to Christianity and the church was more complex. First, the evidence about her faith points in multiple directions. She regularly attended Christian worship services throughout her life. However, the Little House books offer a variety of descriptions of the church and Christianity, some of them with a negative edge. In addition, for most of their adult life in Mansfield, Missouri, she and her husband attended the Methodist Episcopal church

3. Stephen W. Hines, *Saving Graces: The Inspirational Faith of Laura Ingalls Wilder* (Nashville: Broadman & Holman, 1997); *A Prairie Girl's Faith: The Spiritual Legacy of Laura Ingalls Wilder* (New York: Waterbrook, 2018).

4. Miller, *Becoming Laura Ingalls Wilder*, 62, 253, 261.

there without ever becoming members. In fact, I have found no definitive evidence that she ever formally became a member of any church.

There is also disagreement among scholars about how much to credit Wilder with the material in the Little House books and how much to credit her daughter Rose Wilder Lane. The major book-length biography of Rose, *The Ghost in the Little House*, by William Holtz, describes her as a ghostwriter. Holtz argued that Rose was the source of most of what makes the series so beloved. Wilder biographers dispute this depiction. Pamela Smith Hill describes Lane as little more than a skilled editor. William Anderson, John Miller, Caroline Fraser, and other scholars are more comfortable describing the relationship as a collaboration. After reading the original manuscripts of the books, I agree; both women contributed to the final literary product. Rose had rejected traditional Christianity, and those close to her later described her as a Deist (as believing in a supernatural creator who does not interfere with the workings of the universe). Rose also was attracted to Islam for cultural reasons during the years that the two women were working on the books together. Their extensive collaboration further complicates the project of understanding Wilder's faith.

Scholars of religion describe a variety of elements involved in religious belief and practice. Doctrine involves beliefs about God, the world, human beings, and how God interacts with the world and people. Related to beliefs about God are experiences with the transcendent and how they are later described. A third aspect is personal identity. Identity is formed by a variety of influences, including culture, ethnicity, religion, and nationality. Different individuals and groups embrace different influences as central or primary to their identity. Identity is shaped by beliefs about God and the world, and it shapes those beliefs as well. Personal identity is also related to community identity, the group that a person chooses to affiliate with, and in turn how the group influences that person. Finally, practice has to do with how people live in the world, including how their beliefs, identity, and community impact their behavior. Practice includes both ethics—moral decisions based on religious beliefs—and rituals—actions that are repeated in time, alone and with others. I will consider how Laura Ingalls Wilder engaged all these aspects of religion.

This book examines all available sources written by Laura, both published and archival. It also considers other available sources about her life, particularly the writings of her daughter Rose. At times I will admit that I don't know exactly how to describe the motives of the people I am writing about. The challenges I confront in understanding people who are living today and about whom I know a lot make me reticent to speculate on the inner thoughts and motivations of those in the past whom I know only through sources that have survived. I am guided by the work of other scholars, but I ultimately do not agree completely with any one biographer's picture of her faith.

Early chapters rely on Laura's memoir, *Pioneer Girl*, for information about events and developments in her life. I understand that memoirists do not describe everything that happened, and they include what they do describe for particular reasons. However, in areas where it is supported by other sources, I believe that the memoir is a reliable source for the contours of the Ingalls family's experiences. Because the Little House books are fiction, I do not rely on them for biographical details. In later chapters, I examine the original manuscripts and intermediate manuscripts and typescripts that ultimately became the published Little House books. These chapters contribute to the conversation about each woman's involvement in writing the books, and particularly her influence on the books' depictions of the church, Christianity, and faith. As a result, this book shares a (perhaps unavoidable) pattern with other biographies of Wilder: since later chapters consider the writing of the Little House books, which describe Laura's childhood, the reader may feel that the same material is being addressed twice. The final chapters consider Laura's faith after the Little House books were completed and the ways that Rose and others shaped later generations' understanding of her life and writings.

Not everything that is known about Laura Ingalls Wilder's life is included in this book. The most complete biography is Caroline Fraser's *Prairie Fires*. This book also does not focus on how the Little House books were written; John Miller's *Becoming Laura Ingalls Wilder* and Pamela Smith Hill's *Laura Ingalls Wilder: A Writer's Life* both address that question well. Finally, this book does not attempt to set Wilder's life in extensive regional or national historical context. That work is done in both *Becoming Laura Ingalls Wilder* and *Prairie Fires*. The latter presents more extensive and more recent research; the former provides a more straightforward and accurate historical argument.

This book examines Laura Ingalls Wilder's religious beliefs, experiences, identity, patterns of belonging, and behavior. It also works to recreate the Christian landscape of several of the small, Midwestern towns in which Laura lived, particularly Mansfield, Missouri, her home for over sixty years. Laura Ingalls Wilder's engagement with Christianity was complex. There is evidence that she possessed Christian faith of a traditional, mainstream, moderate Protestant nature. Many sources speak to her lifelong church attendance, knowledge of the Bible, and practice of prayer; the most detailed sources address her childhood and later years. In addition, her memoir includes a description of an experience of God's presence. However, I will argue that while Christianity was important to Laura's life, it was not central. This departs from the interpretations of John Miller; Miller argued that her faith was central to her life and worldview. Laura was also influenced by stoic ideas.

While she lived most of her adult life in the Ozarks, her early years in the upper Midwest were formative for her worldview. A "prairie faith" is an apt description of Laura's life and her religious journey. It is my hope that this investigation of Laura's faith will provide greater understanding of her religious life and greater wisdom for ours.

1

Home, on and off the Prairie

Kansas and Wisconsin, 1867–1874

Laura Elizabeth Ingalls was born to Charles and Caroline Ingalls in a log cabin near Pepin, Wisconsin, on February 7, 1867. She spent the first year and a half of her life with her parents and her sister Mary on farmland near extended family. When she sat down sixty years later to write the memoir of her life, however, she first described a place far from Wisconsin. She wrote about her family's sojourn in Kansas. Her memoir, *Pioneer Girl*, provides first glimpses of the formation of Laura's religious world.

Mobility and War: Charles and Caroline Ingalls

Laura's ancestors, the Ingalls and Quiner families, had also moved multiple times. Charles Phillip Ingalls was born in the town of Cuba in western New York, on January 10, 1836. He was the third child born to Lansford and Laura Ingalls, who ultimately had nine other children. During the early 1840s, the family moved to Illinois and bought a farm near Elgin, forty miles west of Chicago. In 1853, they moved again to property close to the town of Concord in Jefferson County, Wisconsin, west of Milwaukee. There the family lived close to the Quiner family, who had also moved from the East. Henry and Charlotte Quiner had seven children and had lived briefly in Ohio and Indiana. Their daughter Caroline was born on December 12, 1839. Henry died in a shipwreck on Lake Michigan in 1844, and Charlotte remarried several years later. The Quiner and Ingalls families helped each other through the yearly cycles of agricultural labor and rural life. Eventually, three Ingalls children married Quiner siblings; Charles Ingalls married Caroline Quiner on February 1, 1860; Henry Quiner and Polly Ingalls were married the previous year; and Peter Ingalls married Eliza Quiner in 1861.

When Charles and Caroline were married, Caroline's mother gave her a book titled *Persuasives to Early Piety* by J. G. Pike. John Gregory Pike was an English Baptist pastor born in 1784. *Persuasives* was first published in England in 1819 and later reprinted by the American Tract Society in New York in 1830. It was his most popular work. Early chapters argue that everyone is sinful and in need of salvation, describe sins to which young people are prone, and explain how to trust in Christ alone for salvation. Then the book presents reasons why people should embrace true Christianity when they are young, answers objections, and presents an impassioned plea for sinners to come to Christ. This volume, with its outline of the good news of Christianity, remained with Charles and Caroline during their family's many moves. They passed it on to their daughter Laura, who also kept it. It now is at the Laura Ingalls Wilder Historic Home and Museum in Mansfield, Missouri.

About a year after Charles married Caroline, the Civil War broke out. As it did most American families, this intramural conflict affected both the Quiner and Ingalls families. Caroline's brother Joseph enlisted in the Union army and was sent to the South to fight. He was shot through the arm at the Battle of Shiloh in April 1862 and died of his wounds a few weeks later. Two of Charles's brothers also volunteered, but they did so in early 1865 when the war was nearly over. The economy of Wisconsin was also shaken by the war; prices for crops fell and prices for transport soared. As a result, small farmers paying mortgages were squeezed. In January 1862, Charles Ingalls's father lost his farm to the bank when he could not make payments.

In addition, central Minnesota was the site of the United States–Dakota War in August and September 1862. Treaty payments from the federal government to the Dakota (Sioux) had been delayed for several years, and in the meantime many more white Americans had moved to the area. Difficult negotiations with federal Indian agents and disastrous interactions with local whites led hundreds of Dakota warriors to attack local settlements, killing settlers and destroying houses and towns. Fear swept through the European populations of both Minnesota and Wisconsin. More than six hundred white settlers and soldiers were killed. It is unknown how many Dakota men and women perished in the fighting. The violence was eventually ended by the United States Army, and more than three hundred Dakota were captured, put on trial, and sentenced to death. The number of condemned was reduced to thirty-eight by President Abraham Lincoln. Their hanging in Mankato, Minnesota, in December 1862 is still the largest mass execution in American history.

In the middle of the Civil War, and in the aftermath of regional panic about Indigenous Peoples, Charles and Caroline Ingalls moved to the western edge of Wisconsin. On September 22, 1863, Charles and his brother-in-law Henry Quiner purchased adjacent tracts seven miles northwest of Pepin, Wisconsin. The cost was $335 for 160 acres of property. They paid $35 in cash and took out a $300 mortgage. They each planned to farm 80 acres. Charles and Caroline's first daughter, Mary, was born in January 1865. Two years later, Caroline gave birth to their second daughter. They named her Laura.

"I Sat on the Doorstep One Day and Watched Them Pass": Kansas

In the second half of 1868, when Laura was about eighteen months old, Charles and Henry sold their property in Wisconsin and purchased land in Chariton County, Missouri. The Civil War had been over for three years, and a man named Adamantine Johnson was selling parcels of land. Charles and Caroline packed their family's belongings into a covered wagon, and the family traveled 400 miles to north-central Missouri. It may be that Henry Quiner's family never left Pepin; they appear in local Wisconsin records in the fall of 1868. Charles Ingalls and his family also did not stay long in Missouri. By the end of 1869, they had moved another 250 miles southwest into Kansas.

Why did Charles and Caroline move their family more than 600 miles from Wisconsin to Kansas? One reason was certainly economic opportunity. Long moves had not been unusual for the Ingalls family's ancestors. Laura's great-great-great-great-great-great-great-grandfather Edmund

Ingalls (nine generations before Laura in direct descent) had traveled across the Atlantic Ocean from Skirbeck, England, to Salem, Massachusetts, during the 1630s. Laura's grandfather Lansford Ingalls was born in Canada and traveled more than a thousand miles when he moved to New York, Illinois, and Wisconsin. A more particular reason was Charles's desire for open land and the opportunity to hunt. Multiple times in her writing, Laura described her father as becoming frustrated when their neighborhood was settled to the point that wild animals became scarce. He must have heard about opportunities in Missouri and Kansas and seen them as places where he could provide for his family while doing what he loved.

During the early nineteenth century, Kansas was part of the area west of the Mississippi River set aside for the use of American Indians. By the middle of the century, much of it had been opened by the federal government to settlement by white Americans, and after the Civil War ended, additional settlers moved into the state. White Americans were mainly drawn to Kansas by the possibilities of obtaining land to farm. There were several ways of getting title to land. One way was by homesteading. If an area of land owned by the US government had already been surveyed, one could use the provisions of the Homestead Act of 1862 to get title to 160 acres for free. A homesteader had to build a house, plant at least 40 acres, and live there five years for at least six months each year. Alternatively, one could purchase land from the federal government. A law passed in 1841 allowed those who had been living on a piece of land to "preempt" others and buy it for $1.25 per acre. This enabled families who lived on land that was not yet surveyed to buy it before land speculators, railroad companies, or others. It also encouraged squatting, or moving to an area before it was legally open to settlement, because it established residency for a preemption claim.

Some land in Kansas was not legally available for white settlement because it still belonged by treaty to American Indians. One such section was the Osage Diminished Reserve, a tract in southeastern Kansas controlled by Osage tribal leaders. It was to this area that Charles Ingalls brought his family in the middle of 1869. They settled on land in Montgomery County, about twelve miles southwest of Independence, inside the Diminished Reserve. Charles likely knew that what he was doing was illegal and that the land still belonged to the Osage. He was also not the only white settler who moved his family to the Reserve during the late 1860s. The US census of 1870 records neighbors coming from Iowa, Illinois, Kentucky, Maryland, and England. It appears that the local Osage band was away hunting, not at their village, when the Ingalls family arrived and chose a location for their home. Charles built a log cabin out of wood hauled from a nearby creek bed, dug a well, and planted a small crop.

Because she was only three to four years old, what Laura actually remembered of life in Kansas may have been mainly images and impressions. Her family probably repeated stories about their time in Kansas as she was growing up, and these stories became part of her memories of the place. The family's time in Kansas provided some of the most vivid recollections in *Pioneer Girl*. In her memoir Laura describes exploring the landscape, investigating the wildlife, and enjoying the wide-open spaces. She relates other memorable events: Her father took her one night to the window to look at a pack of wolves that had surrounded the cabin. Their cabin was menaced by a prairie fire. The entire family was also laid low by malaria. They were saved from death by Dr. George Tann, a black doctor originally from Pennsylvania, who lived in the area and provided necessary medication to them and to their neighbors.

Laura's recollections also relate multiple encounters with American Indians. Osage men often came to their cabin and asked for food or other possessions. They most likely saw this as appropriate, since the Ingalls were squatting on land that rightfully belonged to them. Federal payments to the Osage had been uneven since the beginning of the decade, so some families may have encountered significant hardship. As more white families moved to the area in 1869 and 1870, tensions rose. *Pioneer Girl* includes a detailed incident where two men came to the cabin, required that Caroline Ingalls cook for them, and took all the meat and tobacco when they left. When many Osage returned to their village after having been gone for some weeks, they sang and chanted late into the night. After they left again, Charles Ingalls and the girls went to visit the village. Mary and Laura spent most of a day picking up beads scattered on the ground. They returned to find that Dr. Tann was at the house and that their mother had given birth to their sister, Caroline Celestia Ingalls. Carrie was born on August 3, 1870.

Finally, the memoir describes a large procession of Osage, riding past the cabin:

> I sat on the doorstep one day and watched them pass on their path that went right by the door. As far as I could see, looking one way, they were coming, riding their ponies. . . .
>
> When a woman rode by with a baby in a basket on each side of her pony and they looked at me with their bright, black eyes, I could keep still no longer. I wanted those babies and when Pa said "no": I cried and was very naughty so that Pa picked me up and set me down in the house. "We have a baby," said he. ["]I don't see what you [want] those papooses for."
>
> But I did want them their eyes were so bright.[1]

This youthful desire remained a vivid memory to Laura as an older woman. It is difficult to convey the exact meaning of "wanting those babies" to an audience living 60 years later (when the memoir was written), let alone 150 years later. It sounds like Laura as a child saw the babies as potential possessions and not as human beings. If she was asking for the babies to join their family, the assumption was that her father could simply make that happen, with or without the consent of their parents. Her father rebuked her for her refusal to let the idea go, and he eventually had to impose a punishment. It is probable that this procession was a portion of the Osage leaving for new homes in Indian Territory (later Oklahoma).

The earliest section of *Pioneer Girl* reveals important characteristics of Laura's earliest formation. Charles and Caroline worked together to make a home for their family in a remote part of rural America. They loved their children and sought to make their lives happy and meaningful. Charles worked to protect his wife and children from the dangers of nature and to provide for them materially, even though that provision was often extremely limited. At Christmas, the children took joy in simple gifts: a tin cup and peppermint candy. The first community that Laura interacted with was her tight-knit and caring family.

---

1. Laura Ingalls Wilder, *Pioneer Girl: The Annotated Autobiography*, ed. Pamela Smith Hill (Pierre: South Dakota State Historical Society, 2014), 16–18.

Laura's writings also reveal that the Ingallses were part of a broader community of neighbors who supported the family. Dr. Tann helped them during their struggle with malaria, and he and a neighbor assisted Caroline with the delivery of her third child. The Christmas presents were brought by a neighbor who crossed the raging creek when Charles could not. Tragically, that sense of community did not extend to the Osage men, women, and children who lived so close to them. Cultural differences and conflict over land precluded seeing American Indians as part of their neighborhood community. The Ingalls family had moved to Montgomery County with the assumption that they would some day own the land they occupied, not the Osage. Laura as a young child might desire a beautiful Osage child as a possession, but ultimately they remained outside the circle of any authentic, ongoing community.

There is no evidence that the family interacted with any formal religious body during their time in Kansas. The closest Christian churches were twelve miles away in Independence. Roman Catholic missionaries had reached out to the Osage in previous decades, and they established a mission station in Independence in 1869. A Methodist church also began meeting for worship in Independence several times a month that year. As the white population of Independence and its environs increased, more congregations were organized; by the time the Ingalls family left the area, both Baptist and Presbyterian churches were meeting in the town. It does not appear that the Ingalls family made contact with any of these groups. Laura also does not describe Sunday observance in Kansas, as she does of her childhood in Wisconsin. In fact, Laura does not mention the church, Christianity, or religion in general in this section of *Pioneer Girl*. It appears that the Ingalls family only became involved in a church body and with organized instruction in Christian principles later. In addition, when Laura thought about her earliest years, she did not think about religious practices. She recalled and wrote of her vivid experiences with nature and Indigenous Peoples.

Either in late 1870 or early 1871, the Ingalls family once again packed their belongings into the covered wagon to move back to Wisconsin. *Pioneer Girl* states that soldiers were removing the white settlers from Osage land. The memoir also mentions that her father again owned their land near Pepin because the buyer had not paid. Charles and Caroline's decision to leave Kansas was complicated. It was certainly more complex than what is described in *Little House on the Prairie*, which simply blames the US government. Multiple groups were competing for land and authority in southeast Kansas at the time, and US soldiers had been stationed near the Diminished Reserve, but they never received orders to remove white settlers from Osage land. However, rumors and a report in at least one newspaper suggested they would do exactly that. Osage leaders conducted separate negotiations with the federal government and a local railroad company, as both wanted to purchase the land. The Reserve was officially opened to white settlement in the fall of 1870, and the remaining Osage eventually moved to a reservation in Oklahoma. It was around this time that Laura and her family left Kansas. Perhaps Charles Ingalls decided that the land there would not prove inexpensive enough for his means. At least he determined that the family would be better off returning to Wisconsin.

The Ingalls family traveled to Wisconsin by way of Missouri and, most likely, Iowa and Minnesota. On their way, they drove their covered wagon into a rain-swollen river and got across only when Charles leaped into the water to help lead their horses to firmer footing. After that, they stayed for a time with a family in Missouri, where Charles worked for the owner. According to *Pioneer Girl*, a fire broke out in the chimney of this house and Caroline had to beat it out with a pole. Laura helped to pull Mary and Carrie away from the burning sticks inside the house and was praised by her mother. Both of these stories were included, in different locations and in much more detail, in *Little House on the Prairie*. Eventually, the family completed the journey back to their previous home, the log cabin north of Pepin, Wisconsin.

"On Sundays the Days Seemed Long": Wisconsin

During the 1600s, southwestern Wisconsin was a gathering place where French traders met with a variety of Indigenous Peoples, including the Ojibwe, Potawatomi, Ottawa, Menominee, Meskwaki (Fox), Sauk (Sac), Ho-Chunk (Winnebago), and Dakota. The United States extended its authority into the area during the early 1800s. Local Dakota signed a treaty with the United States and moved west to Minnesota during the 1840s.

After the Civil War, and after the United States–Dakota War, the United States signed treaties with the Meskwaki and Sauk that arranged for their relocation to reservations in Oklahoma. The Ojibwe and Menominee agreed to reservation lands in northern Wisconsin. As increasing numbers of white families moved into the area, members of other American Indian groups often moved north or west.

The town of Pepin had been founded in 1855, though white Americans had been moving to the area since the middle of the 1840s. Pepin sat at the southwestern corner of a large lumbering district centered on the Chippewa River. Lumber gangs cut wood in western Wisconsin and floated it down the Chippewa to the Mississippi. Lake Pepin was a widening of the Mississippi River, which constituted the border between Wisconsin and Minnesota. The location was a good place for a steamboat landing. By the time the Ingalls family returned from Kansas in 1871, the town comprised over a hundred buildings and a population of seven hundred.

Laura's memories of these years growing up in western Wisconsin are recorded in *Pioneer Girl*. These accounts still focus on the nuclear family but also include a broader family circle, additional community members and institutions, and the beginnings of formal religious instruction. Charles Ingalls provided for the family by fishing in Lake Pepin, raising hogs on their acreage, and trapping and shooting wild game in the woods, including bears. In *Pioneer Girl*, Laura described him making bullets, playing games with the children, telling stories, and playing his fiddle for the family in the evening. Caroline took care of the children and the house and did the outside chores in Charles's absence. She taught Laura to knit and later to read.

Extended family was also important to Laura's formation. The Ingalls family lived very close to the Quiners: Uncle Henry Quiner (Caroline Ingalls's brother) and Aunt Polly Quiner (Charles Ingalls's sister) had four children close to Mary and Laura's age: Louisa, Charley, Albert, and Lottie. There was much coming and going between the two farms, and therefore many opportunities for the cousins to play together. In addition, Laura's grandparents Lansford and Laura Ingalls lived about thirteen miles north, and they held a memorable dance at their house that was later featured in *Little House in the Big Woods*. Finally, Peter Ingalls, Charles's brother, was married to Eliza Quiner, Caroline's sister, so their children Peter, Alice, and Ella were "double cousins" as well. They lived near Laura's grandparents.

Other members of the neighborhood community also interacted with the Ingalls children. Thomas and Jane Huleatt headed an Irish family that lived nearby and were close friends of Charles and Caroline Ingalls. The Huleatt family also hosted a dance. Their children Eva and Clarence played house with Mary and Laura, and Caroline and Jane wondered at times if perhaps Clarence and Laura might someday marry. Mary and Laura attended the Barry Corner School, which was close to their cabin. School attendance records written by their teacher, Anna Barry, are on display today at the Laura Ingalls Wilder Museum in Pepin and include entries for Mary and Laura Ingalls and their Quiner cousins.

Laura described her earliest moral and religious instruction in this section of *Pioneer Girl*. Sibling rivalry between Mary and Laura led to an argument about whose hair was prettier, Mary's blonde hair or Laura's brown hair. It escalated until Laura slapped her sister's face. This was observed by her father, who spanked Laura and later told a story about his own childhood disobedience. In another account, their cousin Charley was supposed to be helping his father and uncle with the grain harvest, but instead he cried out for help multiple times when nothing was the matter. His deception meant that the adults did not come when he stepped on a yellow jackets' nest and was stung repeatedly.

Pioneer Girl also gives a detailed account of the family's patterns of Sunday observance.

> On Sundays the day seemed long. We were dressed all in clean clothes with fresh ribbons in our hair and were not allowed to knit or sew or be noisy in our play. . . .
>
> We liked best to look at the pictures in the big paper covered Bible and there were two we always lingered over. One was Adam naming the animals. Adam was sitting on a big rock and all the animals big and little were standing or sitting around him. Adam looked so comfortable. He didn't have to be careful of his clothes for he had none on except a skin around his waist and the animals wouldn't get that dirty even if they did put their paws on him as Wolf was always doing to me. . . .

The other picture we liked was of the Flood with people and animals all mixed together climbing out of the water onto a big rock.

But Sunday at best was a long, tiresome day.[2]

Laura also described a Sunday afternoon where she became too loud while playing with the dog and had to sit in a chair and be quiet. When she threw a tantrum, Pa spoke to her. After dinner, he told her a story about how hard it was for his father to keep Sunday when he had a new sled to try out. The message was that while Sundays may have been challenging for Laura, they were much more difficult for people in previous generations. The account ends with Pa playing "There Is a Fountain" and "Rock of Ages." The first title refers to "Praise for the Fountain Opened," a hymn written in 1772 by William Cowper, commonly known by its first line, "There is a fountain filled with blood." The hymn "Rock of Ages" was written by Augustus Toplady in 1763.

The available sources about this period suggest that the family was not connected to any church, and biographers agree that in Wisconsin they did not attend worship services. Two reasons are normally given: the seven miles to Pepin were too far to travel on a weekly basis, and the Protestant church in Pepin was Methodist, not Congregational, the denomination the Ingalls family later embraced. If one visits the replica cabin on the land where Laura was born and looks to the northwest, however, one can see the church steeple of the Sabylund Lutheran Church in Lund, a rural community about one and a half miles away. The church was founded in 1856 by Swedish immigrants. Several longtime residents of Lund told me that the Lutheran church—and the nearby Marie Lund Mission Covenant Church (founded in 1874, the year the Ingallses left Wisconsin)—held worship services in Swedish into the twentieth century, and likely into the 1930s. As the Ingalls family did not speak Swedish, they could not have worshiped with either of these congregations. One member of the community also said that the Lutheran church moved to this nearby property in 1893.

Some initial contours of the Ingalls family's patterns of religious belief, belonging, and behavior can be drawn from these sources. Their moral system was based on biblical principles. As they raised their children, Charles

2. Wilder, *Pioneer Girl*, 35–36.

and Caroline emphasized obedience to parents and those in authority, kindness to others, and respect for God, his Word, and his day. The most important unit for identity formation was the nuclear family, and that was the case for religious formation as well as moral formation. That formation was done with both instruction and practice. The Bible was read in their house, at least on Sundays, and Laura engaged the text, thinking about the story in terms of her own life. She also said her prayers nightly before going to bed.

"Everything Was So Sweet and Lovely but Me and I Was a Liar"

In 1873, Charles Ingalls decided to move his family yet again, most likely to pursue a new economic opportunity: land on which to raise wheat in an area that was not as heavily settled. He was able to sell his farm for $1,000, and the family lived for several months with Peter and Eliza Ingalls. They too then sold their farm, and both families traveled across the Mississippi River to Minnesota in early 1874. They stayed in an empty house a few months before moving on. The Peter Ingalls family stopped near the Zumbro River in southeastern Minnesota; Charles and Caroline continued west.

Laura later described experiencing a vivid remembrance of sin and forgiveness at the abandoned house. One evening she lay awake listening to her father playing his fiddle, and the song brought back to her something that she had done and never confessed to her parents. Large icicles had grown down from her uncle Peter's house in the big woods, and her mother had told her not to eat them. Laura had eaten a piece and then told a bold-faced lie to her mother when she asked. While Laura had been ashamed at the time, she later forgot the incident. In the empty house, the calm and beauty of the evening led to remembrance and forgiveness.

> This night as I lay watching the firelight and the shadows and everything was still but the murmur of the waters and the fiddle singing, it all came back to me. My heart hurt, because everything was so sweet and lovely but me and I was a liar.
>
> Then my throat filled up so that a big sob popped out of my mouth, and then they kept coming.
>
> The fiddle stopped singing and Ma hurried in to see what was the trouble. It was such a comfort to tell her all about it. She smoothed

my hair and said of course she would forgive me, because I had told her I was sorry and that now I must say a little prayer and ask God to forgive me too. She told me to say "Dear God please forgive me for telling a lie?" And when I did, Ma said she was sure I would never be so naughty again, then she tucked me in kissed me and went away. The fiddle was singing again as I went to sleep.[3]

This account is a poignant description of a parent's offer of forgiveness to a repentant child. Laura remembered that it was not only forgiveness on the part of the parent but also the offer of God's forgiveness to a repentant sinner. This account is one of the few places in any of Laura's writings where sin and forgiveness from God are mentioned.

Laura also wrote of her father's fiddle playing and its relationship to confession and forgiveness in an undated autobiographical sketch.

When Father played on his violin in the twilight, I could no more help confessing, if I had been naughty during the day than I could keep from giving my Father and Mother the love that welled up in my heart, at times, until it was a positive pain.

Many a time I have gone to sleep at night, after being forgiven for some childish sin, with the kiss of my Mother warm on my lips and the music of Father's violin lulling me to dreams.[4]

Children learn their first ideas about religion and the transcendent from their parents. In Laura's case, the combination of music, beauty, and her father's person shaped her early experiences of life, love, and forgiveness. This story adds an episode that includes asking for God's forgiveness to depictions of the family's structures of moral formation, Sunday observance, biblical instruction, and prayer.

Laura's identity and belonging were found first and foremost in her family, because it was a constant community in the midst of geographical mobility. Her parents worked to inculcate Christian morality in their

3. Wilder, *Pioneer Girl*, 61–62.
4. Laura Ingalls Wilder, *A Little House Reader*, ed. William Anderson (New York: HarperCollins, 1998), 161.

daughters. They also observed Christian rituals, including nightly prayers, weekly Sabbath observance, Bible reading, and the singing of hymns. Laura described her first experience of the transcendent in relation to her father's violin playing. On the other hand, while these practices were important to the Ingalls, it appears that Christianity was not absolutely central to their family life. There is very little mention of faith, the church, or Christianity in the section about Kansas, and the family had no connections to an external community of Christian believers in either Kansas or Wisconsin.

The Ingalls family eventually continued west, coming to a stop in Redwood County. They had traveled about two hundred miles from Pepin. Charles settled his family on a farm a mile and a half from the new town of Walnut Grove. It was here that Laura's understanding of the world expanded, and the family's connection with organized Christianity began.

2

Exploring the World and the Church

Minnesota and Iowa, 1874–1879

T he southwest corner of what is now Minnesota was prairie grass-land until the middle of the nineteenth century. Bands of Dakota, Ojibwe, and Ho-Chunk used the land for hunting, gathering, and fishing. The Dakota gave up their claim to most of the region in the Treaty of Traverse des Sioux in 1851 and moved to land along the Minnesota River. The United States did not fully honor the terms of that agreement, and relations between the Dakota and local white Americans erupted in violence in the United States–Dakota War in 1862. Southern Minnesota was fully opened to railroad expansion and white settlement in the aftermath of that conflict. The Winona and St. Peter Railroad, a branch of the Chicago and North Western system, founded Walnut Station in Redwood County in 1873, and the town that grew up around it became known as Walnut Grove. In this town, the young Laura Ingalls had multiple engagements with organized Christianity.

"We Loved to Go to Sunday School": Walnut Grove, Minnesota

In 1874, southwestern Minnesota had few white residents and wide-open opportunities, two things that attracted Charles Ingalls. The land was almost free from trees, except along streams or next to ponds. The soil was fertile Midwestern loam, and the many creeks in the area promised to keep crops well watered. Charles and Caroline filed a preemption claim with the US government for 172 acres that had previously been worked by a Norwegian farmer and, in May, moved into a one-room dugout house the farmer had built into the bank next to Plum Creek. Dugouts were common in the area since timber was scarce and creek banks were plentiful. They were cool in the summer and could be easily kept warm in the winter, but they posed significant challenges for lighting, ventilation, and housekeeping. There is no longer a dugout at the site, which is made accessible to the public by the current owners, but there are reproductions of dugouts at the Laura Ingalls Wilder Museum in Walnut Grove and at the Ingalls Homestead outside of De Smet, South Dakota. A twenty-first-century American would find them small, dark, and confining.

Laura was now seven years old, so her memories of the farm and town provided many stories for *Pioneer Girl*. During their first year on the property, Charles planted and harvested a small crop and prepared to build a larger frame house. Mary and Laura played in and around the creek. They watched its water level rise and fall, depending on local rainfall; they encountered badgers and other wild creatures; and they helped their mother take care of the dugout and their younger sister Carrie. The family spent one winter in the dugout, then in 1875 Charles built a new wooden frame house for the family.

Since the family was now only a few miles from town, they became involved in Walnut Grove community institutions. Mary and Laura walked the two miles to the one-room schoolhouse in Walnut Grove, where they interacted with girls and boys from town and the surrounding farms and found both friends and adversaries. Their best friend was Nettie Kennedy, the daughter of a Scottish family with three other children. Nellie and Willie Owens were the children of a storekeeper in town who treated Laura and Mary poorly. Laura was able to get a small amount of revenge on Nellie and other town girls who had mistreated her by taking them to Plum Creek, where they were scared by a large crayfish (Laura called it a crab) and Nellie got leeches stuck to her bare feet and legs.

The year they moved to the area, Charles and Caroline Ingalls joined with twelve other citizens of Walnut Grove to form the Union Congregational Church of Christ. The group raised money to construct a building, which was dedicated in December of 1874. It was the first church building in town. Laura also remembered that her father donated the money the family had saved for new boots to a fund to buy a bell for the church. Records show that he gave $26.15 to purchase the bell, although this may have included funds collected from other church members. Charles Ingalls also served as a trustee.

Edwin H. Alden served as pastor of the Congregational church during its first years. He was born in 1836 in Vermont and attended Dartmouth College in New Hampshire and Bangor Theological Seminary in Maine. He was ordained in 1864 by the American Missionary Association, an interdenominational Protestant organization that started schools for freed slaves. He served as the administrator of a school in New Orleans in 1864 but returned to Vermont before becoming a home missionary to Minnesota in 1867. He lived in Waseca and preached regularly at churches in New Ulm, Sleepy Eye, Barnston, Walnut Grove, Saratoga, and Marshall. The railroad made possible his cultivation of congregations in so many small towns. The archives of the Laura Ingalls Wilder Memorial Society in De Smet have copies of several articles he wrote about his work for the *Home Missionary*, a periodical of the American Home Missionary Society, which supported Congregational pastors across the country. Alden provides updates on each congregation, asks for prayer and monetary support, and appeals for more pastors to come to plant churches.

The Congregational church in Walnut Grove met for Sunday school weekly, and it held a worship service when Alden was in town. Laura remembered her Sunday school class, taught by Julia Tower: "We loved to go to Sunday school. Our teacher, Mrs. Tower, would gather us close around her and tell us Bible stories and every Sunday she taught us a verse from the Bible that we must remember and tell her the next."[1] Julia Tower, also originally from Vermont, married a man from New York, and they moved to a farm west of Walnut Grove in the middle of the 1870s.

The Congregational church also hosted a Christmas celebration that featured a Christmas tree, the first that Laura had ever seen. It was decorated with colored paper, candy, candles, and gifts. The gifts, donated by one of the other churches that Alden served, included clothes, tools, and toys. Laura received a beautiful fur collar; she was so excited that she

---

1. Laura Ingalls Wilder, *Pioneer Girl: The Annotated Autobiography*, ed. Pamela Smith Hill (Pierre: South Dakota State Historical Society, 2014), 71.

could hardly thank the pastor. Previous Christmas celebrations described in *Pioneer Girl* were simple affairs at home featuring homemade or small store-bought presents. The sights and sounds of prosperity at this community event made a significant impression on the eight-year-old Laura.

Unfortunately for Laura's family, portions of western Minnesota had been victimized by Rocky Mountain locusts, a species of large grasshoppers, during the early 1870s. It is probable that the Ingalls family had heard reports about the threat, but they settled there anyway, as did many other families. The movements of locusts were unpredictable; they might ravage one location while a nearby area was spared. While the family's crops and garden escaped damage in 1874, the next year, just as Charles counted on his wheat crop to support the family and pay for their newly built house, grasshoppers descended on their farm and the broader neighborhood. The wheat crop was destroyed, leaving them with no hope of income. Like the heads of other families in the same predicament in the fall of 1875, Charles walked to eastern Minnesota to get work harvesting the crops of areas unaffected by the locusts. He walked in order to save money on train fare. He returned with funds that supported the family into the next year.

In the late fall, the family moved into town because Caroline was expecting their fourth child. Living in town also made it much easier for the girls to get to school. They all lived in a small house behind the church. Caroline gave birth on November 1 to their first son, Charles Frederick. The family called him Freddy. They moved back to the farm in the spring.

Locusts struck the area again in 1876, prompting Charles to contemplate another relocation. The events of the previous eighteen months made him willing to try something other than farming. William and Mary Steadman, fellow attenders of the Congregational church, had recently bought a hotel in a small town in Iowa. The Ingalls family agreed to move there and to help them with its operation. In July 1876, Charles completed his preemption claim and paid for his farm. Three days later, he sold it and the family prepared for another move, this time to Burr Oak, Iowa, to join the Steadmans.

First, however, they journeyed to southeastern Minnesota, near South Troy, to stay for several months with Peter Ingalls and his family. Laura and Mary experienced both joy and sorrow while their family was living with their relatives. They played with their cousins, did housework, and helped take care of children younger than they were. Laura also remembered walking down to the pasture each afternoon to bring the cows back to be milked. The pasture bordered the Zumbro River, the grass was soft, and the wild plums along the river were sweet. Unfortunately, the family's enjoyment of these days was shattered by tragedy. Laura wrote in *Pioneer Girl*, "Little Brother was not well and the Dr. came. I thought that would cure him as it had Ma when the Dr. came to see her. But little Brother got worse instead of better and one awful day he straightened out his little body and was dead."[2] Freddy died on August 27, 1876. He was nine months old.

Some of the most significant events recorded in *Pioneer Girl* occurred at locations in between the family's long-term residences: crossing a swollen river and dealing with a chimney fire in Missouri on their trip between Kansas and Wisconsin; the scene of remembrance, confession, and forgiveness in the temporary home in eastern Minnesota; and now the loss of their baby brother while staying with relatives. Laura's description of the event is matter-of-fact and unembellished, but one can imagine the deep sorrow this must have brought to Charles and Caroline and their tight-knit family.

"Dark and Dirty": Burr Oak, Iowa

The Ingalls family completed the trip to Iowa in the late fall of 1876. Burr Oak is in northeastern Iowa, less than five miles south of the Minnesota state line and less than fifty miles west of the Mississippi River and Wisconsin. The town had been founded as a stop on the stagecoach line in the 1850s, while white settlers were still moving west to take up farms across northern Iowa and stagecoaches discharged passengers at one of two hotels in Burr Oak. By the 1870s, however, almost all of Iowa's fertile land had been claimed. Railroads had become the primary means of transportation for both people and crops, and the nearest rail line didn't go through Burr Oak but through Decorah, ten miles south. The town's best years were behind it when the Steadman family purchased the Masters Hotel in 1876 from William Masters and renamed it the Burr Oak House. Fewer stagecoaches stopped in the town, and the establishment

2. Wilder, *Pioneer Girl*, 97.

was dependent for its income on long-term boarders and local diners. In *Pioneer Girl*, Laura wrote that Burr Oak "was not a new, clean little town like Walnut Grove. It was an old, old town and always seemed to me dark and dirty."[3] Its population was less than two hundred.

The Burr Oak House was built into the side of a small hill, so that the two front doors were on the main floor but the back door opened on the floor below. The main floor housed a barroom, a parlor, and one room where the Steadman family—mother, father, and three sons—slept. Up a flight of stairs were four rooms for overnight guests. Down a flight were the kitchen, the dining room, and another room where the Ingalls family—mother, father, and three daughters—slept. Bullet holes pierced the dining room door because Will Masters, the son of the previous owner, had once attempted to shoot his wife. The building has been restored by the Laura Ingalls Wilder Park and Museum; one can walk through and experience how small the rooms were.

The Ingalls family worked long hours at jobs that were always tedious and sometimes difficult. Charles helped William Steadman with the operation of the hotel. Caroline made meals for up to twenty people at a time. Mary and Laura went to school during the week and took care of the Steadmans' youngest son, Tommy, on Saturdays and Sundays. In the evenings, they waited on tables and washed the dishes. Early in 1877, the Ingalls family moved to rooms above a grocery store. Charles had extricated himself from the partnership with the Steadmans and worked as the manager of a feed mill. Later the mill shut down, and he supported the family by doing carpentry and other odd jobs around town.

Accounts of local events in *Pioneer Girl* tend toward the stark, disreputable, and scandalous. Older boys at school disobeyed the teacher, who was possibly younger and certainly smaller than they were, but he surprised the ringleader of the group, spanked him with a ruler, and sent the entire group running out of the school building.[4] Later, the saloon in town caught on fire and the town cooperated to put it out. Laura's father asserted that if he could have been sure that only the saloon would burn

3. Wilder, *Pioneer Girl*, 101.
4. Laura and Rose transplanted this incident to upstate New York and made it central to the early chapters of *Farmer Boy*.

and not the surrounding houses, he wouldn't have carried water. A fight between their downstairs neighbors woke the Ingalls in the middle of the night; the man was dragging his wife around by her hair. At the same time, he was holding a kerosene lamp that was spilling and could have set the room on fire. Charles put things right before their home went up in flames. Finally, a local man who had gotten drunk in the saloon woke up, took a drink, then lit a cigar. This action ignited the fumes from the whiskey, and he breathed the flame into his lungs and died immediately. At least that is what Laura heard had happened.

In the early spring of 1877, the family moved to a rented house on the outskirts of town, several blocks from the hotel and next to the Congregational church. The depictions in *Pioneer Girl* of life after this move are more positive. Laura continued to go to school. She greatly valued her teacher's gift for bringing literature alive for the students, and she credited the school in Burr Oak with developing her ability to read and her appreciation of poetry. The family bought a cow, and Laura enjoyed taking it to pasture in the morning and bringing it back at night, looking at the flowers and dipping her feet in the brook on the way. Some weekends she went with a friend to the Burr Oak Cemetery; she appreciated the beauty and tranquillity of the setting. The family rejoiced in the birth of a fourth daughter, Grace Pearl, on May 23, 1877.

Based on their practice in Walnut Grove and De Smet, the Ingalls family likely attended Sunday school and worship services at the Congregational church in Burr Oak. One biographer, Donald Zochert, asserts that Charles and Caroline were church members. A sign at the site of the church says it was established in 1850; the church building was dedicated in 1858; and the church was closed in 1885. The founding pastor, George Bent, also preached for congregations in Bluffton, Iowa, and Lenora, Minnesota. Later pastors continued this pattern. George Sterling was the pastor of the church in 1876 and 1877, while the Ingallses were living in town. Originally from Connecticut and a graduate of Andover Theological Seminary, a Congregational school in Massachusetts, Sterling held several pastorates in the Midwest, including Burr Oak, before returning to New England. Burr Oak housed two other churches during the 1870s: the Methodist church and the First Advent Christian Church. The Advent Christian churches broke away from the larger Seventh-day Adventist movement in 1860, and the Burr Oak congregation was founded in 1869. They were constructing their church building in 1877, and Charles Ingalls may have helped to build that structure. The church closed in 1964, and the building now belongs to the Laura Ingalls Wilder Park and Museum. The Methodist church building stands today on the same site it did during the 1870s. Laura does not mention any of these congregations in *Pioneer Girl*. In fact, the only mention of Christianity or faith in this section of the memoir is one reference to the hymn "There Is a Happy Land, Far Away."

Why did Laura not mention faith or Christianity in this section of her memoir? It is likely that the other dramatic events she recalled from this period crowded out other memories. Maybe George Sterling was not as striking as the other pastors of her childhood, Edwin Alden and Edward Brown. The church in Burr Oak was probably smaller than the Congregational churches in Walnut Grove and De Smet because Burr Oak was a smaller town; maybe it did not hold special events like revivals or a Christmas celebration. In addition, perhaps the family's rhythms of religious practices were unchanged from Walnut Grove so she didn't feel the need to mention them. At any rate, we don't know how Laura experienced Christianity during her years in Burr Oak, or whether participation in the life of the Congregational church might have helped the family deal with the many challenges they encountered.

After almost a year in Burr Oak, the Ingalls family was in dire financial straits. Charles was doing poorly paid, temporary, manual labor jobs, and work often took him away from the family. They were in debt for doctor bills—probably for Grace's birth—and grocery bills, and they were behind on their rent. One afternoon, Laura returned from a visit to the cemetery to find her mother talking with the local doctor's wife, Eunice Starr. Mrs. Starr wanted to adopt Laura, because her daughters had grown up and she wanted someone to help with housework and to keep her from being lonely. While a wealthier family adopting the child of a poorer one was not unheard of during the nineteenth century, such a discussion must have shocked Laura. Caroline maintained that their family could not possibly do without her.

Not much later, Charles asked for extra time to pay their rent; their landlord refused and threatened to seize and sell their horses. So one evening Charles sold their cow to get travel money, then he and Caroline packed all their belongings into their wagon. The family left in the middle of the night and headed back to Walnut Grove. Laura wrote that she knew at the time that if they paid their debts they couldn't leave, because they wouldn't have had money for travel expenses. Charles and Caroline may have thought their decision to leave Burr Oak to avoid paying their debts was justified because their landlord was unreasonable. Baby Grace had joined the family in Iowa, and Laura could count some pleasant memories there, but their sojourn in Burr Oak had been an economic disaster for the family.

"That Is What Men Call God": Walnut Grove Again

When the Ingalls family reached Walnut Grove again, they first stayed with a local family, the Ensigns, who were friends from the Congregational church. Later, Charles was able to build a small house in a pasture near town owned by William Masters. It is unclear whether they rented the space, bartered for labor, or were allowed to live on the land for free. *Pioneer Girl* does not describe this house in any detail. Charles ran a butcher shop for one summer. At other times he worked in a store or did carpentry work for those moving into the growing town. For instance, he helped Masters construct a store building with a meeting hall on the second floor. The Ingalls family lived in Walnut Grove two more years, from 1877 to 1879. Laura turned eleven, then twelve years old. Accounts of these years in *Pioneer Girl* show even more attention to events in the broader community. She describes her experiences with school, paid employment, community scandals, and two different churches.

Mary, Laura, and Carrie all attended the local, one-room school. Laura was a tomboy and enjoyed playing baseball and engaging in snowball fights with the boys, among other activities. The first schoolmaster upon their return was Samuel Masters, whom the children called "Uncle Sam." He had a penchant for absent-mindedly rubbing girls' hands in school; Laura pricked him with a pin once, and he did not do it to her again. Laura clashed with Nellie Owens and with a new girl her age, Genevieve Masters, the daughter of the schoolmaster. Genevieve was born in New York and looked down on the other girls as "westerners." Both she and

Nellie fought to be the leader of the schoolgirls Laura's age, and for a while the group divided. Laura didn't join either crowd and ultimately found that both Nellie and Genevieve were seeking her friendship and she was the leader.[5] Once Mary forcibly tried to keep Laura from participating in snowball fights at recess; Mary ended up being pulled to the door and pelted with snow. Mary later prevailed upon their mother to keep Laura from rough games at recess, although Laura still played on the way to and from school.

School also provided the setting for Laura's first relationships with boys. One boy her age, Howard Ensign, asked her to marry him someday. She considered the request seriously until he cried when she played with the Congregational pastor's son. Several of the girls at school were smitten by another boy, Clarence Spurr, until he was expelled after an altercation with the schoolteacher. A third object of the girls' attention, Silas Rood, was disgraced for making up a story of being attacked by a band of ruffians. Laura's memoir thus provides brief but vivid descriptions of preteen relationship drama in a very small Midwestern town during the late nineteenth century.

During school breaks, Laura worked for the William Masters family's hotel. This was the Masters family who had sold the hotel to the Steadman family in Iowa. The Steadmans had left for Burr Oak, and the Masterses had moved to Walnut Grove and opened a hotel there. Laura was paid fifty cents a week to wait on tables, wash dishes, clean rooms, and help the family's daughter Nannie take care of her baby. When Laura's work was done, she had time to read the family's copy of the *New York Ledger*. The *Ledger* was a weekly newspaper that consisted mostly of serialized fiction but also included poetry, fashion information, and current events. Its circulation was more than 350,000 nationwide during the 1870s. Laura also had time to observe the courtship of Nannie's sister Mattie Masters and a local doctor, Robert Hoyt. The two ultimately tied the knot, but Laura's parents believed that premarital sex led to the necessity of their marriage.

Laura also provided income for the family by staying with multiple families in need of help. She babysat for a local family during Good

5. In the Little House books, Laura combined personality traits from these two girls in the character of Nellie Oleson.

Templars Lodge meetings. Later, she also helped them on Saturdays and Sundays. At some point (the chronology in *Pioneer Girl* is uncertain at times) she began staying with a woman during the week who was sick and possibly pregnant, Sadie Hurley. Finally, she stayed with Nannie and Will Masters for several weeks because Nannie had fainting spells and could not stay alone with their daughter. Laura also helped cook, wash dishes, and clean.

As she had in the section on Burr Oak, Laura described Walnut Grove scandals in her memoir. She was exposed to them because of the family's proximity to town, her work in the hotel, and her presence in other families' homes. She learned that the town milliner often looked sad and downhearted because she had been divorced. Their old neighbor Eleck Nelson operated a saloon in town until it was shut down by the constable because of the amount of drunkenness and fighting there. After its closure, Dr. Hoyt continued to procure whiskey to give to Will Masters, Mattie's brother and Nannie's husband (and the source of the bullet holes in the dining room in Burr Oak). Other scandals became known to the family because Charles was elected justice of the peace in 1879 and heard cases in their front room. The rest of the family retreated to the kitchen, but they could hear what was going on. Laura often sat close to the door.

Laura herself almost became a victim of the societal brokenness in Walnut Grove when she was staying with Will and Nannie Masters. Will was still drinking. One night he came to Laura's bed and leaned over her. She could smell whiskey on his breath. When Laura asked if there was a problem, he told her to lie down and be still. He only left when she threatened to scream for his wife. The attempted assault must have been a horrifying experience for a girl not quite twelve years old. She moved back home with her family the next day. It is not at all surprising that this account was left out of *On the Banks of Plum Creek*, a children's book.

Finally, the church receives significant attention in this section of the memoir. Laura experienced a variety of facets of religious worship, life, and training during these later years in Walnut Grove. She mentions that her family was attending Sunday school and worship services at the Congregational church, where there was now a new pastor, the Reverend Leonard H. Moses. He was born in Maine, attended Wheaton College in Illinois, and served in the Union army during the American Civil War. He pastored Congregational churches in Minnesota and Kansas. Laura does not describe him or his ministry in any detail, although she does mention that she attended school with his children. Moses left Walnut Grove in the fall of 1879, shortly after the Ingalls family did. At some point during these years, Mary became a full member of the Congregational church.

One experience with the Congregational Sunday school was extremely painful for both Laura and Mary. The children of the church were all taken in a large wagon to a Sunday school picnic about two miles from town in a grove next to a creek. Everyone took their own lunch, and it had been announced that there would be lemonade and ice cream. Caroline had given her girls an entire lemon pie, which was Laura's favorite. The children had fun taking turns swinging, playing games, and walking along the creek. Unfortunately, when refreshments were served, the lemonade cost five cents a glass and the ice cream was ten cents a dish. Mary and Laura hadn't taken any money because they hadn't dreamed that there would be a charge, so they had to go without. They agreed that they couldn't have asked their father for money for such luxuries anyway. When lunches were handed out, the lemon pie was missing. Laura later overheard a teacher say that she had saved it for the teachers, possibly claiming that she had made it herself. Laura's day was ruined. She told the other children she didn't want to play because her foot hurt, and she and Mary picked flowers in a place where they couldn't see the costly food. When she reached home, Laura found that she had a large blister on her right heel.

This experience did not keep Laura away from Sunday school or church services, however. In fact, Laura attended Sunday school and weekly services at both the Congregational church (when they held a service) and the Methodist church for an entire year. She went to the Congregational church on Sunday mornings, then joined the Methodists in the second-floor meeting hall of the new Masters building on Sunday afternoons. This was because the Methodist Sunday school was holding a contest:

A prize was offered to the pupil who at the end of the year could repeat from memory, in their proper order, all the Golden Texts and Central Truths for the entire year, which would be two Bible verses for each Sunday of the year. When the time came for the test, we stood up one at a time before the whole Sunday-school and beginning with the first lesson of the year repeated first the Golden Text then the Central truth of each lesson, one after the other as they came, without any prompting or help of any kind. The prize was a reference Bible.[6]

The Methodist church apparently included two Bible verses in their Sunday school lessons each week and challenged children to memorize them. Only Laura and Howard Ensign were able to do it. The church had purchased only one Bible for the contest, but Laura was willing to wait for her Bible because the pastor's wife promised to get her one with a clasp. It appears that Laura went to the Methodist church by herself; *Pioneer Girl* mentions that Mary did not go, and her father attended with her only occasionally. Laura may have pursued this opportunity to establish an identity separate from her family. The contest also certainly appears to have appealed to her competitive nature. As a result, Laura spent a significant time each Sunday in religious instruction and services. She also must have practiced at home on a regular basis to memorize so many Bible verses.

One of the Sunday schools that Laura attended in 1878 gave out cards with Bible verses printed on them. They are about two inches wide and one and a half inches high. The verses are from the King James Version and surrounded by one of three different decorative borders printed in green ink. They could have been printed locally or by a denomination's publishing house. They may have been distributed by the Congregational church or by the Methodist church, perhaps to aid children in its Sunday school's memorization project. Laura kept these cards for years, even as she moved about the country. They are now in the collection of the Laura Ingalls Wilder Historic Home and Museum in Mansfield, Missouri.

Pioneer Girl also describes revival services in both churches. A revival was a series of worship services every evening for one or more weeks. Laura enjoyed singing and watching other people at the Congregational revival meetings, but the meetings at the Methodist church, held the next week in the upstairs of the Masters Building,[7] were more raucous and

---

6. Wilder, *Pioneer Girl*, 136.

7. The Masters Building was purchased by the Laura Ingalls Wilder Museum in Walnut Grove in 2017. It is one of the few remaining buildings Charles Ingalls helped to build, and the upstairs is where Laura sat during these services more than 140 years ago.

uncontrolled. The pastor who led that revival was John Gimson, who was originally from England. His wife was Irish, and they came to America after they were married; they lived in Connecticut and New York before moving to Minnesota.

Laura also attended midweek prayer meetings, and they provide the occasion for a brief meditation about the actions of her previous suitor and fellow contest winner Howard Ensign. He had become a member of the Congregational church after their revival, and he regularly shared about his life and faith at Wednesday night prayer meetings. Laura was uncomfortable hearing others describe their experiences with God: "It someway offended my sense of privacy. It seemed to me that the things between one and God should be between him and God like loving ones [*sic*] mother. One didn't go around saying 'I love my mother, she has been so good to me.' One just loved her and did things that she liked one to do."[8] The account appears between descriptions of the Bible memorization contest and Pa's violin playing during the winter, so there is little direct context for interpreting this reticence concerning talking about God and spiritual things. It seems to be her personal preference, although it is not clear whether she held this opinion during her childhood or when she wrote the memoir. There does seem to be a distinction in the descriptions of the rowdier revival services of the Methodist church and the more staid Congregational revival; maybe she saw Howard Ensign's regular testifying at Congregational midweek meetings as out of place. Her discomfort may also have been connected to an attitude of stoicism and the acceptance of one's situation. Perhaps she thought that one should not complain, boast, or talk about spiritual things too openly. At least by the time she wrote the memoir, and perhaps at the time she experienced Ensign's testimony, she disdained external displays of religious faith and experience.

Several paragraphs later, however, Laura herself provided an account of an experience with God's presence. It occurred when she was staying with Sadie Hurley. Laura knew about her family's economic struggles, and one night she was particularly troubled:

8. Wilder, *Pioneer Girl*, 136. This quotation was also addressed in the introduction.

The rest of the days were lonely and I was homesick. I knew things were not going well at home, because Pa could not get much work and we needed more money to live on.

One night while saying my prayers, as I always did before going to bed, this feeling of homesickness and worry was worse than usual, but gradually I had a feeling of a hovering, encompassing Presence of a Power, comforting and sustaining and thought in surprise "That is what men call God!"[9]

This passage reveals again that Laura prayed regularly before going to bed. Anxiety because of her separation from her family and their financial need may have moved her to especially fervent prayer. It is also likely that this happened during 1878, the year she was attending both sets of services on Sundays and memorizing Bible verses; if so, God and his Word would often have been on her mind. As many Christians in times of distress and need have found, in this moment she felt peace and strength that seemed supernatural. This experience with the transcendent was real enough that she remembered it and did not disdain to describe it in detail years later, despite what she thought about those who talked publicly about their relationship with God. It must have strengthened her for the work that her family needed her to do and the separation she had to endure.

The family experienced an additional trial when Mary became ill in the spring of 1879. It began with a severe headache in the middle of April and led to facial paralysis and diminished eyesight.[10] By the summer she was stronger, but she could hardly see at all. At some point Charles took her to Chicago to be examined by a specialist, and they were told that there was no hope of her regaining her sight. Mary became permanently blind at fourteen years old, and her blindness affected every member of the family. The Little House books relate how Laura acted as Mary's eyes, describing the scenes of their lives to her. Some biographers have suggested that this role trained Laura's ability to notice details, describe them clearly, and

---

9. Wilder, *Pioneer Girl*, 137.

10. A team of medical researchers in 2013 argued that her condition was most likely viral meningoencephalitis. Sarah S. Allexan et al., "Blindness in Walnut Grove: How Did Mary Ingalls Lose Her Sight?" *Pediatrics* 131, no. 3 (2013): 404–6.

perhaps also to remember them. More mundanely, travel and doctor bills added to the family's debts.

Laura left all the events from the year in Burr Oak and most of the events of the later years in Walnut Grove out of the Little House books. Living in these two towns was perhaps the lowest point of the Ingalls family fortunes. Wilder scholars present different ways to interpret the family's poverty and nearness to destitution. Some, including Caroline Fraser, argue that their economic situation must have loomed large in their experience and led to unhappiness and even anguish for Laura. John Miller and others observe that many heads of households in Walnut Grove and Burr Oak were in the same position as Charles Ingalls, buffeted by nature, meager employment opportunities, and other forces beyond their control. It seems clear that although Charles was not able to provide financial stability, he did succeed in creating an emotionally stable environment for his family. In addition, Laura's convictions about God, his Word, the church, and other people were formed and sharpened by these childhood experiences.

"The Things between One and God"

During the late 1870s, in their homes in Iowa and Minnesota, Laura and her family continued to face the challenges of resource privation together. It appears that they all attended religious services together at Congregational churches on Sundays, most likely for the entire period. Living on the farm taught Laura to love the outdoors and to appreciate the many plants and animals in God's creation. Living in town caused members of the family to be pulled in different directions, especially during their time in Burr Oak and their second stay in Walnut Grove. Laura worked outside the home for pay in multiple situations, including several that required her to stay overnight with other families. She also went to services with the Methodists, probably by herself. She was exposed to a variety of personal foibles and actual evils. Mary's blindness caused Laura to take on new roles. The family faced financial ruin more than once. For Laura, these years cannot be described as simple or easy.

We can trace some contours of Laura's patterns of religious belonging during this period. Charles and Caroline Ingalls were charter members of the Congregational church in Walnut Grove, and they may have been members at the same kind of church in Burr Oak. Mary also became a member of the Congregational church in her early teenage years. There is no record of Laura becoming a member of the church during these years, possibly because of her age, though her bonds with the Congregational Sunday school were probably strained by her experience at the Sunday school picnic. At least for one year, she was as comfortable meeting with the Methodists as she was with the Congregationalists. Her answering of the challenge issued by Methodist Sunday school leaders to memorize more than one hundred Bible verses probably endeared her to them. It must also have made her parents unbelievably proud.

During these years Laura also adopted practices that Christians across the centuries have seen as nurturing faith in Jesus Christ. She attended services regularly: worship and Sunday school on Sundays—sometimes at two different churches—and prayer meeting on Wednesday nights. She prayed regularly, most likely every night, and engaged the Bible by learning multiple verses by heart. She also attended special revival worship services, also with two different congregations. Finally, she began to internalize Christian values, especially the Bible's instructions to obey one's parents and to love one's neighbor. It appears that her faith was central to her life at this point in her childhood; it was perhaps the most central role that Christianity ever played during her life.

Laura's reflections about these years give us less in the way of details about her religious beliefs. Her reserved nature and her conviction that the "things between one and God" were best kept private make it a challenge to describe them. Yet, she had a commitment to Christianity, as is evidenced by her regular Christian practices. She believed that God existed and sometimes visited his people with his presence, since she had felt it. The Bible verses she memorized likely provided her guidance in what to believe as well as how to live.

In the summer of 1879, a way out of the family's ongoing financial difficulties in Walnut Grove was provided by Charles's sister Laura Ladocia, or Docia, and her husband, Hiram Forbes. He managed contracts for the Chicago and North Western Railroad as it built west from Minnesota into Dakota Territory and offered Charles a position as bookkeeper, timekeeper for laborers, and manager of the company store. This provided

Charles an opportunity to move to a less-settled area with more wild game and more wide-open spaces and to get paid for it. He accepted the job and left the next day. After he received his first paycheck, he sent money back to the family to pay debts and travel expenses. In the fall, Caroline and the girls rode the train to Tracy, Minnesota, where Charles met them and took them west in a lumber wagon. A new location became the setting for—with new people participating in—Laura's entrance into adolescence, courtship, and marriage.

3

Adolescence and Courtship

Dakota Territory, 1879-1885

In 1803, the United States agreed to purchase the Louisiana Territory from France. The treaty exchanged more than 800,000 acres for fifteen million dollars. The next year, Meriwether Lewis, William Clark, and their Corps of Discovery traveled up the Missouri River and entered what later became Dakota Territory. Their party nearly had a violent confrontation with the Lakota in the central part of what is now South Dakota. During the early nineteenth century, the Lakota, as well as the Cheyenne, Crow, and other groups, circulated on the Great Plains, hunting buffalo. Dakota Territory was organized in 1861. After the United States–Dakota War in 1862, many Dakota from Minnesota were forcibly resettled on reservations in Dakota Territory. In 1868, in exchange for land in eastern Dakota Territory, the Lakota were granted a large reservation west of the Missouri River. The United States unilaterally reduced the size of this reservation multiple times during the rest of the century, including after the Battle of Little Bighorn in 1876.

When the Ingalls family moved into the southeastern corner of Dakota Territory in 1879, they joined what was called the "Great Dakota Boom." This movement was a wave of migration into eastern Dakota Territory during the late 1870s and early 1880s. As railroad lines were built into the territory, white Americans moved with them to obtain land under the Homestead Act. Homesteaders first claimed the land close to railroad tracks and stations, then they occupied the less attractive land farther away. Those who could afford it bought farmland from the railroad. Other migrants came to provide goods and services to the settlers and built homes in small towns with railway stations. In 1880, Dakota Territory had about eighty thousand white residents; five years later the number was three times as many. Thousands moved onto lands that the Dakota had hunted and lived on for decades. The federal government made treaties, maintained reservations, and attempted to compel American Indians to adopt European ways of life.

The landscape in eastern Dakota Territory, now east-central South Dakota, was one of rolling hills and short grasses. One might travel by horse-drawn wagon for significant periods without seeing a tree; they mainly grew near creeks, rivers, or small lakes. Even today, driving east on US Route 14, one can notice a change in the landscape between Walnut Grove, Minnesota, and Brookings, South Dakota. *Pioneer Girl* gives an evocative description of the sunset over this landscape: "The sun sank lower and lower until, looking like a ball of pulsing, liquid light it sank gloriously in clouds of crimson and silver. Cold purple shadows rose in the east; crept slowly around the horizon, then gathered above in depth on depth of darkness from which the stars swung low and bright. The winds which all day had blown strongly, dropped low with the sun and went whispering among the tall grasses, where the earth lay breathing softly under the summer night falling softly over the prairie and tucking them gently in."[1] This passage showcases Laura's ability to use multiple senses to give a feel for a scene in nature. The Ingalls family moved into a shanty for railroad workers near Silver Lake, close to where the town of De Smet would later be built.

"Comfortably Settled": Railroad Camps and the Surveyors' House

In her memoir, Laura remembered being happy to be in the country instead of in a town: "It was very pleasant when we were comfortably settled in the new shanty, with the great, new country clean and fresh around us."[2]

---

1. Laura Ingalls Wilder, *Pioneer Girl: The Annotated Autobiography*, ed. Pamela Smith Hill (Pierre: South Dakota State Historical Society, 2014), 158.
2. Wilder, *Pioneer Girl*, 160.

While it was a benefit to be closer to nature, a late nineteenth-century railroad camp provided rough accommodations among hardworking people. Almost all the laborers were men, and Caroline and the children stayed close to their shanty most of the time. Laura and her cousin Lena were responsible for taking the families' cows to pasture and bringing them back and milking them. Aunt Docia was usually busy cooking for the railroad workers. Charles's job supported his family, although they also took in a boarder to make additional income.

Laura's narrative is dominated by Big Jerry, a colorful character who became good friends with her father. Jerry often ate at the Ingallses' shanty. He had both French and American Indian ancestry, and he was called a half-breed by the men in the camp. Some workers suspected him of being involved with a ring of horse thieves, and some contemporary newspaper reports support that idea, although by Laura's account, Charles never believed it to be so. Laura describes how Big Jerry expressed the workers' displeasure toward a railroad timekeeper they disliked; Jerry led the man and his horse under equipment where they would be covered with dirt. Laura then uses a biblical reference to describe the timekeeper leaving the area "shaking the dust of the west from his shoes—and from all the rest of his clothes."[3] The reference is to Matthew 10:14, "whosoever shall not receive you, nor hear your words, when ye depart out of that house or city, shake off the dust of your feet."[4] Big Jerry made a significant impression on the twelve-year-old Laura.

Pioneer Girl also describes an incident between the workers and Charles Ingalls, their paymaster. Pay came from the Chicago and North Western Railroad two weeks after time sheets had been turned in. Some laborers wanted to be paid in a more timely way and stirred up the entire camp against him. He spoke to the angry men, and they eventually went back to their shanties. A similar uprising at a neighboring camp led to violence and the paymaster being forced to give out money to the workers nine days early. More-detailed fictional versions of these events are presented in *By the Shores of Silver Lake*.

3. Wilder, *Pioneer Girl*, 169.
4. Unless otherwise indicated, biblical quotations in the book come from the King James Version.

Laura's memoir does not mention religious worship services during the several months that the Ingalls family were living in the railroad camp, nor does it refer to acts of religious devotion, such as Sunday observance, Bible reading, or prayer. Worship services may not have been held in railroad camps of this size and type in southeastern Dakota Territory during these years. If worship was held and the Ingalls family attended, it seems that Big Jerry, the danger her father had faced, and the rough and tumble life in the camp crowded other topics out of Laura's memory, or at least out of her writing.

During the fall of 1879, Hiram Forbes's railroad contract had been completed, and most workers moved away for the winter. Apparently, he and Docia did some creative bookkeeping to make money at the expense of the railroad. In *Pioneer Girl*, Laura justified their accounting practices by noting that the railroad had made money at their expense on a previous contract. At this point, Laura and her family did not have to move away, because Charles had been hired by the company to take care of the railroad surveyors' equipment. The Ingalls family moved into what they called the Surveyors' House on December 1, 1879, and lived there for the next four months. They were joined by a boarder named Walter Ogden; the family saw it as wise to have another man around. The Surveyors' House was moved into the town of De Smet in 1884. Today it is maintained by the Laura Ingalls Wilder Memorial Society, which provides tours for visitors.

During this winter and early spring, Charles Ingalls enjoyed the good hunting in the relatively unpopulated area, and the family ate geese and duck and saved the feathers for a featherbed. Laura describes sliding on the ice of Silver Lake with Carrie. One time they encountered wolves. Charles also played the fiddle frequently. *Pioneer Girl* explicitly mentions him playing hymns, including "Sweet Hour of Prayer," "Nearer My God to Thee," "Let the Lower Lights Be Burning," and "The Sweet By and By." The increased leisure time during this winter likely made it possible for the family to pursue religious practices more faithfully than during their time in the railroad camp. It also may be that they continued these practices as before but Laura did not write about them.

On Saturday night, February 28, 1880, the Ingallses were visited by Edwin Alden, whom they had known during their first stay in Walnut Grove, and another Congregational pastor, Stuart Sheldon. In the intervening years, Alden had left the ministry and been appointed by the US Bureau of Indian Affairs as agent at the Fort Berthold Reservation in northern Dakota Territory. While there, he was accused of embezzling money and lying to the Native Americans. He disputed the accusations but resigned in 1879 and returned to the Congregational American Home Missionary Society as superintendent for southern Dakota Territory. The two pastors were exploring places to plant new Congregational churches. The next day, a Sunday, they held a worship service in the Surveyors' House for twenty-five people, according to church records. Those who visit the Surveyors' House can see how crowded twenty-five people would have been in that space, even though a number of those in attendance were probably children, like Laura and her younger sisters. It is remembered in local history as the first Congregational worship service in De Smet.[5]

February 1880 was also the month Charles filed for a homestead. He located the plot, south of where De Smet was later laid out and built, while the family was living in the Surveyors' House. He traveled to Brookings on February 19 to file the homestead claim at the district court. Charles paid a filing fee of a little less than fourteen dollars and hurried home.[6] Because the Surveyors' House was the only place within miles to find shelter, many migrants stopped there during the spring of 1880 and paid the Ingalls family for a meal and a place to stay the night. Charles also purchased two town lots in the newly platted town. He built store buildings on both and then sold one. The family moved to the other on April 3.

"Love Your Enemies": Adolescence in De Smet

Father Pierre-Jean De Smet was a Jesuit missionary born in Belgium in 1801. He was ordained a priest in St. Louis in 1827 and established several missions to western American Indian groups: one among the Potawatomi near Council Bluffs, Iowa, in 1839, and two others among the Salish near Missoula, Montana, in 1841 and 1844. He also was a US government ne-

5. This worship service is transformed in chapter 23 of *By the Shores of Silver Lake*, titled "On the Pilgrim Way." I will discuss this account in chapter 8.

6. The account of Pa's experience at the land office in *By the Shores of Silver Lake* is fictional.

gotiator working with Native American leaders. He acted as a translator and mediator for the meeting at Fort Laramie in 1851 that resulted in the first major treaty between the United States and American Indian groups on the plains. He also served as an emissary to Sitting Bull of the Dakota in 1868. He died in St. Louis in 1873. De Smet was famous enough by 1880 for the Kingsbury County Board to name a new town in his honor.

The Ingalls family spent the next seven years alternately living in the small building on their town lot in De Smet and in the claim shanty on their homestead. They normally moved to town when the weather got cold so that the family could more readily obtain supplies and the children could more easily get to school. When Charles wasn't working to fulfill the requirements of the Homestead Act—fencing the property, breaking the ground, and growing crops—he often worked as a carpenter in town. The family grew as much of their food on the homestead as possible, including turnips, potatoes, beans, tomatoes, corn, and pumpkins. Still, *Pioneer Girl* mentions that sometimes the family lacked cash for necessities, and at times Laura's father went hungry for the sake of his children.

After only half a year on the homestead, the family was confronted by what residents of De Smet called the "Hard Winter of 1880–1881." An October snowstorm caught the family still in the shanty. They moved quickly to town. The area experienced repeated blizzards between December and April. One struck while Laura and Carrie were at the schoolhouse, about two blocks from their house in town, and all fifteen of the schoolchildren were almost lost while trying to walk home in the thick, blowing snow. Trains stopped running to De Smet in January. Food supplies ran short. By April, all the families in De Smet were reduced to twisting hay into sticks to burn and grinding wheat in coffee grinders to make flour for bread.

During this winter, three additional people lived with the Ingalls family. George Masters, the son of Samuel Masters from Walnut Grove, and his wife, Maggie, had come to De Smet early in 1880. Maggie was pregnant too soon after their wedding, and they wanted to have the baby somewhere away from home. They asked to stay with the Ingalls family and were accepted; it may be that the Ingallses remembered the support they had received from the extended Masters family in Minnesota. Their baby was born before the fall, but George put off traveling back east to Walnut Grove. Eventually, the family was caught by the bad weather.

Pioneer Girl depicts George as unwilling to help with the chores and taking more than his fair share of the family's food. When writing *The Long Winter*, Laura deliberately left the Masters family out of the story.

As food supplies in De Smet began to run out, Almanzo Wilder acted to help save the lives of many in the town. Almanzo[7] had grown up on a prosperous farm in northern New York near the town of Malone, less than twenty miles from the Canadian border. He was the fifth of six children born to James and Angeline Day Wilder: Laura, Royal, Eliza Jane, Alice, Almanzo, and Perley Day. The Wilder family had moved to Spring Valley in southeastern Minnesota during the early 1870s. Almanzo, his brother Royal, and his sister Eliza Jane filed on homesteads near De Smet in 1879. The Homestead Act required filers to be twenty-one years old, and Almanzo reported his birth year as 1857, although some evidence from census records suggests that he might actually have been born in 1859. The three siblings moved to Dakota Territory early in 1880, and Royal opened a general store in town. When food supplies in town ran low, Almanzo and Oscar "Cap" Garland drove sleighs to a homestead south of De Smet, bought sacks of the occupant's seed wheat, and brought them back to town. This purchase enabled families to hold out until trains finally got through to De Smet in May.

During the early 1880s, the Great Dakota Boom meant more and more white settlers moved to De Smet and the homesteads surrounding it. They built important businesses and community institutions as well as buildings. Early businesses in De Smet included the railroad depot, a lumber yard, a livery stable, several general stores, and a saloon. The saloon was the only business that never ran out of stock during the Hard Winter, according to *Pioneer Girl*. They were followed by grocery stores, a drug store, a hotel, and a furniture store. For Laura, who had turned fourteen during the Hard Winter, then fifteen in February of 1882, the most important institutions were the school and the Congregational church.

The one-room schoolhouse in De Smet was one of the first community institutions built. *Pioneer Girl* describes Laura and Carrie's interactions with

---

7. The second *a* in his name was pronounced with a short *a*, as in "man," not "awe." Characters on the television series *Little House on the Prairie* pronounced the name incorrectly.

friends and teachers there. Like many teenagers, Laura was self-conscious about her looks. She worried that she was short, plump, and wore clothes that showed her family's financial straits. Still, she developed close friendships with several girls at school, especially Mary Power and Ida Wright Brown, the adopted daughter of the new pastor of the Congregational church. Cap Garland and other teenage boys were potential romantic partners. Laura's antagonist during these years was Genevieve (or Genoitm) Masters, who had moved with her family from Walnut Grove to De Smet. As described by Laura, Geneive schemed to get Cap Garland's attentions, worked to ingratiate herself with the teacher, and poked fun at Laura's appearance and clothes. The schoolteacher, Almanzo Wilder's sister Eliza Jane, also figured significantly in Laura's teenage challenges. *Pioneer Girl* relates that Eliza Jane was unable to maintain discipline in the school and was unjust to Laura and Carrie. Laura fared much better under Frank Clewette and especially Ven Owen, teachers of later terms at the school.

During these years, Laura wrote poetry, which she saved. Some poems describe the prairie landscape while others give Laura's feelings about school, her family, chores, love, and patriotism. It is perhaps in relation to these interpersonal challenges at school that Laura wrote a poem titled "Love Your Enemies":

> Love your enemies.
> Oh, my God! how hard is that command
> To keep.
> To love one's enemies, love must be
> As broad as the ocean,
> And as deep.
> We can not do it,
> Oh my God! unless thou help us
> In thy love.
> Oh give us strength to do thy will
> Great God of earth
> And heaven above.[8]

8. Laura Ingalls Wilder, *A Little House Reader*, ed. William Anderson (New York: HarperCollins, 1998), 186–87.

The poem describes Laura's beliefs in God's existence and his rule over his creation. It also evidences an understanding that his command to love one's enemies was enduring, that people are unable to do so in their own strength, and that therefore reliance on God was necessary. It appears that she drew on these beliefs and on prayer as she confronted challenges common to adolescent girls. Her poem expresses both her struggles and her faith.

The Congregational church in De Smet was founded shortly after settlers had arrived in significant numbers. The Ingalls family expected that Alden would pastor the new church, especially after he had presided over the area's first worship service. There may have been additional Sunday services after this at the Surveyors' House and in the front of the Ingalls family's building in town. The church also met in the railroad depot for several months. Meetings were led by Horace Woodworth, a retired pastor who worked for the railroad.

Rev. Edward Brown arrived during the early summer of 1880 with a letter from Alden introducing him to Charles Ingalls as a retired pastor who was going to homestead. Brown had previously been a schoolteacher and a lawyer, and then had pastored churches in Minnesota, Ohio, and Wisconsin. When he arrived, however, he announced that he had come to be pastor of the Congregational church. Alden subsequently arrived with his own plans of leading the congregation. Alden had the Home Missionary Society's authority to organize the church, but, because Brown had already established himself in the community, Alden relinquished the congregation to him in May. The organizational meeting of the First Congregational Church was held on June 20, 1880. There were eight charter members, including Charles, Caroline, and Mary Ingalls. Articles of incorporation were drawn up in October, also signed by the three Ingallses. The church met in the schoolhouse once it had been built. The Congregational church building was constructed in 1882, and the first worship service was held in the new building on August 30.

An early membership list shows that Mary, at age seventeen, was a charter member along with her parents, but Laura, at age fifteen, was not. The other seven charter members were adults: the pastor and his wife, Charles and Caroline Ingalls, Silliman Gilbert and his wife, and Visscher Barnes, a local attorney and the first clerk of the church. It does seem significant that Mary was the only unmarried individual and must have been the only charter member younger than twenty years old. We learn later in the memoir that Barnes was married, but apparently his wife was not a charter member; it may be that she was unable to attend the organizational meeting and joined later. At any rate, the membership list provides evidence that Laura had not officially joined the church at this point in her life.

Laura kept at least one of the cards from the Sunday school in the Congregational church in De Smet, like she kept cards from Sunday school in Walnut Grove. This card is more ornamental than those. In a circle on the left side of the card is a picture of a church dimly seen across a snowy field framed by trees. Flowers frame the lettering on the card. It reads: "I hereby pledge myself—God helping—to abstain from all Alcoholic beverages, including wine, beer and cider; from Tobacco in every form; and from all profane, questionable, and obscene language."[9] This card was most likely aimed at high school–aged Sunday school students. Church leaders saw alcohol, tobacco, and swearing as contrary to the Christian life and encouraged teens to avoid them.

Another poem that Laura wrote during this period shows her internalization of the major teachings of the church. Titled "Praise Ye the Lord," it provides a window into the foundational beliefs Laura held as a young woman.

> Praise ye the Lord
> For His goodness and mercy!
> Goodness and mercy unto us He has shown.
> His loving eye watches in tenderness over us,
> However far from His path we may roam.
> Praise ye the Lord!
>
> Praise ye the Lord
> That unto the weak He gives strength!
> Strength when sorely oppressed by the strong.
> The oppressed always conquer, for He always aids them,

9. *Laura's Album: A Remembrance Scrapbook of Laura Ingalls Wilder*, comp. William Anderson (New York: HarperCollins, 2017), 24.

'Though their heart may be faint, and the struggle seem long.
Praise ye the Lord!

Praise ye the Lord
That He cares for our troubles!
Troubles that to Him must seem very small.
That He sees, understands them, and pitieth His children,
Like as a Father, who comes at their call,
Praise ye the Lord!

Praise ye the Lord.
That He pardons and forgives us!
Pardons all who repent and turn from the wrong!
Oh! Praise ye the Lord, for His goodness and mercy
Praise Him in heart and praise Him in song.
Praise ye the Lord! [10]

In this poem, Laura declares that she believes that God is good and merciful. He is on the side of the weak and oppressed, and he helps them. His eye is particularly on those who belong to him. Finally, he is a forgiving God, pardoning those who repent. All these truths rightly elicit praise from his people. The poem appears to be patterned after the first two-thirds of Psalm 103, though the order is slightly different. In that psalm, David praises God for his goodness (vv. 1–5), his work for the oppressed (v. 6), his giving of the law (v. 7), his forgiveness (vv. 8–12), and his compassion (vv. 13–14). As a teenager, Laura creatively interacted with biblical themes and made them her own.

While the Congregational church was an important community for the Ingalls family, *Pioneer Girl* provides an unflattering portrait of Rev. Brown and his wife. Brown is portrayed as a greedy, unkempt, and at times rude man who often stopped by their house unexpectedly so that he could eat with the family. During one of these visits, Caroline had made beans with a small piece of meat to flavor them. Brown served himself a large amount of beans and took the entire piece of meat. Brown's

10. Wilder, *A Little House Reader*, 187–88.

wife is described as spending most of her time writing articles for church newspapers. As a result, her house was dirty, and her personal appearance was unkempt. While Laura befriended their adopted daughter Ida Wright, Laura disliked Ida's parents. A column that Laura later wrote for the *Missouri Ruralist* in 1917 gave a more positive interpretation of Mrs. Brown's activities: she had been writing to earn money to buy Ida additional clothes. The point of the column is that at times outside observers do not really understand why people do what they do. There is no such positive turn for Rev. Brown in any of Laura's writings.

Other humorous church-related events are also mentioned in *Pioneer Girl*. Laura often watched the baby of Mr. Barnes, the clerk of the church, so that he and his wife could attend the evening worship service. It appears that the Ingalls family, or at least Laura, did not attend the evening service. Mr. and Mrs. Barnes were more strict practitioners than the Ingalls family. On one occasion, Mr. Barnes surprised his wife by taking a train home on Sunday, after she confidently asserted that he would never travel on the Sabbath. An extended anecdote late in the memoir features a kitten being chased by a dog into the sanctuary during a Sunday morning worship service. The kitten found refuge under Laura's hoop skirt, climbed up the hoops on the inside, and later escaped.

The Congregational church was also the site of the beginning of the most important romance of Laura's life. Previously Alfred Thomas, a young lawyer in De Smet, had expressed interest in courting Laura, and Ernest Perry, the son of a homesteader, had taken her to several parties in the country. A revival meeting at the church was the occasion for Almanzo Wilder to ask to walk her home. She accepted. Almanzo was known throughout the community as one of the young men who had saved the town by bringing back wheat during the Hard Winter. Her parents eventually came to approve of the match. She was sixteen years old.

Bessie and Manly: Work and Courtship

Just as Laura had been paid to work outside of the home in Walnut Grove, she did the same to help support her family in De Smet. In two instances, relationships with those outside the family directly engaged their religious beliefs. During the summer of 1881, she sewed for Martha

White, the mother-in-law of Chauncey Clayson, who owned a dry-goods store. Mrs. White made shirts for the single men of the community. Frequent arguments between White and Clayson made Laura's time at their house unpleasant. Furthermore, the family was prejudiced against Roman Catholics: "For some reason, there was a scare about the Catholics getting control of the government and the awful things they would do to protestants [*sic*]. The daughter would wring her hands and pace the floor declaring that the Catholics should never take her Bible away from her. Then a comet appeard [*sic*] in the sky and both women thought it meant the end of the world and were more frightened than ever. But I couldn't see how I could be afraid of both comet and Catholics at the same time so I worried about neither."[11] The Great Comet of 1881 became visible in the Northern Hemisphere in June. Its appearance was mentioned by local publications, including the *Brookings County Press*.

Laura is perhaps the only writer to connect its appearance with anti-Catholicism, which had a much longer history in the United States. Prejudice against Roman Catholics was common in eastern cities during the early nineteenth century, when large numbers of Irish and German immigrants came to America. At times, it flared into open violence. During the late 1800s, Roman Catholic immigrants particularly came from Italy and eastern Europe. Anti-Catholic sentiment spread to the Midwest along with white settlement; it was common but often less virulent in small towns and rural areas. It seems that the derisive tone with which Laura dismisses anti-Catholicism in her memoir is the voice of her teenage self. The family of one of her friends, Mary Power, were Roman Catholics, and there is no evidence of anti-Catholic sentiment on the part of her parents. These influences likely kept her from the irrational fear of members of other denominations expressed by others at the time, both in De Smet and elsewhere.

During the early spring of 1883, Laura again worked as a seamstress. This time it was for Martha McKee, who was married to James McKee, a dry-goods dealer. The McKee family also had a homestead near Manchester, west of De Smet. In March, April, and May, the McKees paid Laura to live on their homestead and help Martha and their eight-year-old daugh-

11. Wilder, *Pioneer Girl*, 237.

ter, Mary. The Homestead Act required residence on the claim for no less than six months of the year. James McKee came to visit his family during weekends. Laura did not appreciate several of his religious convictions.

> Sunday's were stupid for Mr McKee was a very strict Scotch Pres-
> betrlan [*sic*]. Mary and I were not allowed to play, there must be no reading other than the Bible and we must not laugh aloud.
> He used to lecture me for the good of my soul, trying to persuade me to join the church and at the same time explaining to me his doctrine of foordination [*sic*].
> My reply, varied a little, always was, if that were true, I was already saved, or not saved, so why bother about it and he would shake his head and say "Oh! My! My! That Laura Ingalls!"[12]

Presbyterians held on to rigorous observation of Sabbath restrictions longer than some other American denominations. This passage displays Laura's disdain for what she saw as overstrict Sunday observance; it appears that she was used to a more relaxed mood on Sundays at her home. This passage also indicates that she was not yet a member of any church. Finally, it shows that she rejected the doctrine that God ultimately decides who is saved eternally, known as predestination, God's sovereignty, or foreordination. It was held by Presbyterians and other Protestants in the Reformed tradition, those who follow the teachings of John Calvin. Laura's playful response apparently was both frustrating and endearing to McKee.

Late in 1883, Laura became a schoolteacher for a rural school. A family friend who knew that Laura was a good student introduced Louis Bouchie to the family. Bouchie offered twenty dollars a month for two months to teach five students. She applied to the county superintendent of schools, who administered a teacher examination and gave her a third-class teacher's certificate, even though she was not yet eighteen years old, as required by law. In December and January, she taught in an abandoned claim shanty that had been turned into a one-room schoolhouse about six miles southwest of De Smet.

12. Wilder, *Pioneer Girl*, 284.

The two months of teaching at the Bouchie School were difficult for multiple reasons. First, it was her first teaching position. Second, one of the students was older than she was; he challenged her authority, and she had to learn how to keep order in the school. Third, she stayed in a claim shanty with Louis Bouchie; his wife, Oliv; and their small child. Oliv may have suffered from depression or some other form of mental illness, for she refused to talk to Laura and often sat instead of doing chores. In one chilling account, Oliv menaced her husband with a butcher knife in the middle of the night. She also threatened to take her own life. Laura was saved from spending weekends in this house by Almanzo Wilder, who faithfully appeared on Friday afternoons in his sleigh to take her home for Saturday and Sunday. This weekly respite and the support of her family enabled her to complete the teaching assignment. She was even able to motivate her oldest student to obey, study, and learn. The county school superintendent visited the school and approved of her management. This experience built her courage and self-confidence, and she also received the forty dollars promised in the contract.

During her trials at the Bouchie School, Laura feared that she was not good company for Almanzo and that she was only using him to get home to her family. She chose to be brutally honest and told him that she would not ride with him after the term was done. When he persisted in inviting her for pleasure rides on Sunday afternoons, she decided to continue the relationship. Much of her courtship with Almanzo was conducted in horse-drawn sleighs or buggies on Sunday afternoons. She did not attend the evening worship service, so they often took long rides across the plains, at times traveling more than fifty miles. For a short time, Almanzo included another young woman from his rural neighborhood, Stella Gilbert, on these drives. Laura eventually told him that he would have to choose between Stella and her; Almanzo did not pick up Stella after this ultimatum.[13]

Sometime during 1884, Almanzo bought Laura a thick, hardbound collection of poetry and prose. It was titled *Golden Thoughts on Mother, Home, and Heaven: From Poetic and Prose Literature of All Ages and All Lands*. Most of the selections are by nineteenth-century authors, hymn-

---

13. In *These Happy Golden Years*, Nellie Oleson is the third wheel in these accounts.

writers, or pastors; some are from classical authors and Shakespeare. There are three sections, one on mother, one on the home, and one on heaven. Each section begins with an illustration, a few brief quotes, and a poem by Fanny Crosby, the popular nineteenth-century hymn-writer. The introduction is by Theodore L. Cuyler, a conservative Presbyterian minister in New York City, who explains: "The *Mother* is the fountainhead of the *Home*. The home is the fountainhead of society and of the Church of Christ. And no influences in the universe contribute so much toward guiding immortal souls *Heavenward* as the Home and the Mother."[14] The front and back covers are lavishly decorated. The gift exemplifies Almanzo's resources and generosity and Laura's enjoyment of literature. While it contained more than 450 pages and weighed nearly three pounds, the book traveled with Laura and Almanzo during their many relocations. It is now in the collection of the Laura Ingalls Wilder Historic Home and Museum in Mansfield, Missouri.

Almanzo and Laura's relationship was also built at events held at one of the churches in De Smet. Churches in small towns provided a variety of social events that brought together individuals and families from both the town and the rural areas surrounding it. One was a singing school held on Friday evenings at the Congregational church. Historian John Miller provides this description of the nineteenth-century "singing school": "These 'schools' were organized less for the purpose of learning how to sing than for entertainment and for the financial benefit of the teachers who charged their 'students.' Most of the participants were young couples, and the classes might just as well have been called 'sparking schools.'"[15] Laura called Almanzo "Manly," and he called her "Bessie," to distinguish her from his older sister Laura. On September 4, 1884, Almanzo and Laura attended a ladies' aid ice-cream social at the Methodist church. On the buggy ride home, Almanzo asked her if she would accept an engagement ring from him. She said yes.

Their engagement lasted almost a year. In December, Almanzo decided to return to De Smet from visiting family in Minnesota instead

14. *Golden Thoughts on Mother, Home, and Heaven: From Poetic and Prose Literature of All Ages and All Lands* (New York: E. B. Treat, 1878), 7.

15. John E. Miller, *Becoming Laura Ingalls Wilder: The Woman behind the Legend* (Columbia: University of Missouri Press, 1998), 68.

of traveling to see the World's Fair in New Orleans with family members. During the spring of 1885, Laura was close to finishing high school, but she accepted another teaching position instead. She had previously taught an additional term, during the spring of 1884. In 1885 the school had seven students, and she was paid thirty dollars a month for three months. During her tenure, a prairie fire threatened the schoolhouse, and she and a friend helped to fight it off. *Pioneer Girl* also describes several terrible storms during the year before their marriage. One knocked the half-finished Roman Catholic church building off its foundations. The other spawned tornadoes and their resulting strange stories: individuals were lifted high into the air and landed unhurt, and portions of buildings remained while other parts disappeared.

In early August of 1885, Almanzo asked Laura if they could move up their wedding and have it quietly at the residence of Rev. Brown's family. He did this to preempt the plans of his sister and mother, who wanted him to have a more expensive church wedding. On August 25, at eleven o'clock in the morning, Laura and Almanzo were married at the Browns' home with only the pastor's wife, his daughter Ida, and her fiancé, Elmer McConnell, in attendance. They had arranged with Pastor Brown beforehand that Laura would not have to promise to obey Almanzo in her vows. They then went to the Ingalls family homestead for their wedding dinner, and to their house on Almanzo's homestead north of De Smet.

While Laura was coming of age, her family was celebrating multiple milestones as well. Mary enrolled in the Iowa School for the Blind in Vinton, Iowa. Since the Dakota Territory had no such school, the territorial government paid for Mary's tuition in Iowa; the family had to pay for her clothes, supplies, and transportation to Vinton and back. Charles Ingalls also added to the original claim shanty a second and then a third room, one of which was a sitting room. Finally, Charles proved up on his homestead, sending in the necessary paperwork and receiving title from the US government in 1886, the year after Laura and Almanzo were married.

Faith and the Little Town on the Prairie

Between 1879 and 1885, Laura Ingalls entered adolescence, courtship, and marriage as the town of De Smet was established and grew. Her family was one of the first that settled there, and they helped make the town what it became. Her father helped construct many buildings in the town, and the family provided support for local businesses, the Congregational church, and other community institutions. At the time Laura and Almanzo married, De Smet had somewhere between the 116 people counted in the 1880 census and the 541 in the census of 1890. The town had a roller-skating rink and, by 1886, an opera house. De Smet was as successful as many other towns founded on railroad lines in the upper Midwest during the late nineteenth century.

During her adolescent years, Laura also became as successful as many other young women in her station of life at that time. She had developed into a confident and self-assured young woman. She had completed most of the academic work necessary for a high school diploma from a late nineteenth-century, Midwestern, small-town school. She had successfully taught three terms at rural, one-room schools. With her help, her family had gained title to their homestead claim. For much of her childhood she had been able to enjoy the wide-open Midwestern landscape. While she enjoyed town life, she had a deeper love for the outdoors; Laura's most lyrical descriptions in *Pioneer Girl* describe experiences in nature. Finally, she had married one of the most eligible bachelors in De Smet. Almanzo had built her a small house with many of the comforts of home on his homestead north of town.

During these years, Laura's Christianity was nurtured by her family and by the Congregational church in De Smet. Poems she wrote provide the most explicit descriptions of her beliefs: God exists, he is good, he provides for the weak, he cares for his people, he pardons their sins, and he enables them to do impossible things. Therefore, the proper response for all humans, and particularly for those who know him, is worship and praise. It appears that she rejected the formal doctrine of God's sovereignty or predestination.

In terms of belonging, Laura's parents and sister Mary had become members of the Congregational church, but it appears that Laura had not. As she was now eighteen years old, it appears that not becoming a member of the church was a deliberate choice. Perhaps her—and her family's—ambivalent relationship with Rev. Brown was involved in that decision. She remained a regular attender, and perhaps she had internalized some identity as a Congregationalist. At least her identity involved being a Christian and a Protestant. Her Protestantism did not appear to lead to significant anti-Catholic prejudice. School had connected her with students whose families attended other churches. It is likely that she found community with those in the church she attended.

Laura's patterns of behavior included attendance at Sunday school and Sunday morning worship services; she did not attend the evening worship service. She participated in church activities, including fund-raisers and fellowship events sponsored by the women of the church. Perhaps one can assume that her practices of reading the Bible and of praying before going to bed, mentioned earlier in *Pioneer Girl*, also continued. She also interacted with biblical texts and the beliefs that flowed from them in poetry; this most likely worked to confirm them in her heart as well as in her mind. In De Smet during the late nineteenth century, for families like the Ingallses, family, church, and school cooperated to form young adults with Protestant, Christian character.

These influences and what we know of Laura's responses to them suggest that Laura's faith was genuine. Christianity appears to have been as important to her life as it had been when she was an early teen, although she did not attend as many religious services as she had in Walnut Grove. It also does not appear that other members of her family attended Sunday evening or midweek services. While the Ingalls family had faced many financial uncertainties, Laura may have seen God as being faithful to provide everything that they really needed. The new Wilder family soon faced challenges that were novel for both Laura and Almanzo, as events during their early marriage tested their faith and character in new and different ways.

4

Trials

Dakota, Minnesota, Florida, 1885–1894

L aura Ingalls was eighteen years old when she married Almanzo Wilder in 1885. He was in his late twenties, either twenty-six or twenty-eight, depending on the documents one believes most reliable. They began life together as husband and wife just as the climate of eastern Dakota Territory became dryer and more variable than it had been during the previous half decade. Fortunately for the new couple, Almanzo had lived on his homestead for the required five years, so all he had to do was complete the final government paperwork to gain title to the land. He was also attempting to prove up on a tree claim; the government offered homesteaders an additional 160 acres if they maintained at least 10 acres of trees for five years. Unfortunately for the newlyweds, the Wilders had to tend the young trees while the weather became more arid and more unpredictable.

"The First Three Years and a Year of Grace"

Sometime during the 1930s, while the Little House books were being written and published, Laura wrote a draft of a short novel for adults. She titled it *The First Three Years and a Year of Grace*. It describes events from the first four years of their marriage. While Laura mentioned the idea of writing an adult novel to her daughter Rose, she never showed Rose the manuscript and never sought to get it published. Rose looked at the manuscript after Laura's death but also decided not to pursue publication.

Eventually, it was published as *The First Four Years* in 1971, after Rose's death in 1968. Few changes were made to the handwritten manuscript.

The content of this volume is more like *Pioneer Girl* than the Little House books. Almanzo is called Manly, the name that Laura actually used for her husband. The tone is also wry or world-weary, not earnest. Perhaps most striking, at the beginning of the book, Laura tells Manly that she doesn't want to marry a farmer, and they agree that they will try farming for three years and continue only if they are successful. Why is this work so different from the Little House books in both tone and content? One reason is that Laura did not collaborate with Rose on this volume. It also appears that Laura envisioned a different audience for the book. One cannot assume that everything in *The First Four Years* happened exactly as described, but the manuscript does provide the overall contours of the early years of the Wilders' marriage.

Those years began happily. There were many things for the newlyweds to enjoy together. First and foremost, there was their first house, built by Almanzo on their homestead. It was a beautiful house, carefully constructed to serve the needs of his future wife. There were three rooms, like the Ingalls family's home on their homestead. It featured a pantry with conveniently located shelves and cupboards. A window in the kitchen enabled Laura to look out at the prairie landscape. Laura and Manly also continued leisure activities that they had enjoyed when they were courting, especially buggy rides on Sunday afternoons during the summer and sleigh rides during the winter. They both owned saddle ponies, and Almanzo taught Laura to ride sidesaddle. They worked together to raise oats, wheat, and hay.

The Wilders almost immediately faced agricultural challenges that led to financial reverses. Their first wheat harvest was small because the weather had been dry; low prices compounded the monetary shortfall. A subsequent wheat crop was beaten into the ground by hail during the summer; another was destroyed by a hot wind right before harvest. Still another was scattered by a dust storm shortly after planting. At one point, their haystacks and barn burned to the ground. The trees on their tree claim died from summer heat and lack of moisture. The couple went deeply into debt for farm equipment, horses, and furnishings for the house. Laura also discovered that Almanzo still owed five hundred dollars from the building of their home. Each year, they counted on the income from the following year's wheat crop to right their economic position. One crop after another failed. The Wilders renegotiated their loans several times, then mortgaged their homestead and moved to a smaller house on the tree claim. They eventually had to sell the homestead and its beautiful house.

Other life challenges compounded their financial woes. Laura became pregnant about halfway through the first year of their marriage, and she suffered from morning sickness during the first few months. A daughter was born in early December 1886. They named her Rose after the prairie roses that graced the plains in the summer. She grew to be a vigorous girl, ready for all kinds of mischief and loved by her parents and extended family. In February of 1888, both Laura and Almanzo contracted diphtheria, and Rose was sent to live with her grandparents in De Smet. In March, Almanzo had still not recovered fully, and he disregarded the doctor's warnings against doing too much work. He woke up one morning and could not walk; his legs were completely numb. Laura went to town for the doctor. While the exact medical diagnosis is not completely clear, it appears that he had had a stroke. Almanzo walked with a limp for the rest of his life, and he was substantially weaker after this illness.

Two additional catastrophes confronted the young family during the summer of 1889. On July 11, Laura gave birth to a ten-pound baby boy. Something was wrong, however, and he died on August 7. He was never named. He was buried in the De Smet cemetery; the gravestone reads "Baby Son of A. J. Wilder." For the rest of their lives, Laura and Almanzo avoided talking about him publicly. Two weeks later, on August 23, their house on the tree claim burned to the ground when Almanzo was gone from home. *The First Four Years* reports the episode: "Burying her face on her knees she screamed and sobbed, saying over and over, 'Oh, what will Manly say to me?' And there Manly found her and Rose, just as the house roof was falling in. . . . The silver wedding knives and forks and spoons rolled up in their wrappers had survived. Nothing else had been saved from the fire except the deed-box, a few work clothes, three sauce dishes from the first Christmas dishes, and the oval glass bread plate around the margin of which were the words, 'Give us this day our daily bread.'"[1] After the conflagration, the Wilders stayed with Laura's family briefly, then lived with a nearby homesteader. Soon Almanzo and Laura's cousin Peter

1. Laura Ingalls Wilder, *The First Four Years*, in *The Little House Books*, ed. Caroline Fraser (New York: Library of America, 2012), 2:794.

Ingalls had finished a new tarpaper shanty on the tree claim. By November they had decided to move to southeastern Minnesota to be near Almanzo's parents. They began to make plans for leaving De Smet in the spring.

"Give us this day our daily bread" is one of the petitions of the Lord's Prayer, given in Matthew 6:11 and Luke 11:3. It is one of the very few references to Christianity in *The First Four Years*. Sunday buggy rides and sleigh rides are mentioned in the initial chapter, but Sunday is not mentioned again in the book. The final "Year of Grace" could contain a reference to God's grace, although the more direct meaning of the term in the narrative is an additional year on the farm granted by Laura to Manly. There are no other discussions of faith, the church, or any type of religious practice anywhere in the book, even though Laura and Almanzo experienced some of the most devastating developments of their lives: crop failures, debilitating disease, the death of their only son, and the loss of almost all their possessions. In many ways, their response to these developments appears stoic, not particularly Christian. Like many in the region during the period, they accepted their reversals of fortune and looked for ways to support their family. The manuscript has no questions about the justice of God's acts, no statements of trust in God's provision, and no resolutions to go forward in reliance on his strength. We might assume that she and Almanzo continued to attend the Congregational church in De Smet with the rest of Laura's family. The lack of any mention of faith in relation to these events indicates that Christianity had become less of a vital influence on Laura's life during the early years of her marriage.

Spring Valley and Westville

One farming endeavor had been successful for the Wilders during their years on the homestead: a herd of sheep they owned in conjunction with Laura's cousin Peter, who homesteaded nearby. In the spring of 1890, Almanzo sold the herd for five hundred dollars, which helped the family to settle accounts. Instead of proving up on the tree claim, they purchased the land from the federal government by preemption. They had already decided to leave the area where they had confronted so much sorrow. Accompanied by Peter, they headed for Spring Valley, Minnesota, on May 30. This began a search for a permanent home that mirrored her parents' travels.

When Laura, Almanzo, and Rose moved there, Spring Valley was a town of nearly 1,400 inhabitants, about two and a half times bigger than De Smet. In western Fillmore County, bordering Iowa on the south, the town is only about forty miles northwest of Burr Oak, Iowa, where the Ingalls family had lived fifteen years earlier. By 1890, Spring Valley was served by two railroad lines, which made it a hub for supplying goods and services to farmers in the area. Having moved to Minnesota during the 1870s, Almanzo's family were well established by the early 1890s. His parents, James and Angeline Wilder, lived in a spacious two story, L-shaped house on the northern edge of town. Laura, Almanzo, and Rose had their own bedroom and sitting room on the second floor.

The elder Wilders were members of the Methodist church in Spring Valley, which worshiped in a large brick edifice built in 1878. James Wilder had contributed fifty dollars to its construction. More than two thousand dollars had been raised, and the congregation had purchased twenty-one stained-glass windows imported from Italy. The Wilders attended Sunday worship services there while in Spring Valley. The building still stands and serves as the Spring Valley Methodist Church Museum: A Laura Ingalls Wilder Site. Visitors can view the stained-glass windows and a variety of historical artifacts from the area.

While living with Almanzo's parents, and after pondering what to do next, the couple decided to try a warmer climate to see if it improved Almanzo's condition. They apparently briefly considered moving to New Zealand, perhaps because of their success with sheep raising. However, during the fall of 1890, Peter Ingalls headed south in response to promotional materials about land available in the Florida panhandle. Railroads were built into the region during the late nineteenth century, and both railroad companies and local businesses advertised for farmers and others to build the population in the area along the Choctawhatchee River. Land could be obtained under the provisions of the Homestead Act. Peter claimed a homestead north of Westville, Florida, in Holmes County, several miles south of the Alabama border and about seventy-five miles north of Panama City on the Gulf of Mexico. He also married a local woman, Mary or Molly McGowan. Peter wrote letters to Laura that described the warm weather and encouraged her and Almanzo to come try farming there.

In spring of 1891, the Wilders held an auction in Spring Valley to sell a variety of Laura and Almanzo's possessions, including a number of horses they had raised. In late summer, they sold the tree claim outside of De Smet, which was the last piece of land that they owned. On October 5, they headed southeast by train to the "piney woods" of Florida. They traveled more than one thousand miles to join Peter and his new family.

The Wilder family's experiences in Florida have been pieced together from statements made by Laura later in life, research in public records, and oral history evidence from descendants of Peter Ingalls. Rose also wrote a short story titled "Innocence" about a family—a mother and father and their only daughter—who had moved to the piney woods. The story was published in *Harper's Magazine* and received an O. Henry Prize in 1922. Its descriptions are exaggerated, and it repeats many stereotypes about both southern whites and African Americans, but it does provide a feeling for the culture shock the Wilders must have felt when they moved to the rural South. Even the landscape and the southern flora and fauna were strange to those who had known only the open prairies of the upper Midwest. It is unclear whether Laura and Almanzo lived with Peter and his family or whether they had their own house. The Wilders never filed for a homestead or purchased any land in the area.

Peter Ingalls and his family worshiped at the Mount Ida Congregational Methodist Church, in Mount Ida, a rural neighborhood, north of Westville, where they lived. Peter, his wife, Mary, and his son Alexander are buried in the cemetery behind that church. It is striking, although it seems completely coincidental, that the church in Florida was Congregational Methodist, given the Wilders' association with Congregational churches in the upper Midwest and their later attendance at the Methodist church in Missouri.

The origins of the Congregational Methodist Church were in Methodism, not in Congregationalism. Methodism, founded by John and Charles Wesley during the early 1700s, was brought to America later that century and spread widely, especially in the South, during the early 1800s. Methodist churches were planted by missionaries who served multiple congregations, and pastors were assigned to congregations by the conference, or regional church leadership body. The Congregational Methodist Church was founded in 1852 by Methodists in Georgia who wanted their congregations to be able to call their own pastors, as was the case for the Presbyterian and Baptist churches around them, rather than having to accept pastors sent by the Methodist hierarchy. By the late 1800s, there were Congregational Methodist churches throughout the South. The Mount Ida church was in existence by the fall of 1891, and local sources show that Peter Ingalls and his family were members, but there is no mention of the Wilders. It is not certain that Laura, Almanzo, and Rose attended worship services at this church, at another church, or at any church while they were living in the neighborhood.

The main reason behind the Wilders' move to the South was their hope that the warmer weather would improve Almanzo's health. Unfortunately, the hot and humid weather of Florida was difficult for Laura to tolerate. At one point, she attempted to help Peter plant corn while holding a black umbrella to protect herself from the sun. He convinced her to go inside and let him finish the planting. It also appears that opportunities for successful agriculture did not materialize for Almanzo and Laura. The Wilder family returned to De Smet in August 1892, ten months after having moved to Florida. Peter Ingalls and his family remained, and many of his descendants still live in the area.

Unlike some of the interludes between major destinations when Laura was growing up, we do not know of significant life developments during the Wilders' stays in Spring Valley and Westville. One can imagine that Laura and Almanzo had to work together to navigate relationships with in-laws in the first location and differences in regional culture in the second. Their marriage was also tested by their lack of economic success and the challenges of raising a young child in unfamiliar surroundings. It is likely that the Wilders attended worship services in both locations, and perhaps those church communities provided support to the young couple. As they searched for a place and a way to make an independent living, they decided to return to De Smet.

Last Years on the Prairie

The Ingalls family had experienced many changes during the seven years since Laura and Almanzo were married in 1885. Charles Ingalls had established ownership of his homestead southeast of town. However, he then built a more substantial house on Third Street in De Smet, and he, Caroline, and their three daughters moved into it in 1887. They did not live again on the homestead, and they ultimately sold it in 1892. Charles had opened a store in town named Ingalls & Co. He also served as justice of the peace and continued to work as a carpenter and at other jobs. Mary finished her schooling at the Iowa College for the Blind in 1889 and again lived with her parents, helping her mother keep house and making hammocks and beaded items. Carrie began an apprenticeship at the local newspaper, the *De Smet Leader*, after finishing high school. She continued to work there during her early twenties. Grace was a fifteen-year-old high school student in 1892.

Laura and Almanzo purchased a small house about a block away from Laura's parents in which the family lived, with a cookstove, a kitchen table and chairs, and their beds. North and South Dakota had become states in 1889. The weather in eastern South Dakota remained dry, and prices for agricultural products continued to be low, so there was not widespread opportunity for farmers. Almanzo took whatever work he could find in town, including painting and carpentry. Laura sewed for a local dressmaker from six in the morning to six at night, six days a week. She received a dollar a day. When Rose wasn't in school, she stayed with her grandmother and her aunt Mary. On Sundays when Laura, Almanzo, and Rose visited the Ingalls family, Mary played hymns on the organ. The Ingalls family had a more prosperous life compared to the Wilders, but, like many small town residents during the period, their position was at times precarious.

Understanding Laura's life and writing requires some understanding of Rose and her relationship with her parents. Later in her life, Rose wrote about many events from her childhood. She revealed that she always believed that she had started the fire that destroyed their house on the tree claim. In fact, she was not even three years old, and Laura and Almanzo never blamed her for it; somehow Rose decided that it was her fault. It is also clear that Rose was headstrong and precocious. She had her photograph taken in Spring Valley at age four or five, and later described the event in this way: "I remember the picture-taking well, was impressed by the photographer's stupid pretense that there was a little bird in the camera. The photographer also kept putting my right hand on top of the left, and I kept changing them back because I wanted my carnelian ring to show. And in the end I won out."[2] Rose also claimed that at age seven she had read both *Robinson Crusoe* and *Gulliver's Travels*, and that she regularly read the weekly

---

2. Rose Wilder Lane, "I [One]," in Laura Ingalls Wilder, *On the Way Home: The Diary of a Trip from South Dakota to Mansfield, Missouri, in 1894*, with a setting by Rose Wilder Lane (New York: Harper & Row, 1962), 3.

Chicago Inter-Ocean, a compilation of news from the daily *Inter-Ocean* that was sent to rural and small-town residents across the Midwest.

In another remembrance in later life, Rose recalled this anecdote from when she was five years old and spent time with her grandmother, Caroline Ingalls, and aunt Mary:

I said dreamily, "I wish I had been there when Christ was crucified." My sincerely, deeply pious grandmother was (I now realize) deeply touched by this tender, young piety; I can recall the tone of her voice saying softly "Why dear?" I replied "So I could have cursed him and been the Wandering Jew."

I'm sure I recall the incident because of the inexplicable effect, upon my grandmother, of these candidly innocent words. It was like an earthquake, a silent one. She said nothing. Somehow the air sort of crashed, terrifically.[3]

The Wandering Jew was a legend that was retold in multiple forms in both eastern and western Europe. The idea was that a Jew had cursed Christ during the crucifixion and been condemned to remain alive and wander the earth until Christ's second coming. The character was included in works by American authors during the nineteenth century, including Nathaniel Hawthorne and Mark Twain. Rose's desire certainly shocked Caroline Ingalls, and it is difficult to imagine a five-year-old saying it. While these accounts were her adult memories of her childhood, they do provide a view of an oppositional nature that apparently manifested at an early age.

During their time in De Smet, Laura, Almanzo, and Rose attended church with Laura's family at the Congregational church. The building was only a few blocks from both the Ingalls family's home and the house where the Wilders were living. There is no evidence that either Almanzo or Laura officially became members of the church. Laura did become a member of the Order of the Eastern Star (OES), an organization in support of the Lodge or Freemasons. Women are not allowed to become Masons, but they can join the Eastern Star if a close relative is either a Mason

---

3. Rose Wilder Lane, "Memories of Grandma's House," in Laura Ingalls Wilder and Rose Wilder Lane, *A Little House Sampler: A Collection of Early Stories and Reminiscences*, ed. William Anderson (Lincoln: University of Nebraska Press, 1988), 57–58.

or a member of the Eastern Star. Many residents of small towns joined a lodge during the late nineteenth century. De Smet Masonic Lodge #55 was organized in 1883, and Charles Ingalls became a member three years later. The Bethlehem #13 Chapter of the OES in De Smet was formed in 1891; Caroline and Carrie Ingalls were charter members. Laura was initiated into the Eastern Star at the end of 1893, but Almanzo did not join a lodge until after their next move. Laura demitted her membership in July of 1894 because she and Almanzo had decided to relocate once more. This time, their destination was southwestern Missouri.

Laura wrote later in life, "When we came to Missouri in 1894, we were looking for a place where the family health might make a good average, for one of us was not able to stand the severe cold of the North, while another could not live in the low altitude and humid heat of the Southern states."[4] Railroads and businesses were advertising agricultural opportunities in the Ozark Mountains, "The Land of Big Red Apples." Mansfield, Missouri, in Wright County, billed itself as the "Gem City of the Ozarks." One of the Ingalls and Wilder families' neighbors, Frank Cooley, had taken a tour of the Ozarks paid for by a railroad company; he returned with enthusiastic descriptions of the area. The Wilders decided to pack up their possessions and travel with Frank, his wife, Emma, and their two sons, Paul and George, to Mansfield.

Rose wrote a story about her family's journey to Missouri that was found among her papers and later published by William Anderson in *A Little House Sampler*. It includes an evocative description of the family's last night in De Smet. Laura, Rose, and Almanzo bathed, dressed in their Sunday clothes, and walked to the Ingallses' house for their last meal with Charles, Caroline, Mary, Carrie, and Grace. After dinner they all sat on the porch and Charles played his fiddle until after it was dark. Rose only mentions the titles of two songs, but one must imagine that Charles played some hymns that evening. On Tuesday, July 17, 1894, the Wilders and Cooleys left De Smet, heading south.[5]

4. Laura Ingalls Wilder, "What Makes My County Great and Why I'm Proud to Be a Citizen," *Missouri Ruralist*, December 1, 1923, in *Laura Ingalls Wilder, Farm Journalist: Writings from the Ozarks*, ed. Stephen W. Hines (Columbia: University of Missouri Press, 2007), 293.

5. Rose Wilder Lane, "Grandpa's Fiddle," in Wilder and Lane, *A Little House Sampler*, 67–70.

Trying Times

During the first nine years of their marriage, the Wilders confronted life-altering challenges. Their dream of owning and farming their own land near her family was destroyed by debt, disease, and bad weather. They watched their son die before he was a month old. Laura also saw her husband changed into a weaker man who walked with a limp. They traveled hundreds of miles and lived in three different states, searching for economic opportunity. Their situation was shared by many during the late 1800s, especially in the wake of the Panic of 1893. The Panic was felt keenly in the agricultural Midwest. In response to their trials, Laura and Almanzo turned to their extended families.

The Wilders attended a Congregational church in South Dakota, a Methodist church in Minnesota, and likely attended a Congregational Methodist church in Florida. It appears that neither Laura nor Almanzo was a member of the church in any of these locations, while Laura did officially join the Eastern Star in 1893. Evidence that she read the Bible often and said daily prayers before going to bed is given in sources addressing her childhood. Perhaps we can assume that these practices continued. Otherwise, we know little about Laura's beliefs, religious identity, or patterns of Christian behavior during this period. There are no sources about whether her beliefs or practices changed in response to the immense challenges that she and her husband faced.

Like her parents, like many in the Midwest during the late nineteenth century, and like many families across American history, Laura and Almanzo were willing to launch out into the unknown to better their lives. They participated in the local community and its institutions in each location where they lived, but they were also willing to cut ties with a particular place to seek greater opportunity elsewhere. It had taken several significant moves before the Wilders were able to get established in one location for the long term. The community where they ultimately became settled was Mansfield, Missouri.

5

New Beginnings

Missouri, 1894-1911

The three Wilders and the four Cooleys left De Smet on July 17, 1894, arriving in Mansfield, Missouri, six weeks and two days later. Laura kept a diary of the journey, writing daily in one of two small memorandum books. Laura was not normally a diarist, but several times as an adult she maintained one while she was traveling. It is likely that she wanted to remember what she had seen and thought about while she was in unfamiliar surroundings. She saved the diary, and Rose found it among her papers after Laura died in 1957. Rose edited it and had it published, along with a "setting" she wrote herself: a prologue and epilogue that describe what she remembered of the time before and after the trip. The slim volume of one hundred pages appeared in 1962 as *On the Way Home: The Diary of a Trip from South Dakota to Mansfield, Missouri, in 1894.*

Life on the Road

Like the Wilders, many other Midwestern families were launching out into the unknown during this period. The Panic of 1893 unsettled the economic conditions of communities across the country. Dry and unpredictable weather in the plains and prairie states had also forced many farmers to seek opportunity in new locations. As a result, Almanzo and Laura met numerous travelers during their journey from De Smet to Mansfield. Groups stopped to exchange information. Like the Cooleys and Wilders, some families were leaving North or South Dakota for Nebraska, Kansas, or Missouri. Others traveled the opposite direction.

The Wilders had one covered wagon that contained all their possessions. Almanzo had also packed dozens of asbestos fire mats that he could trade for food and other supplies on the way. When placed on a stove or fire, one of these mats prevented a pot or pan from scorching. The money they had earned to buy a farm in Missouri was hidden in a lap desk that Almanzo had made for Laura. She also carried a revolver in case protection of their lives or property was necessary. Frank and Emma Cooley had their assets in two wagons, one driven by Frank and one normally driven by their nine-year-old son, Paul. Emma drove this wagon when they were in more populated areas. During the trip, Rose became very good friends with Paul and his younger brother, George, who was eight. Sometimes she rode between them on the seat of the wagon Paul was driving; she was seven years old.

Laura's diary is the earliest significant amount of her writing that is available. It provides many early examples of Laura's ability to make a scene come alive in the reader's mind. Unfortunately, in *On the Way Home*, Rose added words, changed constructions, and at times altered the meaning of what was written in the original diary. While the published book has the feel of the Little House books, the original diary sounds more like a twenty-seven-year-old woman reflecting at the end of a day on the road. Some descriptions are spare and simple; she noted local price levels, whether crops looked good or bad in the area, and the temperature in the wagon (until they lost the thermometer). Some descriptions of landscape and nature are more elaborated, detailed, and poignant. Riding along the Nebraska side of the Missouri River prompted this reflection: "What is it about a large body of water that always affects a person? I never see a river or lake but I think how I would like to see a world made & watch it through all its changes."[1] A week later, she reflected after she and Almanzo had waded in the Platte River: "The water was lovely, warm & clear. The sand was warm & soft but shifting & would run away right under my feet

1. Laura Ingalls Wilder, Diary, July 24, 1894, folder 33 (unpaginated), Wilder, Laura Ingalls Papers, Microfilm Collection, State Historical Society of Missouri, Columbia, Missouri; and *On the Way Home: The Diary of a Trip from South Dakota to Mansfield, Missouri, in 1894*, with a setting by Rose Wilder Lane (New York: Harper & Row, 1962), 28.

& if I stood still it would drift over my feet. I stood still until one foot was covered just for fun."[2] Laura's writing exhibits a keen eye for detail and the ability to compose clear and evocative descriptions.

The Wilders and the Cooleys did not travel on Sundays. They set up camp on Saturday night and did not leave until Monday morning. They rested, visited with local people or other emigrants, or repaired equipment. This contrasted with many other emigrants they encountered who were on the road on Sundays. For instance, on August 5 they camped between Lincoln and Beatrice, Nebraska, and Laura recorded that five emigrant wagons had passed by. The next Sunday they had entered Kansas and camped west of St. Mary's, and they encountered nine wagons. The following Sunday, the Wilders and Cooleys were close to the Missouri border. The men worked on the Cooleys' stove while the women and children went to a nearby creek. August 26 was their last Sunday on the road. They had entered the Ozarks and camped just outside the small town of Everton. Laura noted that she had spent the day reading, writing, and sleeping.

While the Wilders and Cooleys observed Sunday as a day of rest, there is no record that they attended worship services on any of these Sundays. There were churches they could have attended along the way. For instance, the last Sunday they were traveling, they stayed near Everton, Missouri, where there was a Cumberland Presbyterian church. There were multiple churches in Lockwood and Greenfield, which they had traveled through on Saturday. Greenfield had Methodist, Presbyterian, and Baptist churches. There were also country churches: Laura mentions camping next to one southeast of Topeka, Kansas, on August 14. Perhaps they were unwilling to walk into a strange church in a small town, or maybe the Wilders did not worship at one of these churches because they were not Congregational. It appears that while the Wilders saw Sunday as a day of rest, they did not prioritize worship when they were not at home and familiar with the congregation.

As they entered the Ozarks, Laura's descriptions became more and more positive. On Saturday, August 25, after driving almost all the way across Dade County, Missouri, she wrote: "Well, we are in the Ozarks at last, just at the beginning of them & they are beautiful. We passed along

2. Wilder, Diary, July 31, 1894, folder 33 (unpaginated); *On the Way Home*, 37.

the foot of some hills & could look up the sides. . . . The trees & rocks are lovely. Manly says we could almost live on the looks of them."[3] On Thursday of that week, she noted: "The farther we go east, the better we like it. Parts of Nebraska & Kansas are nice, but Mo. is simply glorious. There Manly has interrupted me to say, 'it is a beautiful country.'"[4] They reached Mansfield the following day at a little before noon, and other emigrant wagons had arrived at about the same time. Their six-hundred-mile journey was finished. Laura had written in the diary each and every day, but her record keeping ended with the completion of their travels.

The Wilders camped outside of town and immediately began to look for a farm that was suitable. Rose's epilogue in *On the Way Home* describes their camp as a "Sunday camp": "After the long boredom of so many dull days that we hardly remembered De Smet, now every day was Sunday without Sunday's clean clothes and staid behavior. The camp was a Sunday camp; the Cooley's [*sic*] wagons on one side, ours on the other; in the grove between them the table and chairs were set and the hammock hung in the shade."[5] This selection gives some idea of how Rose remembered Sundays had been observed during the trip. The camp was set up more deliberately, the children were required to wear Sunday clothes, and there were restrictions on what could be done. Still, several Sundays in Laura's journal describe wading in nearby creeks, so there was some leisure in addition to rest.

Rose's epilogue also describes what happened the day that Almanzo and Laura found the farm they wanted to buy. They returned to camp and dressed in their best clothes to go to the bank and sign the mortgage documents. Then the unthinkable happened: they discovered that the money that was kept in the lap desk was gone. Rose mentions just a single one-hundred-dollar bill that was lost, but there might have been more. Laura and Almanzo searched without success, then they asked Rose if she had touched the money or told anyone else about it. Rose denied doing either. Years later she recalled how angry, insulted, miserable, and afraid she felt. The money was not found for several weeks, and no details are recorded

3. Wilder, Diary, August 5, 1894, folder 33 (unpaginated); *On the Way Home*, 65.
4. Wilder, Diary, August 29, 1894, folder 33 (unpaginated); *On the Way Home*, 68.
5. Rose Wilder Lane, "III," in Wilder, *On the Way Home*, 75.

about how exactly it was recovered. On September 21, 1894, three weeks after arriving in Mansfield, Laura and Almanzo obtained a mortgage to purchase the forty-acre farm southeast of town and took possession. Laura named the farm Rocky Ridge.

Rocky Ridge and Mansfield

In the 1890s, Mansfield, Missouri, was a small country town. During the centuries before Europeans arrived, the Ozarks had been home to a variety of Native groups, including the Osage, Delaware, and Shawnee. Both Hartville, the county seat of Wright County, and Mountain Grove, the largest town in the county, had been founded before the Civil War. During the war, Missouri was devastated by regular armies and irregular forces on both sides of the conflict. Wright County was not spared; a significant battle was fought at Hartville. Physical, emotional, and economic wounds healed during the following decades. The Kansas City, Fort Scott, and Memphis Railroad built tracks through southern Missouri in 1881. The company founded the town of Mansfield the next year. Mansfield, like De Smet, was created by the railroad and existed as a regional center where farmers, woodcutters, and other producers could market their goods and buy supplies. At the center of town was the railroad station and the Bank of Mansfield. The population of Mansfield was between three hundred and four hundred when the Wilders arrived.

Rocky Ridge was about a mile southeast of the town square. When the Wilders signed the mortgage, it took a significant amount of imagination to see the farm as a promising venture. The house was a log cabin with no windows. Only four acres of land were cleared, and these had been planted with two hundred apple trees. The previous owner had purchased an additional eight hundred apple trees that waited for more land to be prepared. Almanzo and Laura immediately began to cut down trees using a two-person crosscut saw; they sold the wood in town for firewood. Laura raised chickens and sold eggs as well. Income from these sales paid for food and materials to expand farm operations. They planted small corn crops and tended a garden. The remaining apple trees were planted. Within the first few years, Almanzo had bought a pig and a cow, and the family had built a more snug, two-room house with windows and a loft for

Rose to sleep in. The original log house became a stable. Laura managed the family finances, and the family lived frugally.

Rose attended school in Mansfield. Classes met in a brick building with four classrooms. Because of the distance involved, Almanzo bought a donkey for Rose to ride to school. They named the donkey Spookendyke. At times it refused to move while Rose was mounted, and she had to walk along with it the entire way. Rose was gifted academically, and she read all the available books at the schoolhouse quickly. In small towns, educational communities are often where young people learn about social and economic distinctions in the local population; the school in Mansfield was no exception. Children from wealthier families who lived in town had better clothes and did not have to walk a donkey to school. There were other children from the country who attended school in Mansfield, but Rose does not seem to have identified with them. Her mental acuity and her lack of connections to other children can be seen in her creation of an entire language that she spoke to Spookendyke. In later recollections, Rose described feeling her family's poverty deeply. On the other hand, she also remembered comfort and security at home even while confronting discomfort and social insecurity at school.

In early 1898, the Wilders moved to a rented house on the east side of Mansfield. This made it possible for them to access additional sources of income. Frank Cooley had died of pneumonia in December 1897, and Almanzo purchased his team and wagon and took over Frank's delivery service, picking up products from the railroad station and taking them to stores or homes. This led to a job with Waters Price Oil Company; Almanzo delivered oil, kerosene, and linseed oil to farms in the area. This work allowed him to sit down for much of the day. On occasion they sublet a room in the house to either N. J. Craig, cashier at the Bank of Mansfield and later founder of the Farmers and Merchants Bank, or John Quigley, who supervised local railroad construction. The Wilders rented out the farmhouse at Rocky Ridge and continued to develop the farm's potential as they had opportunity.

In the summer of 1898, Almanzo's parents visited Mansfield. After James Wilder had sold the farm in Spring Valley, Minnesota, he and his wife were traveling to Crowley, Louisiana, to live near their daughter Eliza Jane. She had married a widower who owned a rice plantation. At the end of their visit in Mansfield, Wilder gave Almanzo and Laura enough money to buy the house in town where they were living. The purchase enabled them to devote more of their income to the improvement of the farm. Living in town also provided the Wilders with additional opportunities to participate in community life, including the life of the church.

The preeminent Christian denominations in the Ozarks were the Baptist, Christian (Church of Christ or Disciples of Christ), Methodist, and Presbyterian churches. Congregationalism had not penetrated rural southwestern Missouri, although there were some Congregational churches in Springfield. The religious landscape of Mansfield is outlined in Mansfield's local weekly newspapers during the late nineteenth and early twentieth centuries: the *Mansfield Mail* from 1895 to 1906, the *Mansfield Press* from 1908 to 1911, and the *Mansfield Mirror* after 1912. Each paper listed the churches and their worship times. In 1895, three churches met in Mansfield: Christian, Cumberland Presbyterian, and Methodist Episcopal. By the turn of the century, the Christian church was no longer listed and apparently had stopped meeting. The Cumberland Presbyterian church had been founded in Mansfield during the early 1880s, and its church building was completed in 1883. The Methodists began meeting twelve years later.

Mansfield's Methodist Episcopal church was founded in February 1895, less than six months after the Wilders purchased Rocky Ridge. It was the result of a series of revival services held in the Presbyterian church building led by a Rev. Worthen, in cooperation with Rev. E. G. Cattermol. Cattermol was the pastor of the Methodist Episcopal churches in Seymour, about twelve miles west of Mansfield, and Rogersville, about eighteen miles west of Seymour. The next year, the Methodist conference appointed a pastor to serve Seymour and Mansfield. The Mansfield congregation had twenty-six charter members. It is likely that they worshiped in the Presbyterian church building until their building was completed in 1899. The church was part of the Methodist Episcopal Church (MEC), not the Methodist Episcopal Church, South (MECS), which had split from the MEC in the 1840s because of disagreements about slavery. Most churches in Missouri had left the MEC to join the MECS at that time. By the last years of the nineteenth century, after the Civil War had settled the question of slavery and sectional tensions had decreased across the nation and in Missouri, there was less animosity between the members and leaders of the two denominations. There were also congregations of a separate Methodist denomination in the state, the Methodist Protestant Church (MPC).

At some point after it was organized, the Wilders chose to attend the Mansfield Methodist Episcopal church. Regional differences between the Ozarks and the upper Midwest probably meant that aspects of the worship, community, and practices of Mansfield's Methodist Episcopal church were new and different for the Wilders. Historian John Miller noted, "While many aspects of the culture were familiar to them—religious revivals, Fourth of July celebrations, pie suppers, band concerts, workings, social visiting, and the like—there was also much that was new."[6] "Singings," or all-day hymn sings, were held on Sundays during the summer. The largest was conducted in Hartville the first week of July, and it featured church choirs and smaller ensembles. The local newspaper also advertised singings in many rural churches. These events demonstrated that religious life in Mansfield and surrounding communities was to some extent interdenominational. At the same time, individual congregations maintained distinctive beliefs, identities, and institutional structures.

Laura and Almanzo's names do not appear on lists of charter members in church histories. Since the Methodist church in Walnut Grove where Laura had worshiped for a year was part of the MEC, there may have been similarities with the church in Mansfield. Almanzo's family had also been staunch Methodists. Laura participated in the Methodist ladies' aid society and helped to organize a Christmas bazaar to raise money after the completion of its new church building in 1899. She baked for church events and may have served as a substitute teacher for a Sunday school class. Later church membership rolls from the period do not exist, but biographers agree that Laura, Almanzo, and Rose never officially became members of the church.

It was common for churches in small Midwestern towns to have worship services less frequently than every Sunday. Many congregations did not have enough members to support a full-time pastor. In the late 1890s,

6. John E. Miller, *Becoming Laura Ingalls Wilder: The Woman behind the Legend* (Columbia: University of Missouri Press, 1998), 102.

neither of the churches in Mansfield had a preaching service (a worship service with pastor who preached a sermon) every week. In late 1895, the Cumberland Presbyterian church had preaching at eleven in the morning and seven in the evening on the fourth Sunday of each month. The Methodist Episcopal church had preaching on the second Sunday of the month at the same two times. There was a "Union Sunday School" that met at ten in the morning every Sunday. By the first years of the new century, each church was conducting its own weekly Sunday school. The Presbyterian church had preaching on the first Sunday of the month, and the Methodist church on the second and fourth Sundays. In 1909, the Presbyterian church again had worship services on the fourth Sunday and the Methodist church on the first and third Sundays. Early that year, a Baptist church began meeting for services on the third Sunday of the month. Its Sunday school met every Sunday at 2:30 in the afternoon, so it is likely that the Baptists held both Sunday school and worship in the Presbyterian church building. The Baptist church dedicated its own building in May of 1911.

Attendance at weekly Sunday school meetings may have been less than attendance at the preaching services. Articles frequently appeared in the local newspaper promoting the importance of Sunday school, which could mean that some members were not coming. During these years, there is no evidence for whether Laura, Almanzo, and Rose attended Sunday school when there was not preaching.

Between 1896 and 1910, the pastor who served the Mansfield Methodist Episcopal church also served the church in Seymour, which was older and likely had more members. Each church had preaching two times a month. During these years, the St. Louis Conference, the regional Methodist governing body, added the membership of both churches into one figure: in 1896, this total was 147, and in 1910, it was 218. During intervening years, membership figures fluctuated. Payments to the district (the local Methodist governing body) and to the conference were based on membership, so there was motivation for churches to keep accurate membership rolls. Pastors in the St. Louis Conference were appointed to their churches at its meeting in March. Methodist churches had a long tradition of itinerant ministry, going back to John Wesley, founder of the movement in England, and Francis Asbury, one of the first two Methodist bishops in the United States. This meant that pastors often served multiple churches and were moved by the conference to new pastorates after one to three years of service. As a result, ten different pastors served the church in Mansfield between its founding in 1895 and 1911. (Their names are given in the appendix.)

Early pastors who served the Mansfield Methodist Episcopal church were young and had few years of pastoral experience when they arrived: J. S. Meracle had served just one year as a pastor, Francis Leckliter was a probationary pastor (not yet a member of the conference) when he served, and Charles Tippin had just two years of experience. Succeeding pastors had longer terms of service. William Yount had been a pastor in the conference for eight years, John Frazier and John Slusher both had almost twenty years in the ministry, and Burrel Jones had served as a pastor for almost thirty years.

Pastors also had a variety of regional backgrounds. Some were longtime residents of Missouri. Yount was born in the northeastern Ozarks; Tippin was born in 1857 in Indiana, though his family relocated to southwestern Missouri when he was a child. As longtime residents of the Ozarks, they were probably comfortable preaching to the congregation in Mansfield, even with its two transplanted Congregationalists from South Dakota. By contrast, Slusher, Jones, and Frazier were all from outside Missouri. Slusher was from near Jasper, Arkansas, about 120 miles south of Mansfield, but still in the Ozarks. Jones was from Paducah, Kentucky, about 250 miles east of Mansfield, though he moved with his family to Arkansas when he was young. Finally, Frazier had originally been a member of the Newark Conference of the MEC, serving a church in Raritan, New Jersey, before taking pastorates in Nebraska, New Mexico, Arkansas, and Missouri. After serving in Mansfield, he transferred back to the Newark Conference. These ministers would have brought their experience of different places to their work in Mansfield.

Although apparently Almanzo and Laura did not become members of the Methodist church, they did officially join the Masonic Lodge and OES in Mansfield. Laura was a charter member of the new Eastern Star chapter in Mansfield when it was founded in 1897. She was also immediately elected to be Esther, one of its ceremonial officers. Almanzo became a member of the Lodge in Mansfield the next year and joined the Eastern

Star several years later. Almanzo and Laura attended meetings together on the first and third Friday of each month.

In the United States during the twentieth century, there has been some disagreement about whether Masonic lodges and the Eastern Star should be seen as religious organizations. Members maintain that the Lodge is a fraternal organization and not a religious one. Faith is one of the values of the institution, and each lodge has an altar, most often with a Bible placed on it. However, for lodges where the majority of members are of another faith, a copy of the Torah, Qur'an, or Vedas may be placed on the altar. The Eastern Star was created in the 1850s by Rob Morris, a Christian and a Freemason, who named many of the officers and some of its rituals after women in the Bible. Members of the Eastern Star are required to believe in the existence of a supreme being, but nothing more. Neither organization makes claims about salvation. On the other hand, some Reformed and evangelical churches during the twentieth century argued that organizations like the Masons and Eastern Star, because of their altars, religious language and imagery, and secret ceremonies, were incompatible with Christianity. Such churches discouraged members from joining the Lodge or OES and barred members of such organizations from serving as officers.

Laura and Almanzo were members of the Eastern Star until 1931, and they often served as officers. Almanzo served as warder, a minor officer of the organization, in 1905. In 1899, Laura was elected associate matron, the next year she served as conductress, and in both 1902 and 1903 she was chosen to be the worthy matron, or presiding officer, of the Mansfield chapter. Laura became a deputy grand lecturer for the Grand Chapter of the Eastern Star in August 1904. The Grand Chapter was a statewide organization; she visited the chapters in her district and reported on their standing to the Grand Chapter meeting in St. Louis in September 1905. She was elected to local offices each year for the rest of the decade. In 1909 she was again worthy matron, and the chapter held a "watch meeting" the evening of December 31 at her direction. Watch meetings, or watch night services, had been held, especially in Methodist churches, since the 1700s. They featured hymn singing, Bible reading, prayer, and invitations to those gathered to commit themselves to godly living. These gatherings were also meant to be an alternative to New Year's Eve parties that featured drinking or other unwholesome activities.

Transitions

Laura was called away from her work in her household and community
in early 1902. Her mother or one of her sisters had written that her father
was dying of heart disease. She took the train to South Dakota and arrived at the Ingalls home in De Smet on May 27. Laura's sisters Mary and
Carrie still lived in the house on Third Street with their parents. Carrie
continued to work for the *De Smet News and Leader*. Grace had finished
high school, taught several terms of country school, and then married a
farmer who lived west of De Smet in 1901. Charles Ingalls died on June 8,
1902, surrounded by his wife and four daughters. His funeral was held at
the Congregational church two days later. He was eulogized in the *News
and Leader* as a pioneer, a faithful member of the Congregational church,
and a member in good standing of the De Smet Lodge and Order of the
Eastern Star. Those who knew the Ingalls family testified that although
they didn't have much in the way of material things, Charles had always
been a respected member of the community. Laura stayed several additional weeks with her family and then returned to Mansfield.

At some point, in an undated manuscript, Laura wrote down some of
her earliest memories of him: of his eyes, his hair, his arms, his voice, and
especially his violin playing. Charles Ingalls's strength and love for his
family had provided guidance, safety, and meaning to Laura's childhood.
It appears that his periodic failures as a material provider for his family
were overshadowed in her mind by his ability to provide emotional and
psychological security. She also admired him for his consistent attempts
to provide in whatever ways were possible to him at the time: agriculture,
wage work, business, or civic office. His example inspired her, and her
memories of him were instrumental when she later began writing the
story of her life.

The Wilder family's residence in Mansfield itself brought benefits to
Rose. She no longer had to take a donkey to school, she was no longer
a "country girl," and her family's additional income enabled her to wear
clothes that were closer in quality to those of other students. She remained
an outsider, however, awkward in social situations and without many
friends. She also had intelligence that reached beyond many of her peers—
and perhaps some of her schoolteachers. Rose looked down on many of

her teachers, ridiculing them in notes she wrote to herself. She often faced discipline for opposition to authority. A few times she did not finish the school year; it is not clear if this was at her insistence or if she was expelled. The school in Mansfield was not equipped to educate students past junior high school. Ninth-grade classes were first offered in 1900; Rose turned fourteen in the middle of that year. Tenth grade was added the next year. Rose discovered that a family who had moved into Mansfield had a bookcase full of books; she borrowed and read them all.

Laura's relationship with her daughter was complicated and often involved conflict. In letters and diary entries written later in life, Rose complained that she had not received enough affection from her parents. Both she and her mother had dominant personalities, and therefore when they disagreed on a course of action, both were likely to dig in their heels. John Miller describes their relationship this way: "Laura always considered that what she did was best for Rose and that she was doing it for Rose's own best interest, and not for her own. But the mother's idea about what constituted her daughter's best interest did not always coincide with Rose's. Add to that a large degree of certitude and self-righteousness on Laura's part, heavily reinforced by religious belief, and we arrive at a situation in which the mother's stifling presence could frequently seem overwhelming to the daughter and make her want to get out from under her mother's strict rules and regulations."[7] I am not as convinced as Miller that religious belief was central to Laura's worldview, but I agree that it could have nurtured certitude and self-righteousness. Laura attempted to form Rose into a young woman equipped to face life, based on Laura's own upbringing and ideas about proper behavior. It is likely that Rose rejected her mother's efforts for the same reasons that many young women do: At times it was because she had developed a different opinion about what was appropriate. At other times, she rebelled just because she wanted to. As Rose navigated her teenage years, it appears that Almanzo and Laura often found it challenging to encourage, correct, and discipline their daughter.

Almanzo's sister Eliza Jane visited Mansfield in the summer of 1903 and invited Rose to return with her to Crowley, Louisiana, to study at the high school there. Laura and Almanzo allowed Rose to go. Crowley was

7. Miller, *Becoming Laura Ingalls Wilder*, 105.

a town of around four thousand people located about seventy-five miles west of Baton Rouge. It sat on an expanse of level land that was used for rice farming. Eliza Jane's husband had passed away, and Rose lived with Eliza Jane and her son. Rose never exactly fit in at the high school; she was more interested in her own writing and a romantic relationship with a young man in his midtwenties who owned a carriage. Still, in just one year, she completed all the courses that the school offered beyond what she had taken in Mansfield. She wrote a poem in Latin and recited it at the graduation ceremonies. Then she returned to Mansfield in the summer of 1904, having completed her formal education at age seventeen.

Rose immediately sought a way to support herself and pursue broader horizons. She found it in learning how to operate a telegraph. The daughter of the railroad stationmaster, a former classmate at the Mansfield school, taught her the basics of the new communications technology. In late 1904, she accepted a job as a telegrapher in Kansas City. During the next five years, she worked in telegraph offices in Kansas City, Missouri; Mount Vernon, Indiana; and San Francisco, California. Rose's relocation to California was occasioned by a budding relationship with Claire Gillette Lane, a traveling salesman. Rose and Gillette were married on March 24, 1909, and made a brief trip to Mansfield in 1910 so that he could meet her parents. Rose became pregnant later that year. On November 23, the couple was living in Salt Lake City when Rose went into premature labor. "Infant Lane" was stillborn and was buried the next day. Later that winter, Rose apparently had a surgical procedure in Kansas City that may have left her unable to have children.

Once Rose had moved out, Laura and Almanzo had time to consider their future. Their frugality and hard work had enabled them to add more land to the farm: an additional twelve acres in 1897 and forty more in 1899. They also saved money to expand the farmhouse. In 1911, the Wilders sold their house in town for five hundred dollars and moved back to Rocky Ridge. In between her work at the Mansfield house and on the farm, Laura had designed her ideal farm home. The final plan included ten rooms, four porches, and a rock fireplace. Windows opened to the countryside in all directions, with large ones in the parlor. Almanzo hired contractors to provide the heavy labor of constructing an addition that dwarfed the original house. He did much of the finished carpentry himself, creating built-in bookshelves in the library and a multitude of storage spaces in the kitchen. They used wood and stone from their own land as much as possible. The work was completed in 1914. The result was completely suited to Laura and Almanzo's tastes and desires. Almanzo was around five feet four inches tall, and Laura was probably no taller than five feet. He built the countertops, cupboards, closets, and bookshelves to fit their stature. Visitors who tour the farmhouse at Rocky Ridge Farm today can see the Wilders' vision for human flourishing in a rural setting.

New Beginnings and Endings

A picture was taken of Laura in her work clothes on the porch of their house in town sometime during the first decade of the century. On the back of the photograph, she wrote, "Just as I am, without one plea." This was the first line of "Just as I Am," a hymn written by Charlotte Elliott in 1835. The hymn expresses thanks to God for salvation from sin, help in conflict, healing and provision, and enduring love. Maybe Laura was thinking of all these things when she jotted the note on the back of the picture. Perhaps the phrase was just a way of saying, "This is what I look like." At any rate, the familiar hymn came to her mind when she looked at the photograph and turned it over to write on the back.

By 1911, Laura and Almanzo's household was generally stable financially, though that stability required consistent frugality. Almanzo was not strong, and their farm operation was not a commercial producer of row crops. Apple trees planted in the 1890s began to bear in the first two decades of the new century. Almanzo grew hay and corn, mainly to feed his cows and pigs. Laura cared for a large flock of chickens and helped Almanzo with farm work when necessary. Eggs brought necessary cash to the farm. Ten years of living and working in town had also contributed to their resources. They had worked hard to build and then remake their home on Rocky Ridge.

They had also made efforts to establish themselves in Mansfield society. They attended the Methodist Episcopal church and therefore participated in the congregation's life, even if they had not officially joined. They were important members of the Eastern Star, particularly Laura; she normally occupied a leadership position in either the local chapter or the state organization. They also participated in other voluntary, civic, and religious events common to many early twentieth-century small towns. Their upbringing in the upper Midwest set them apart from those who were originally from the Ozarks, but it seems they had reasons to feel part of their community.

Gratitude for their relative material success and standing in the community may have competed in their thoughts with concern about how well they had done raising their daughter. Rose's headstrong nature must have brought them grief, especially during her teenage years. She left home as quickly as she could, even before finishing high school, and was determined to forge her own path in the world. Meeting Rose's husband only after she was married may have caused them pain; hearing of her stillborn son must also have been difficult. The chapter of their life devoted to child rearing ended during the first decade of the twentieth century, but their ongoing relationship with their adult daughter shaped the rest of their lives.

As was the case during Laura and Almanzo's early marriage, there is little evidence in Laura's words about her religious beliefs, belonging, and behavior during this period. Were hymns a fixture of life in the Wilder home the way they had been for the Ingalls family? How much did Laura and Almanzo's Christian beliefs contribute to Rose's desire to leave home? Did the family attend Sunday school regularly, or go to the Methodist church only when the pastor was preaching, once or twice a month? Might their regular participation in the ceremonies of the Eastern Star have impacted their view of the world? Teresa Lynn, author of *Little Lodges on the Prairie*, argues that Laura joined the Eastern Star because it was generically Christian and because it provided an outlet for her abilities. The organization required that members believe in a supreme being, but otherwise members could be affiliated with any church.

What does seem clear is that Laura and Almanzo had decided to attend and therefore to identify with the Methodist Episcopal church. Perhaps they chose that church because Methodist teachings were closest to their own. Laura's dislike of Presbyterian doctrines like predestination and practices like strict Sunday observance suggests that this was at least part of the reason. Perhaps it also was because Laura had experience with Methodists growing up in Walnut Grove, and because of Almanzo's family's ties to Methodist churches. Apparently, their membership in the Lodge and Eastern Star was not an obstacle to their connections with the Mansfield Methodist church, like it might have been for other, more conservative or evangelical denominations. Participating in worship and in activities the Methodist church sponsored, especially those surrounding the construction of its new building in 1899, cultivated a circle of like-minded friends and a place in the community. In a small town with multiple churches, this was significant.

On the other hand, Laura was willing to formally become a member of the OES in Mansfield, while she did not join the Methodist Episcopal church. She also served as an officer and even a state officer for the OES. Such leadership positions were not available to women in the MEC until decades later. Perhaps this was part of the reason she did not join. She did use her influence to have the Eastern Star hold a New Year's Eve service like those often held by Methodist churches. Laura and Almanzo's membership in the Eastern Star may have been more important to them than their participation in the Methodist church. One way to describe the distinctions drawn in her engagement with Christianity was that Laura's faith was important to her, but it was not absolutely central to her life.

Laura turned forty-four in February of 1911. Her adult daughter had left home, the renovations were under way on the farmhouse, and she and her husband were enjoying a certain amount of financial stability. It appeared that their days of traveling to find economic opportunity were over. Laura had turned to writing at least several times before. As a teenager she had composed both prose and poetry. She had regularly recorded observations about the family's trip from South Dakota to Missouri in 1894. Undated fragments of writing suggest that she from time to time wrote about her life and experiences. During the second decade of the new century, she began writing regularly to share her ideas with others and earn additional income. By the 1920s, she had gained a readership for her observations about farming, life, and faith.

6

Writing about the Farm, the Good Life, and God

1911–1924

etween 1911 and 1924, Laura Ingalls Wilder published more than
150 columns, articles, and features for the *Missouri Ruralist*, a regional farm newspaper. This was a substantial accomplishment for
a farmer's wife with many responsibilities. The publication that she
wrote for and the concerns she addressed in her writing were shaped by
broader American economic, political, and social developments, including
Progressive reforms and the Country Life Movement.

Progressive reformers attempted to respond to rapid changes in American society during the late nineteenth century, including industrialization,
urban growth, and foreign immigration. They often were experts, trained
in universities as social scientists and connected to urban businesses, community organizations, and governmental entities. They founded settlement
houses to integrate immigrants into American society, led campaigns for
better government, and called for changes to the educational system.
Eventually, Progressives influenced both American political parties.

Country Life Reformers included professors at agricultural colleges,
employees of the US Department of Agriculture, and editors of farm
newspapers. They were concerned about economic and cultural changes
in rural America. As easily obtained land dwindled, farmers adopted more
capital-intensive agricultural methods, such as the use of fertilizer, silos,
machinery, and better livestock breeds. This led to increased prosperity,
and in general, farmland and crops commanded high prices. Even as rural

life improved, however, many country people were leaving the farm. Some were unsuccessful farmers or those who could not afford new technology, but reformers were also concerned that unsatisfactory ways of life caused the children of farmers to relocate to urban areas. Ironically, the methods reformers advocated to preserve rural society often meant making rural lifestyles more like life in the city. Such solutions included labor-saving devices, new organizations for farmers, and the updating of rural social institutions, such as the rural family, rural school, and rural church.

Perhaps the most important way that reformers delivered their recommendations to rural people was through the farm press. The total circulation of farm newspapers nationwide exceeded 17 million in 1920; that year the US farm population was 31.5 million. A farm newspaper was the periodical most likely to be received by rural midwesterners, and farmers from across the economic spectrum subscribed. Agricultural papers created a forum for debates about farming and rural life, providing a voice for both urban-based reformers and rural people themselves. The circulation of farm newspapers and their presence in the homes of rural midwesterners suggest that these discussions were important to many rural people.

Most American farm newspapers were regional in scope. The *Missouri Ruralist* became the farm newspaper of record for the state of Missouri during the 1910s. It was founded in Sedalia, Missouri, in 1902, and it was purchased by Arthur Capper, a newspaper publisher from Kansas, in 1910. The *Ruralist*'s circulation in 1911 was slightly more than ten thousand; by 1920, it had grown to ninety thousand. There were about 263,000 farms in Missouri that year. While it is probable that not all the paper's subscribers lived on farms, it is possible that between a quarter and a third of farmers in Missouri regularly received the paper.

Regional farm newspapers normally included a Home Department aimed at farmers' wives and other women living in rural areas. Home Departments contained instructions for gardening, poultry raising, and homemaking; recommendations for labor-saving devices; and advice on moral issues related to life on the farm. Most Home Departments had a home editor, who was often a woman. Some home editors took an active role in shaping the topics and voices found on the page; others simply wrote a regular column and left the rest of the content to the editor of the paper.

The Missouri Home Makers' Conference was held at the Missouri State Agricultural College in Columbia on January 10–13, 1911. It was part of the "Farmers' Week in the College of Agriculture," an event that brought together Missouri farmers, agricultural educators, and Country Life reformers. One of the papers read at the conference was "The Small Farm Home," by Mrs. A. J. Wilder from Rocky Ridge Farm, Mansfield. Laura most likely did not attend the event; instead, someone else read the paper she had written. It argues that a good life can be had on a farm if one has access to five acres and modern conveniences, such as gasoline engines, running water, rural mail delivery, and circulating libraries. This was completely in line with the recommendations from Country Life reformers that rural people should adopt modern ways of life to stay on the farm. Wilder made the argument her own by using examples from Rocky Ridge. Apparently, someone from the *Missouri Ruralist* was in the audience when the paper was read. On February 18, 1911, the *Ruralist* published the paper verbatim as a feature story titled "Favors the Small Farm Home."

Between February 1911 and June 1915, Wilder published eight more articles and one poem in the *Missouri Ruralist*. The byline of the next two articles was just A. J. Wilder, but they were composed by Laura, not Almanzo, although they were written from his point of view. They read much like Laura's other columns and nothing like the few available sources written by Almanzo. Both were feature articles. "The Story of Rocky Ridge Farm," published on July 22, 1911, described the improvements they had made to the property during their years of ownership. "My Apple Orchard" appeared almost a year later, on June 1, 1912; it described Almanzo's methods for planting trees, trimming them, and controlling insects and other pests. The front cover of the issue featured a large picture of Almanzo in front of an apple tree. Laura was published again in June 1913; the piece presented labor-saving ideas for rural women. Briefer columns in February and April 1914 gave instructions for developing women's clubs in the country and beauty tips. In June 1914, a feature article described the development of a Missouri farm by a family transplanted from St. Louis. It particularly highlighted the work of the woman of the house, who proved a skilled farm manager while her husband continued to work in the city. Finally, two columns in early 1915 provided suggestions for egg production and food preparation.

A poem by Laura was published in between the first and second features that Laura wrote for the *Ruralist*. Titled "The People in God's Out-of-Doors," it appeared on April 15, 1911:

> I love to listen to the bird songs every day
> And hear the free winds whisper in their play,
> Among the tall old trees and sweet wild flowers.
> I love to watch the little brook
> That gushes from its cool and rocky bed
> Deep in the earth. The sky is blue o'er head
> And sunbeams dance upon its tiny rivulete [*sic*].
> I love the timid things
> That gather round the little watercourse,
> To listen to the frogs with voices hoarse,
> And see the squirrels leap and bound at play.
> Then, too, I love to hear
> The loud clear whistle of the pretty quail,
> To see the chipmunk flirt his saucy tail,
> Then peep from out his home within the tree.
> I love to watch the busy bees,
> To see the rabbit scurry in the brush
> Or sit when falls the dewy evening's hush
> And listen to the sad-voiced whippoorwill.[1]

The way this poem evokes the sights and sounds of living things echoes passages from the diary she kept in 1894. It also previews the affectionate descriptions of nature in her later writing. As poetry, however, it is much more highly organized: it can be divided into four stanzas, the first consisting of three lines and the others consisting of four lines. Each stanza begins with "I love" in the first line. The middle two lines of each stanza (the second and third of the first stanza) rhyme, the first and last do not. God is not mentioned in the poem itself, but the title suggests that she

---

1. Laura Ingalls Wilder, "The People in God's Out-of-Doors," *Missouri Ruralist*, April 15, 1911, 12; also in *Laura Ingalls Wilder, Farm Journalist: Writings from the Ozarks*, ed. Stephen W. Hines (Columbia: University of Missouri Press, 2007), 16–17.

wanted it remembered that he designed the "people" described. Wilder's second publication for a regional farm newspaper was a celebration of the natural world and the animals in it; it might also be understood as giving praise to the God who created them.

"West from Home"

At the end of 1915, Laura began a period of much more consistent and sustained production of articles and columns for the *Ruralist*. During the next five years, she wrote between twenty and twenty-five pieces for the publication each year. Since the paper was published twice each month, this meant that something by her was in almost every issue. From 1921 to 1924, her production slowed; her regular columns were shorter, and between ten and fifteen appeared each year. Still, this output was more regular than what had been published during the years before 1915.

Laura's more concerted program of writing was launched by a trip to visit Rose in California in the fall of 1915. Laura had multiple motivations for the visit. Rose had asked her mother to come see the Panama-Pacific International Exposition in San Francisco that year, and Laura was curious. Rose also hoped Laura and Almanzo might consider moving to a farm in California to be closer to her. Laura wanted to talk to Rose about writing. Rose was developing her writing abilities at the *San Francisco Bulletin*. She had begun as an assistant to the editor of the paper's Women's Department, but she was now taking her own paid assignments. She had also begun working on serialized biographies of early aviator Art Smith and silent movie star Charlie Chaplin. Both mother and daughter thought that Rose could teach Laura how to be a better writer. Rose was still married to Gillette Lane, though Laura saw signs that their marriage was in trouble. Rose later wrote that she had already given up on their marriage, but that she and Gillette attempted to make things look good while her mother was visiting.

While she was traveling, Laura sent a series of letters back home to Almanzo. The letters narrate what she and Rose did together, and they provide detailed descriptions of what Laura had heard and seen. She asked Almanzo to save her letters so that she could read them later and perhaps write about them for publication. He did. After Laura's death in 1957 and Rose's death in

1968, Rose's heir Roger Lea MacBride found them. In 1974, Harper & Row published an edited collection of the letters titled *West from Home: Letters of Laura Ingalls Wilder, San Francisco, 1915*. They are also available in their entirety at the Herbert Hoover Presidential Library in West Branch, Iowa.

Laura boarded a train heading west in Springfield, Missouri, on September 21. Inspired by seeing parts of the country that she and her husband had never seen before, Laura wrote extended descriptions of the landscape she could see through the train window. She also gave an account of the many stops and transfers necessary to reach the West Coast. Once she arrived in California, she sent Almanzo detailed narratives of happy trips to the ocean, long visits to the exposition, and extended walks around Berkeley, Oakland, and San Francisco. Rose did prevail upon Laura to travel with Gillette to the Santa Clara Valley to see about the possibility of buying a farm there, but Laura and Almanzo ultimately decided against moving to California. They probably had not seriously entertained the idea. Land there was five hundred dollars an acre, many times what it cost in Missouri. The weather was also too hot. Laura could think of no compelling reason to begin completely anew at this point in their lives.

The only description in the letters of something directly related to Christianity is a discussion of two pictures of the crucifixion in a room of French art at the fair: "There, on each side, was a painting of Christ crucified, the only pictures of the kind I ever saw that were not horrible. These were wonderful. Between them in the center of the room was a bronze statue of Sorrow, a woman weeping. The most realistic thing. It almost made me cry to look at it. At the end of the room, covering the whole end wall with the Christ on each side and the weeping woman before it, was a painting of the armies of France."[2] It appears that the French government was attempting to recruit American sensibilities in support of their side in the Great War, since the United States was still neutral at this point during World War I. The display was also meant to showcase the work of French artists. The Christian—more specifically, the Roman Catholic—imagery proved moving for Laura. However, she speaks almost as eloquently about other exhibits,

2. Laura Ingalls Wilder to Almanzo Wilder, October 14, 1915, box 13, folder 184, Rose Wilder Lane Papers, Herbert Hoover Presidential Library, West Branch, Iowa; also in *West from Home: Letters of Laura Ingalls Wilder, San Francisco, 1915* (New York: Harper & Row, 1974), 148.

including wood from different parts of the world, animals from Australia and New Zealand, and a large, mechanized display for Keen Cutter knives. In general, Laura was interested in people from other cultures, technological advances, and the beauty of the surroundings at the fair.

The letters can be used to reconstruct Laura's activities on many individual days of the trip, so one can consider if she attended services on Sundays. There is no evidence from the letters that Laura attended a Sunday worship service in California. In a letter written the evening of Sunday, August 29, she describes resting most of the day, because she and Rose and Gillette had gone to the beach at Lands End the preceding day. That Sunday evening, they visited the fair to see the fireworks. On September 21 she reported that the previous Sunday they had ridden streetcars around the city. The following Sunday, she and Rose rode a water ferry to Berkeley to see the city and visit the Greek Theater at the University of California. On Monday, October 4, she sent a postcard to Almanzo that said she had gone to a movie the previous night. Finally, on October 14, she recounted that on the most recent Sunday, Rose had written most of the day and then she and Laura had headed for the beach. During their six-week trip from South Dakota to Missouri, the Wilder family rested on Sundays, but there is no evidence they attended worship. It appears that this was generally the case for the eight weeks that Laura stayed with Rose in San Francisco. Laura was most likely to attend worship when she was settled in a community. Rose had not connected with a church and was not interested in Sunday worship.

An article in the *Missouri Ruralist* from the following year indicates that Laura did attend at least one religious service in San Francisco. In it she describes a few scenes from the recent Mansfield Agricultural Fair and Stock Show, and then this scene: "a Chinese Salvation Army meeting, on a street corner in San Francisco's Chinatown. The crowd was large and all Chinese except myself and escort. Altho [*sic*] Chinese was the only language spoken and I could not understand a word, I could follow the exhorter's meaning and by the expressions on the faces about me could tell the state of mind of his audience."[3] She also listened to those gathered sing "Onward, Christian Soldiers" in Chinese. The point of the piece that connects it to the other

3. Laura Ingalls Wilder, "Our Fair and Other Things," *Missouri Ruralist*, November 5, 1916; *Laura Ingalls Wilder, Farm Journalist*, 88–90.

vignettes is that often connections can be formed between people even if they can't hear or understand the language spoken; it just requires empathy and attention to others. In an early letter to Almanzo, written on Tuesday, September 7, Laura mentioned visiting Chinatown but did not say which day she and Rose had gone there. It could have been Sunday, September 5. Salvation Army services were sometimes held outside.

The financial arrangements underpinning the trip were complex. It seems that earlier, Laura and Almanzo had loaned $250 to Rose and Gillette for a real estate venture. During the entire trip, Laura reported to her husband that Gillette was hoping to close a deal or obtain a job that would enable him to pay them back, and perhaps even to pay off the mortgage they had on their property. The job or deal never came through. Rose paid Laura five dollars every week to compensate for the egg and butter money Laura would have made back home on the farm. Money was tight for both Rose and her parents. Laura and Almanzo generally responded to financial challenges by pursuing strict frugality. Rose tended to alternate between periods of thriftiness and extravagance. These patterns continued for most of the rest of their adult lives, and at times they became sources of conflict.

Laura did talk with Rose about writing. Rose believed that her instruction would lead to magazine publications or even a novel, which would provide increased income for her parents. Laura was inspired; one letter to her husband related her hopes that magazine or story writing would pay better than articles for a farm newspaper. Closer to the end of her time in California, Laura adopted a more limited vision. She wrote Almanzo that observing the work that Rose put into writing made her more content to raise chickens. The trip was cut short after Laura fell from the side of a streetcar and spent several days in a hospital with a concussion. When she returned to Rocky Ridge later that fall, she brought with her a greater understanding of what was required to write for publication, additional ideas for articles for the *Missouri Ruralist*, and new energy for the task.

"The Lack of Christianity Has Brought Us Where We Are"

Wilder's articles and columns for the *Missouri Ruralist* address a wide variety of topics. During the early 1910s, and then again during the early 1920s, many articles were features about successful farmers. Wilder also wrote a regular column in the newspaper's Home Department; she was listed on the paper's masthead as its home editor. Originally, each piece had an individual title, but in 1919 the column became The Farm Home; this was changed to As a Farm Woman Thinks in 1921. Columns provided tips for raising chickens, advice for effective farm management, and guidance for other aspects of farm wives' work. Moreover, Wilder regularly addressed moral, political, economic, and family topics. She frequently reflected on the role of women in the home and in society. She also addressed developments in World War I, which the United States participated in from April 1917 to November 1918. While at times she reflected on national events, more often she was concerned with everyday life. Laura's columns often described an event in her life, an interaction with a neighbor, or another vignette, and then used that account to teach a lesson.

John Miller, who considered Laura's writings for the *Ruralist* in multiple works, summarized their moral and intellectual underpinnings:

> Many things drew Laura's ire, among them selfishness, overreliance on experts, the tendency to find fault with others, negative—as opposed to friendly—gossip, swearing, relativistic ideas, and the failure to follow Christian precepts. If a single lesson stood out, it was the necessity of love, a message she derived no doubt both from the warm and loving family environment that she had grown up in and from her own experiences as an adult. The commitment to love was strengthened by her religious beliefs. While seldom mentioned explicitly in her columns, biblical teachings lay at the core of her thinking.[4]

The chief theme of the columns was everyday morality. Laura did not often make direct references to God, to Christian doctrines, or to the Bible itself. By my count, only 28 of the 170 different articles and columns printed in the *Ruralist* explicitly mention God, Christianity, or the Bible. An examination of those references can help us build a more complete understanding of Laura's adult belief system.

First, Laura believed that humans were flawed and prone to sin against one another. People's own faults and weaknesses are what cause problems

---

4. John E. Miller, *Becoming Laura Ingalls Wilder: The Woman behind the Legend* (Columbia: University of Missouri Press, 2007), 131.

between neighbors, between groups in society, and between countries. A column titled "Getting the Worst of It" describes a conversation about the price of eggs between a country woman who sells them and a woman who lives in town. They fail to come to an agreement because of selfishness, and Laura provides this commentary: "After all, it is thru [*sic*] some fault or weakness of our own that . . . most of the evils of life come to us. It is as if our strength of character and virtues formed a guard around us, but a fault or weakness of character makes an opening thru which our punishment comes."[5] Two years later, she identified selfishness as the cause of conflicts about boundaries in Europe, troubles between labor and capital in the United States, and arguments between individuals. The column goes on to address Christianity directly in relation to the many problems facing humankind:

> Here and there one sees a criticism of Christianity because of the things that have happened and are still going on. "Christian civilization is a failure," some say. "Christianity has not prevented these things, therefore it is a failure," say others.
>
> But this is a calling of things by the wrong names. It is rather the lack of Christianity that has brought us where we are. Not a lack of churches or religious forms, but of the real thing in our hearts.[6]

Some have called World War I a failing of Christianity, because the nations in Europe who fought so brutally against each other were all historically Christian nations. Here Laura argued that the cataclysm was caused by an absence of genuine Christianity. She defined "the real thing" as overcoming selfishness, dealing justly with others, and loving others the way that we already love ourselves. Laura believed human beings are sinful and by nature find it difficult to treat one another with love.

The columns show that Laura also believed that God's laws, as revealed both in the Bible and in the world, were enduring. Following God's laws brings good things to people; abandoning his rules leads to problems and

5. Laura Ingalls Wilder, "Getting the Worst of It," *Missouri Ruralist*, March 5, 1917; in *Laura Ingalls Wilder, Farm Journalist*, 104.

6. Laura Ingalls Wilder, The Farm Home, *Missouri Ruralist*, December 20, 1919; *Laura Ingalls Wilder, Farm Journalist*, 208.

evil. One column from June 1919 argues that German leaders did not keep their word during the war, and therefore their word was not trusted after the war. Laura compares this to the story of her cousin Charley who "cried wolf" while her father and uncle were harvesting; as a result they did not come quickly when he later stepped in a yellow jackets' nest.[7] In a column several years later, Laura mourned after learning that a nineteen-year-old boy was charged with murder but also noted that boys who are not taught God's law early in life will break it later on. She then equated laws discovered in nature with those revealed in God's Word: "If we break a law of nature we are punished physically; when we disobey God's law we suffer spiritually, mentally and usually in our bodies also; man's laws, being founded on the ten commandments, are really mankind's poor attempt at interpreting the laws of God and for disobeying them there is a penalty."[8] The overall point of the column is that child rearing is important, because the way children are trained will determine how they live later in life. This corresponds to Proverbs 22:6, which she references. In other columns, she quotes from Exodus 20:8–11, Proverbs 15:1, Proverbs 27:1, Matthew 7:12, and Matthew 25:40. All these Scripture passages give instructions on how to live.

Laura also asserted the importance of thanking God for his goodness. She wrote about gratitude regularly in meditations on Thanksgiving in November issues of the paper. Some exhortations to thankfulness are general; others specifically say thanks are to be given to God. A column from November 1916 tells the story of a vehement childhood argument with her sister Mary over whether sage should be used in the stuffing for the goose that her father had gone to hunt. Both children realized their presumption and lack of gratitude when their father returned empty-handed.[9] Seven years later, she wrote of the importance of thinking about God himself when giving thanks. The column is brief, and it begins by noting that many cultures have had a harvest celebration to give thanks to a "Higher Power." She suggests that this is because in fact the Christian God exists. She concludes, "even more than for material blessings, let us, with humble hearts, give thanks for the revelation to us and our better

7. Laura later used this story in *Pioneer Girl* and *Little House in the Big Woods*.

8. Laura Ingalls Wilder, As a Farm Woman Thinks, *Missouri Ruralist*, May 1, 1922; *Laura Ingalls Wilder, Farm Journalist*, 269.

9. Laura later included this story in *Pioneer Girl* and *By the Shores of Silver Lake*.

understanding of the greatness and goodness of God."[10] This is one of the most explicit considerations of God published in the *Ruralist*.

Finally, Laura also often meditated on the meaning of Christmas. The first article that does so, in 1916, is perhaps the most striking. She begins by imagining the origin of Christmas in the pagan world of Europe centuries before. Since the sun was treated as a god, the shortening of the days in late fall led priests to sacrifice a child every December 24. Doors in the village were left unlocked so that the priests could come and take a child from one of the villagers, and families must have listened in terror for footsteps on Christmas Eve. Then, "How happy they must have been when the teachers of Christianity came and told them it was all unnecessary. It is no wonder they celebrated the birth of Christ on the date of that awful night of sacrifice . . . nor that they made it a children's festival."[11] Fascinatingly, the focus for this meditation is not Jesus Christ but Santa Claus. The title of the article is "Before Santa Claus Came," not "Before Jesus Came." Saint Nick dominates the last paragraph: "Instead of the stealthy steps of cruel men, there came now, on Christmas eve, a jolly saint with reindeer and bells, bringing gifts. This new spirit of love and peace and safety that was abroad in the land did not require that the doors be left unbarred. He could come thru [*sic*] locked doors or down the chimney and be everywhere at once on Christmas night, for a spirit can do such things."[12] It is unclear where this story that contrasts the pagan and Christian conceptions of the winter celebration originated. It is striking that Christian teachings about the work that Jesus Christ came to do are not mentioned in the article. When she wrote in the *Ruralist* about Christianity explicitly, Laura was much more likely to simply address God, his laws, or his goodness in general.

One would not necessarily expect articles in a farm journal to reveal a complete description of Laura's understanding of the Christian belief system. Nevertheless, since Wilder does reference selfishness, God, and the Bible at different points, it is notable that she rarely mentioned for-

10. Laura Ingalls Wilder, As a Farm Woman Thinks, *Missouri Ruralist*, November 15, 1923; *Laura Ingalls Wilder, Farm Journalist*, 292–93.

11. Laura Ingalls Wilder, "Before Santa Claus Came," *Missouri Ruralist*, December 20, 1916; *Laura Ingalls Wilder, Farm Journalist*, 95.

12. Wilder, "Before Santa Claus Came"; *Laura Ingalls Wilder, Farm Journalist*, 95.

giveness, salvation, or Jesus Christ. Because Jesus Christ is hardly ever mentioned, Christianity as depicted in the *Missouri Ruralist* articles seems to center on moral actions. A Christian is someone who does the right thing. The Bible is given as the standard of what is right and wrong, but one can also grasp God's commands from living in the world. The Bible calls everyone to treat others as they desired to be treated. Christians are to love God and love their neighbors.

Community, the Church, and Other Writing

During the 1910s and early 1920s, Laura and Almanzo raised what they could on the farm and remained active in Mansfield community events. Almanzo tended the trees on Rocky Ridge and marketed the apples each year. He also raised some corn, wheat, and hay, mostly to feed to his horses, cattle, and pigs. At times he sold strawberries and blueberries. Almanzo helped to organize the Mansfield Agricultural and Stock Show in 1912. At various times during the 1910s, he served as one of the show's superintendents of the cattle, sheep, swine and goats division or the horses and mules division. He also won prizes from the show for the best sheaf of millet in 1913, red Durham steer in 1913, Durham cow in 1914, sheaf of Sudan grass in 1916, timothy and orchard grass in 1921, and Missouri pippin apple in 1922. Laura took care of her chickens and served as one of the show's superintendents for the poultry division several times during the 1910s. In 1914, she won first prize for brown leghorn chickens.

The Methodist Episcopal church in Mansfield continued to be where Almanzo and Laura worshiped. Twelve pastors served the church between 1911 and 1924. (Their names are given in the appendix.) The conference changed which circuit included Mansfield from time to time, but usually the Mansfield church shared a pastor with the church in Seymour (about twelve miles west), Ava (nearly fifteen miles south), Hartville (about twelve miles north), or a combination of three of the four towns. In 1914, the Methodist conference meeting was moved from March to September or October. Also that year, Mansfield Methodist church changed its frequency of preaching from twice a month to just once each month.

The landscape of Christian worship in Mansfield changed again in 1913, when a revival held in town led to the formation of a Church of Christ. This congregation may have included members who attended the Christian church listed in Mansfield's newspapers during the 1890s. By the middle of 1915, the monthly preaching schedule was as follows: the Church of Christ on the first Sunday, the Baptist church on the second, the Methodist Episcopal church on the third, and the Cumberland Presbyterian church on the fourth Sunday of each month. All four churches held Sunday school every Sunday morning.

By far the most colorful Methodist pastor during the 1910s was Guy Willis Holmes. He was named the pastor of the Mansfield, Ava, and Seymour churches in September 1916. Holmes, who had previously pastored in St. Louis and served as a missionary to Cuba, lived in Seymour and had an expansive vision of what the churches he served could accomplish. Holmes unveiled the "Top Notch Campaign" at a banquet in Mansfield on New Year's Day 1917, attended by members from all three of his churches.[13] Holmes told those gathered that with effort and God's grace, they could increase their membership, Sunday school attendance, giving, and subscriptions to the conference newspaper. He conducted a two-week-long revival in Ava that resulted in twenty-two conversions and held revival services in Hartville that continued for several weeks and resulted in forty reported conversions. He also became active in local community events, speaking at public school assemblies in Mansfield and helping to start a Boy Scout troop in Seymour. In spring of 1917, he delivered the baccalaureate addresses for multiple high schools and spoke at the Mansfield Memorial Day observance.

Holmes found additional opportunities for his energy after the United States entered World War I in April 1917. That summer he recruited enough young men to organize a company of the Missouri National Guard and was named its lieutenant. In August he was promoted to captain and made a chaplain in the army. He never left Missouri, however, because he did not pass the final medical examination. During the war, he preached sermons exhorting his hearers to buy Liberty Bonds and contribute to the Red Cross, a chapter of which was formed in Mansfield. Laura and

13. "Big Booster Banquet," *Mansfield Mirror*, January 4, 1917, 1.

Almanzo did both. In February of 1918, Holmes was named the federal food aid administrator for Wright County. For the rest of the year, rules for farmers, stores, and individuals were published in the newspaper over his signature. Staples like flour and sugar were rationed, farmers had to market their wheat immediately, and threshing machine owners were required to provide weekly reports. After the war, in February 1919, he preached a sermon that honored the memory of President Theodore Roosevelt, who had died the previous month; it was printed in the *Mansfield Mirror*. In the early fall, he took a course on rural sociology at Northwestern University in Evanston, Illinois. At the conference meeting, he was assigned to the Methodist church in Joplin, Missouri.

Subsequent pastors returned to the pattern of serving for just one year at a time. In January 1922, J. W. Paterson became assistant pastor of the church, and again there was preaching two Sundays every month—the third and fourth Sundays. It appears that Paterson, a retired Methodist pastor who lived in the area, preached one of the Sundays. In 1922, conference statistics also divided the appointments; the membership of the Mansfield church alone was seventy-five. W. A. Gray served as pastor of the Mansfield church by itself from 1922 to 1923. After Gray, congregants in Mansfield again shared their pastor with a congregation in another small town.

How did Laura and Almanzo experience Christian fellowship and the Mansfield Methodist church during these years? The church experience of Methodists in Mansfield, like Methodists in other small towns in the region, must have been shaped by the transiency of the pastors. It would have been challenging for a pastor to get to know members when he was only in town one weekend a month for just one year. This arrangement likely influenced the identity and formation of both members and regular attenders like Laura and Almanzo. Laura does not mention any of the pastors in her correspondence, so we don't know what she and Almanzo thought of Holmes and his striking career as pastor and volunteer war leader. The Wilders later came to oppose what they saw as federal government overreach during the New Deal; it is not clear whether they resented the US Food Administration's rules and regulations during World War I.

It appears that the Wilders continued to attend worship, at least on the one or two Sundays a month when there were preaching services. We do not know if they attended Sunday school during these years. Continued periodic exhortations from church leaders in the *Mirror*—many from the interdenominational Wright County Sunday School Association—suggest that many in the county did not attend Sunday school regularly. There were regular dinner fund-raisers of the Methodist ladies' aid society, but Laura's name does not appear on the lists of ladies' aid society officers published during the 1910s.

There is some evidence that Laura and Almanzo attended other worship services in southwestern Missouri. They often went to the yearly "singing" in Hartville, which brought thousands to the county seat. It also appears that they sometimes attended services at churches in rural areas. In August of 1937, Laura sent a set of what she called "Character Sketches" to Rose. She had written them during the 1910s and had just rediscovered them. She thought that perhaps Rose might use them for future writing. They are about rural communities named Mt. Zion and Mt. Pleasant, where families educated their children and residents cared for one another during hard times. The pastor of the local Missionary Baptist church was essential to community life, visiting, giving counsel, and performing baptisms, weddings, and funerals. As a result, families prospered and homes were modernized. Laura contrasted these neighborhoods with other areas where the church declined, and community life and property values declined as well. She ended the sketches by noting that her descriptions "seem to show the influence of country churches on the surrounding communities. Cause or effect take your choice."[14] Up until this sentence, it appears that Laura was cataloguing the ways that a vibrant church contributed to the peace and prosperity of these rural neighborhoods. The final sentence complicates this message somewhat, but the overwhelming feeling created by the six handwritten pages is that the church and its faithful and engaged minister were the cause of the communities' accomplishments.

Laura also wrote an account of a special Sunday at the General Baptist church in a rural community named Prairie Hollow. There was a morning worship service, a potluck luncheon of delicious food, an afternoon service with the sacrament of the Lord's Supper, and a time when mem-

---

14. Wilder to Lane, August 19, 1937, unpaginated, box 13, folder 193, Rose Wilder Lane Papers.

bers washed each other's feet. The afternoon sermon emphasized service, which connected well with the humility expressed in the foot washing. Wrote Laura, "The earnestness, the devoutness of this congregation of hard working people put a hope in my heart that in spite of the confusion and contention abroad on earth, 'God is still in His Heaven' and 'all will be right with the world.'"[15] While undated, the piece mentions that people arrived at the church via cars, buggies, wagons, horses, and on foot, and this suggests that it could have been during the 1920s. The reference to confusion and contention could also have been to World War I. The quotes are the last two lines from a song by Robert Browning in his verse drama *Pippa Passes* in 1841 and later printed in a collection of Browning's poetry in 1848. It is likely that Laura learned these lines in school; they were commonplace in the late nineteenth century. In both the sketches Laura sent to Rose and this account, the spirit with which Laura writes of rural people shows her respect for them and for the Christianity they professed, even though it was of a different type and denomination than what she practiced.

During the 1910s and early 1920s, the *Mansfield Mirror* reported on local people's visits to see others. This was common in small-town newspapers during the late 1800s and early 1900s. The Wilders appear in these listings, both as visiting and receiving visitors. Of the visits mentioned in the newspaper, most appear to have occurred on Sunday afternoon. Of forty-two visits involving Laura and Almanzo between 1914 and 1922, twenty-five happened on Sunday and eleven on another day of the week. No date was given for the remaining six. This suggests that the Wilders used Sunday for visiting as well as for worship. Adding the evidence of these visits to the depiction in *Pioneer Girl* of the Ingalls family's pattern of worshiping only on Sunday mornings, it may be safe to assume that Laura and Almanzo did not attend Sunday evening worship services.

Laura remained active in the leadership of other community organizations. She was an officer in the Mansfield Eastern Star chapter during most of the 1910s and early 1920s. During World War I, Laura served on several committees for the local Red Cross Society, helped roll bandages

15. Laura Ingalls Wilder, *A Little House Reader: A Collection of Writings by Laura Ingalls Wilder*, ed. William Anderson (New York: HarperCollins, 1998), 117.

and make hospital garments, and contributed both a rooster and eggs to a Red Cross auction. When Mansfield celebrated the return of local soldiers in May 1919, Laura was on the committee responsible for refreshments. She also served on the Committee of Agriculture, Farming, and Produce of the Mansfield Chamber of Commerce in 1921.

Laura was also instrumental in the founding of two women's clubs. During the early twentieth century, women's clubs gathered in members' houses to discuss educational topics, current events, public affairs, and their lives. Refreshments were also shared. The Athenian Club was made up mostly of women from Hartville; Laura was one of several members from Mansfield who traveled north for monthly meetings. The Mansfield members of the Athenians also hosted meetings of the group; when Laura hosted on August 7, 1919, the women discussed Shakespeare. The Justamere Club was created in 1919 by and for women from Mansfield. When Laura hosted the club on August 14, 1919, Rose was visiting and spoke about her time living in New York City. Laura wrote the club's song, "We Are All Friends," in early 1920. Most months she attended the meetings of both clubs, and she hosted each group periodically. She served as the president of the Justamere Club from June of 1921 to June of 1922.

Laura undertook a paid position of service to the regional community when she became the secretary-treasurer of the Mansfield National Farm Loan Association at its first meeting in July 1917. The Federal Farm Loan Act of 1916 created the first national program that made loans to individual farmers. The government provided money to regional federal land banks, which in turn made it available to local associations. Farmers could borrow money from the local association at interest rates significantly lower than those offered by most banks at the time. Farmers who obtained loans were required to pay dues and buy stock in the association, and many years the association paid a dividend on stock. Laura signed up her friends and neighbors for loans and filed the paperwork for the mortgages in Hartville on a weekly basis. She wrote about the opportunities available in the *Missouri Ruralist* and placed ads in the *Mansfield Mirror*. Laura was reelected secretary-treasurer by the association every year between 1917 and 1928.

Finally, Laura participated in some local political organizations. She and her friend Maude Reynolds, also a member of the Justamere Club, often attended Wright County Democratic Party meetings in Hartville during the late 1910s and early 1920s. Laura also served as chair of the Pleasant Valley Democratic Women's Association and as secretary of the women's division of the Wright County Democratic Committee in 1919. This put her in the minority; most residents of and elected officials from the Ozarks were Republicans during the period. During the late nineteenth century, the Democratic Party was the party of limited government, and this was still the case in rural areas during the early twentieth century. It is likely that Laura and Almanzo were drawn toward the Democrats because of this commitment to less government, and it provides continuity with their later resentment of government action during the New Deal.

Like her mother, Rose had been busy since their time together in 1915. Her work writing for San Francisco newspapers had led to highly fictionalized serial biographies of Charlie Chaplin in 1916, Henry Ford in 1917, and Herbert Hoover in 1920. In 1918 she and Gillette Lane formally ended their marriage, and she left San Francisco and moved to New York City. There she did freelance writing and collaborated with Frederick O'Brien on his book *White Shadows on the South Seas.* In 1920, she was hired by the Red Cross to go to Europe and write about its relief efforts there. During the next three years, she traveled across the Continent and into the Middle East. She visited London, Paris, Rome, Vienna, Prague, Warsaw, Budapest, Sarajevo, Athens, Istanbul, Cairo, Jerusalem, Damascus, Beirut, and Baghdad. She especially enjoyed the time she spent in Albania, both in the capital of Tirana and in travels to the mountains. She reveled in the country's natural beauty and the company of the people she met there. Almost all the areas she visited were torn by war and cultural change. Rose returned to Rocky Ridge in December 1923 with her mind and spirit full of images and memories. She was thirty-seven.

Before her trip to Europe, Rose had assisted Laura in getting an article published in a national magazine. "Whom Will You Marry: The Farmer's Wife Says" appeared in *McCalls* in 1919. Rose knew the editor of the magazine, which was running a series about marriage to men in different walks of life. Rose secured the assignment on the perspective of the farmer's wife for her mother. She also rewrote the article significantly, for in a letter to Laura she breezily defended her decision to remove one section and rework others. The article's publication impressed Laura's friends in Mansfield, and it was noted in the *Mansfield Mirror.* Rose's return to Rocky Ridge made it more possible for her to encourage Laura to seize additional writing opportunities, and to mentor Laura's work.

Faith, the Broader World, and Rural Life

Laura Ingalls Wilder was in her forties and fifties during the second and third decades of the twentieth century. During this time, she knew what she believed, and her columns in the *Missouri Ruralist* shared her ideas about farming, human nature, and ways to love your neighbor. She had grown up in a variety of rural areas and small towns in the upper Midwest; she had visited one of the up-and-coming urban areas of the Far West during her trip to San Francisco in 1915; and she had seen people and cultures from many other parts of the world at the Panama-Pacific International Exposition. Ultimately, she was content to return to her husband, their dog, and their farm outside a small town in the Ozark Mountains. She remained active in community activities, especially the Mansfield Agricultural and Stock Show, the Order of the Eastern Star, local women's clubs, and the Mansfield Farm Loan Association. During World War I, both she and Almanzo volunteered to support the war effort.

Laura's Christian beliefs, as revealed in her *Missouri Ruralist* articles, emphasized God's law and the evils that come from breaking it. She asserted that all people are flawed and selfish, but she also maintained that all are called to compassion, fair dealing, and love for their neighbors. She offered observations based on her own upbringing and world affairs, but most often she related these topics to everyday duties. Her writing did not often feature explicit references to God, Christianity, and the Bible. These patterns of engagement suggest that while Christianity formed an important part of her worldview, it was not absolutely central to it. In addition, whether it was because of the emphases in her ideas about Christianity or the nature of the publication, these writings did not mention the work of Jesus Christ, forgiveness, or personal salvation.

Almanzo and Laura attended the Mansfield Methodist Episcopal church, mostly on Sunday mornings. They also often used Sunday for visiting with neighbors and friends. It is unclear how they related to the many pastors who served the Methodist church during the 1910s and early 1920s. We might assume that Laura continued reading God's Word and praying on a daily basis, but there is more documentary evidence from the period for her regular participation in the Eastern Star and Justamere Club.

Histories of American Christianity during the early twentieth century often discuss whether someone was a fundamentalist or a modernist. Modernists, or liberals, were led by pastors and other intellectuals who believed that Christianity should be updated to include the insights of modern science and critical approaches to the Bible. They were connected to the Social Gospel, pastors' efforts in cities to minister to the disadvantaged; these leaders emphasized social action and de-emphasized eternal salvation. Modernists often rejected supernatural accounts in the Bible. During the early twentieth century, fundamentalists opposed these efforts within Protestant denominations. They argued that sin and salvation must be preached and that the supernatural was a vital part of the Christian message. Those who followed their teachings later became known as evangelicals. Laura's approach to Christianity can't be placed easily into either the modernist or the fundamentalist camps. Laura's religious beliefs and practices were conventional across a great range of moderate Protestantism. Laura reflected a kind of Christianity that was entirely typical for many Protestants, especially in rural areas, during a period when historians emphasize conflicts between fundamentalists and liberals.

Rose stayed at Rocky Ridge with Almanzo and Laura intermittently for the rest of the 1920s and early 1930s. She hoped to support her parents by her writing. Her presence brought both joys and challenges to all three members of the family. Events in Laura's life and Rose's encouragement led Laura to think about new directions for her writing, including a turn to autobiography.

7

From Memoir to Children's Literature

1924–1935

In February of 1924, Laura Ingalls Wilder turned fifty-seven years old. In April, she received a telegram informing her that her mother had passed away. Caroline Quiner Ingalls died in De Smet on Easter Sunday, April 20, somewhat unexpectedly. She was eighty-four. Laura reflected on the experience of learning of her mother's death—and on the role of memories—in her regular *Ruralist* column several months later.

"Mother Passed away this morning" was the message that came over the wires and a darkness overshadowed the spring sunshine; a sadness crept into the birds' songs.

Some of us have received such messages. Those who have not, one day will. Just as when a child, home was lonely when mother was gone, so to children of a larger growth, the world seems a lonesome place when mother has passed away and only memories of her are left us—happy memories if we have not given ourselves any cause for regret.

Memories! We go thru life collecting them whether we will or not! Sometimes I wonder if they are our treasures in heaven or the consuming fires of torment when we carry them with us as we, too, pass on.

What a joy our memories may be or what a sorrow! But glad or sad they are with us forever. Let us make them carefully of all good things, rejoicing in the wonderful truth that while we are laying up for ourselves the very sweetest and best of happy memories, we are at the same time giving them to others.[1]

This was Laura's column in its entirety. It has been interpreted by Wilder biographers in strikingly different ways. Caroline Fraser focuses on the negative words in the first three paragraphs of the piece: "darkness," "sad ness," "lonesome," "regret," and most importantly, "consuming fires of torment." She sees the article as communicating that Laura was haunted by memories of her childhood, that she had many regrets, and that when she thought of her mother, she experienced deep sorrow. This interpretation is key to one of the themes of Fraser's biography, *Prairie Fires*: that Laura's childhood was essentially one of privation and difficulty, but the Little House books transformed her negative memories into a positive story of family perseverance. John Miller emphasizes the final paragraph of the column, arguing that it shows that Laura wrote the piece not to convey that she had anguished memories but to encourage her readers to better living. He argues that, like most of Laura's farm newspaper articles, this column should be seen as optimistic. While it acknowledges the darkness and sadness in the world, Laura asserts that everyone can work to create pleasant memories in and for the future. Miller notes that in all the articles and columns in the *Missouri Ruralist* where Laura describes her childhood, her recollections were happy.

Given the didactic nature of Laura's writing for the *Ruralist*, I believe that Miller's interpretation of this column is more likely to be correct. In addition, it appears that after "Memories!" the piece is no longer about mourning her mother; it shifts to reflections about the nature of remembering. While she grieved her loss, she also attempted to use it to encourage positive change in her own life and in her readers' lives. This is often what Laura did in her *Ruralist* columns. "Treasures in heaven" is a reference to Matthew 6:20, though she does not use the phrase the way Christ used it in the Sermon on the Mount. Other than that, Laura did not mention God, Christianity, or faith in the piece. Fraser and Miller

---

1. Laura Ingalls Wilder, As a Farm Woman Thinks, *Missouri Ruralist*, June 1, 1924; also in *Laura Ingalls Wilder, Farm Journalist: Writings from the Ozarks*, ed. Stephen W. Hines (Columbia: University of Missouri Press, 2007), 309–10.

agree that the death of Caroline Ingalls was likely one of a series of developments between 1924 and 1929 that led Laura to write a memoir of her early life. In addition, as problematic as her relationship with Rose became at times, Laura would not have succeeded in her writing endeavors without her daughter's instruction and encouragement.

Family, Church, Community, and Writing

Rose returned to Rocky Ridge in time for Christmas in 1923. During the fall of the following year, Laura wrote an article about the design and construction of their farmhouse kitchen, and Rose got it accepted by *Country Gentleman*, a national magazine for rural people. It appeared in January 1925 as "My Ozark Kitchen." As she had for Laura's previous national publication in *McCalls* in 1919, Rose significantly edited—and possibly rewrote—portions of this article before submitting it to her agent. When the deal was accomplished in November 1924, Rose was staying with friends in New York, and she wrote a lengthy letter to Laura with detailed instructions for how to write additional material that would be accepted by national magazines. She argued that Laura could be making thousands of dollars a year if she just listened to her advice. Rose had promised her parents that she would pay them five hundred dollars a year to help them stay on the farm; because her own income was not consistent, at times this became a burden that she resented. Laura and Rose collaborated on a second article for *Country Gentleman* that appeared as "The Farm Dining Room" in June of 1925.

On December 15, 1924, the *Missouri Ruralist* published Laura's last column, ending their thirteen-year publishing relationship. In it, she described the first school that she taught and Almanzo's coming to pick her up in his sleigh to take her home for Christmas. This return to a story from her teenage years may be additional evidence that Laura was hoping to do more writing about her childhood. Perhaps at this point she also aimed to get more material into the *Country Gentleman* or another magazine that paid better than the *Ruralist*. However, the two articles in 1925 were the extent of Laura's national publications during the decade.

Two months later, Laura pursued a different paid position. On February 26, 1925, the *Mansfield Mirror* announced that she was a candidate for the office of tax collector of Pleasant Valley Township. It is likely that she chose to run because the job paid three hundred dollars a year. The election was on the last day of March, and a letter that Laura wrote to the voters ran several times in the *Mirror*; it stressed her service as secretary-treasurer of the Mansfield National Farm Loan Association since 1917. She ran as an Independent Farmer against both a Republican and a Democrat, even though she had previously had connections to the Democratic Party. When the votes were reported at the beginning of April, she had come in third. If she had won, the position's salary would have been a welcome contribution to the family's income. Caroline Fraser notes that the job may also have made it less possible for her to devote time to autobiographical writing.

In June of 1925, Laura wrote a letter asking her aunt Martha Carpenter, Caroline Ingalls's older sister, for recipes for an article she was hoping to write for the *Ladies' Home Journal*. She also asked for as many stories as Martha could remember about her youth in Wisconsin. She said she was interested in them for her own writing, and perhaps Rose could make stories from them. Aunt Martha complied, sending Laura several letters full of recipes and stories. The article never appeared, but the materials her aunt sent may have sparked Laura's memory and provided even more motivation to write down the stories she could remember from her own childhood.

During her time staying with her parents at Rocky Ridge, Rose often argued with Laura. One can imagine that being almost forty years old and living with her parents was a challenge for Rose. During the previous five years, she had lived for extended periods in New York, Paris, and Tirana, Albania, places where adventure was nearby. She had visited Italy, Austria-Hungary, the USSR, Turkey, Egypt, Syria, and Iraq. Now she was living on a farm near a small town in southwestern Missouri. Mother and daughter shared many personality traits, but they also disagreed on foundational ideas about what constituted the good life. Rose wanted to provide economically for her parents and occupy a position of decision-making authority. Her cash flow was uneven because it was dependent on her ability to write and sell her short stories and serials to national magazines, newspapers, or other publications. She also worried about being a failure and disappointing her mother. These geographic, economic, and psychological realities heightened tensions between Rose and Laura; they also increased Rose's anxiety when she suffered writer's block. As a result, after little more than a year and a half on the farm, Rose was making plans to return to Europe. To make her parents' lives easier in her absence, she purchased a used Buick in New York and had it shipped to Mansfield. Both Laura and Almanzo learned to drive, and the car did make getting around easier for them. They named it Isabelle.

In the fall of 1925, Rose convinced Laura to take a trip in Isabelle to California with her and Helen Boylston, a friend Rose had met in Europe who had been living at Rocky Ridge since the spring. Helen's nickname was "Troub," short for Trouble, and she did most of the driving. Laura wrote letters to Almanzo from a number of places along the way. The letters described the landscape of the plains and mountains and commented on their driving and lodging arrangements. The three women spent a few weeks in San Francisco and Los Angeles before returning home. Like Laura's prior trip to California, none of the letters mention church attendance. They traveled on Sunday in Kansas, in Utah, and in California. They reached San Francisco on a Sunday. They arrived at their hotel at noon, got their mail, wrote answers, walked through Chinatown to Little Italy for dinner at 7:00 p.m., went to a movie, then headed back to the hotel. As during all her previous travels, Laura did not prioritize Christian worship when she was not at home.

In one letter to Almanzo, Laura also considered the future financial underpinnings of their household, comparing the contributions of selling their cream and Laura's work as secretary-treasurer for the Mansfield Farm Loan Association. She indicated that if it were possible, she would resign from her position as secretary-treasurer. Three years later, in 1928, she did step away from her work for the Association. During her ten years in the office, she had helped local farmers borrow close to a million dollars. The money she earned had helped to keep her and her husband on the farm. It was another indication that she was preparing to do some other work.

At the same time, Rose's restlessness continued. During the second half of the 1920s, she invested an increasing amount of her earnings from writing in the stock market. Between 1925 and 1929, the value of her portfolio, like those of millions of Americans, skyrocketed. Rose even got her parents to invest some of their savings in the market with the same Wall

Street firm she used. With her balance sheet well in the black, Rose decided she could leave the country to pursue new dreams. She and Troub Boylston left the United States for Europe in 1926. First they lived in Paris and studied Italian, Russian, and Albanian. Then they bought a Ford that they named Zenobia and drove it through France and Italy to Albania, the country that Rose loved. Rose spent thousands of dollars in Tirana on food, servants, and modifications to the house where she and Boylston lived, and which they did not own. When she could, Rose did some writing that sold and provided some income, including *Cindy*, a novel that brought her $10,000. Perhaps not unexpectedly for someone with Rose's constant longing for transcendent experiences, her life in Albania did not ultimately bring her lasting feelings of meaning, purpose, or peace. By late 1927, the situation between Albania and Mussolini's Italy had become tense, Rose missed the United States, and opportunities presented themselves to move out of the rented house and book passage to America. In January of 1928, Rose arrived back at Rocky Ridge.

Once again, Rose was living with her parents. A daily diary she kept consistently from 1928 to 1930 gives us some indication of the Sunday practices of different members of the household. Multiple times in her Sunday entries, Rose notes that her parents attended Sunday school. Several of these days were not on the first or third Sunday of the month, which indicates that Laura and Almanzo attended Sunday school at the Methodist church in Mansfield even when there was not preaching. Rose only mentions attending once herself, and that entry makes a cynical comment about the Sunday school class. During Sunday afternoons and evenings, Laura and Almanzo participated in a variety of activities with Rose, including visiting, picnics, driving to events, and eating at a restaurant in Mansfield or another nearby town. This supports the idea that the Wilders did not attend Sunday evening worship services.

The worship schedule at the Methodist Episcopal church stabilized during 1924 with preaching on the first and third Sundays of every month. This continued into the 1930s. The Baptist church also had preaching on those Sundays, and the Cumberland Presbyterian church held worship services on the second and fourth Sundays. The Church of Christ had preaching services only one Sunday each month, the first Sunday, until 1927, and the fourth Sunday after that, but in 1929 the church disappears from the *Mansfield Mirror* listings. Almost every year during the late 1920s and early 1930s, the *Mirror* reported on revival meetings at most of Mansfield's churches. It also describes visiting foreign missionaries, homecoming Sundays, and special services on Easter, Thanksgiving, and Christmas.

During the 1920s, two pastors served the Mansfield Methodist church for longer than just one year. George Wells served the Methodist churches in Ava and Mansfield from 1924 to 1927, and Christopher VanZant served the churches in Hartville and Mansfield from 1927 to 1929. The early 1930s saw a return to yearly appointments. J. E. Owen served only the church in Mansfield in 1930 and 1931. As a result, there are statistics for just the Mansfield church that year: sixty-five members. The names of other pastors are given in the appendix.

Holley Day served as pastor of the churches in Seymour and Mansfield from 1933 to 1937. During the first three months of 1934, the *Mirror* announced that the Mansfield Methodist church was hoping to get one hundred people to attend Sunday school. The newspaper provided weekly attendance figures that fluctuated from a low of thirty-two in January to a high of eighty-seven in February. The goal was never attained, but the drive reaped free advertising from the newspaper, and it likely encouraged Sunday school attendees like the Wilders.

After Rose had returned from her second European sojourn, it again became difficult for her, Troub, Laura, and Almanzo to be living in the same house. As a result, Rose decided to build her parents a new house on the back of their property. There is no evidence that they had asked for a new house, and they had constructed their farmhouse to suit their own desires, but Rose prevailed upon them to accept the gift. This meant that Laura and Rose would not have to live under the same roof or share the same Ozark kitchen. Rose was making some money from writing, and her stock investments continued to pay dividends and increase in value. She chose a Sears Roebuck house, but instead of buying the kit of materials from the mail-order company, she bought only the plans and had a local architect modify them to her specifications. She then hired a local contractor to build it under her supervision and made additional alterations during construction. When the house was completed in late 1928, it had cost $11,000, more than five times what the Sears kit alone cost. She had to borrow $2,500 from her parents to finish it. They moved into what became known as the rock house in December 1928. It sat on the other side of a ridge from the farmhouse. Rose then undertook significant remodeling in the farmhouse, where she lived at times with Troub Boylston, at times with Catherine Brody (another friend and writer), and often with a live-in housekeeper, for the next seven years.

Laura learned in late 1928 that her sister Mary Ingalls was very ill. Mary had been visiting her sister Carrie Ingalls Swanzey at her home in Keystone, South Dakota, when she suffered a stroke. After she experienced a second stroke, Carrie wrote Laura that the end was near. Mary died on October 17 at age sixty-three.

About a year after Mary Ingalls's death, the US stock market crashed. Initially, like many Americans who owned stock investments, Rose and her parents believed that the disruption was temporary and that their portfolios would recover. During the next several years, they ultimately came to understand that there was no quick fix for the nation's economic problems. As individuals, families, businesses, and governments worldwide scrambled to respond to the new realities and plan for the future, Laura turned to memories of her past.

"*This Is What Men Call God*": Pioneer Girl

Sometime during 1929 or early 1930, Laura began to write the story of her early life. She wrote using pencil and inexpensive tablets of paper and named the memoir *Pioneer Girl*. The first-person account began with her memories of Kansas and continued until her marriage. There were no divisions or chapter headings. The work was meant for publication, but it was also a document for Rose, because Laura indicated sections that were meant for Rose's eyes only. The manuscript included a collection of lifelike descriptions of nature, landscape, people, and events from her childhood. Laura walked from the rock house to the farmhouse and gave the tablets to Rose on May 7, 1930.

Rose took the handwritten manuscript and typed it, double spaced, while doing some editing. The process took only about ten days, so the editing was not extensive. She then sent the resulting typescript to her agent in New York, Carl Brandt. Unfortunately for Laura, the summer of 1930 was a challenging time for American publishing, as it was for the American economy in general. The stock market had not recovered, so many American businesses and individuals were left with greatly reduced assets. Rose's and her parents' brokerage accounts in June of 1930 were worth about half what they had been twelve months before. Brandt ultimately sent back the manuscript to Rose, saying that he didn't think that it could be placed.

Rose decided to edit the manuscript more heavily and try again. She also inserted a story about Laura's father stopping at the house of—and then participating in the effort to find—the Benders of eastern Kansas, a family of notorious serial killers. In 1873, at least ten bodies were found on the killers' homestead, but the Benders had moved on and were never found. It is not clear whether this account was part of Laura's memory of Kansas or even of family lore. It is likely that Rose added it in hopes of giving the manuscript greater appeal. When Brandt again declined to market it, Rose traveled to New York herself to meet with contacts in the magazine business, in effect acting as her mother's literary agent. Rose also switched agents, giving her new agent, George Bye, a third, typed revision of the work. Bye could not get any magazine or publisher interested in *Pioneer Girl*.

Before traveling to New York in early August 1930, Rose took some of the stories told by Charles Ingalls from *Pioneer Girl* and created a manuscript she hoped could become a children's picture book. Her diary referred to it as a juvenile, but it does not say to whom she sent it on August 18. She also did not tell her mother. In February of 1931, an editor at the children's division of Knopf publishers expressed interest in this book, if it could be turned into a book for beginning readers. Rose wrote Laura from New York, explaining the situation and providing instructions on how to do what the publisher was requesting. The manuscript had to be longer, include more details about pioneer life, and be written in the third person. Laura changed the point of view, wrote the additional material, and brought the complete handwritten manuscript to Rose, who was back at Rocky Ridge, on May 8. Rose typed it and the two of them met to go over the manuscript a few times at the end of that month. The finished typescript was in the mail on May 27.

Rose continued to work to get a publishing outlet for *Pioneer Girl* sporadically during the next several years, but the book was not published until 2014. Laura consulted the manuscript as she wrote the Little House books, and Rose used narratives and accounts from it to write two books of her own. The volume that appeared in 2014 as *Pioneer Girl: The Annotated Autobiography* presents Laura's handwritten draft. In 2021, the three typescript versions of *Pioneer Girl* were printed in parallel columns in *Pioneer Girl: The Revised Texts*. One can trace the changes made by Rose in her efforts to get the book published. For most of the original manuscripts' descriptions of the church, Christianity, and faith, all three drafts are essentially the same. Some accounts are dropped in later drafts as Rose attempted to streamline the narrative. There are no substantive changes to the passage about Laura's dislike of Howard Ensign's testifying at the Congregational prayer meeting. The description of her experience with God's presence has some changes to punctuation, and "That is what men call God" is changed to "This is what men call God."[2] Both constructions have been quoted in books about Wilder's life.

In June of 1931, after the children's book was in the mail and Rose had turned again to her own writing, Laura and Almanzo decided to take a trip to South Dakota. They drove and took their dog Nero with them. A diary that Laura kept during the trip was published in 2006. The Wilders left on June 6 and experienced hot, dry, and dusty conditions for the three and a half weeks that they were away from home. They first went to Manchester, South Dakota, west of De Smet, and stayed with Laura's youngest sister, Grace, and her husband, Nate Dow. Both Dows were in poor health, Nate with asthma and Grace with diabetes. While staying there, Laura and Almanzo drove to De Smet almost daily to speak with former acquaintances, visit their parents' house in De Smet, and drive past Charles Ingalls's homestead. After a week and a day, they left Manchester and drove to Keystone in the Black Hills of western South Dakota, where her sister Carrie lived with her husband, Dave Swanzey, and his son Harold. The Swanzeys took the Wilders sightseeing, including to Mount Rushmore, which was in the process of being transformed into the presidential monument. Laura and Almanzo then returned home. It took six days to travel to De Smet but only five days to drive back to Mansfield and Rocky Ridge.

2. Laura Ingalls Wilder, *Pioneer Girl: The Revised Texts*, ed. Nancy Tystad Koupal (Pierre: South Dakota State Historical Society, 2021), 192–93.

In this diary, the church or Christianity is mentioned only two times. First, Laura recorded driving past German Catholic churches in eastern Nebraska. While staying with the Dows, she noted that the Presbyterian ladies' aid society in De Smet was holding a food sale. When the Wilders had traveled from De Smet to Mansfield thirty-seven years earlier, they had used covered wagons and stopped every Sunday. During this trip, Almanzo and Laura drove on Sundays. On Sunday, June 7, they drove 277 miles north and west to Eureka, Kansas. Three weeks later they were on their way home, and they drove 233 miles from Phelps City, Missouri, to south of Higginsville. While staying in Manchester on Sunday, June 14, they visited De Smet and went to the Ingallses' old house on Third Street. Laura does not record that they attended any worship service, but they likely worshiped at the Congregational church, several blocks from that house, if there was preaching that Sunday. The following Sunday was the day they visited Mount Rushmore. As was the case during the road trip Laura took with Rose six years earlier, neither worshiping in a church nor observance of Sunday seems to have been a primary concern for the Wilders when they were on the road.

When Laura and Almanzo returned to Rocky Ridge, perhaps they brought back with them a new perspective on Laura's childhood, family, and life story. They and Rose had reasons to be optimistic that Knopf would publish Laura's first book. Maybe Laura was also thinking about future books for children, drawn from her life experiences and the writing she had already done.

"Now I Lay Me Down to Sleep": Little House in the Big Woods

The road to publication of that first book, however, was still not a smooth one. In September 1931, Marian Fiery, the editor of the children's department at Knopf, accepted the manuscript and promised to deliver a contract for three books. Then in November, Knopf decided to close its children's department entirely. As the Great Depression deepened, many businesses saw cost savings as the best way to weather the storm. Somehow Virginia Kirkus, an editor in the children's department at Harper & Brothers Publishers, came to read the manuscript. It may have been sent to her by George Bye, or Fiery may have shared it with her. By the second week of December 1931, Kirkus had read it and loved it. Harper's gave Laura a contract. Laura and Rose corrected page proofs in late January 1932, and author's copies of the book, now titled *Little House in the Big Woods*, arrived at Rocky Ridge by the end of March. The book sold well and received positive reviews in the *New York Times* and other newspapers. Laura was sixty-five years old.

In *Little House in the Big Woods*, Christianity is mentioned two times. One chapter elaborates on the section in *Pioneer Girl* about Sunday observance in Wisconsin. There are detailed descriptions of baths on Saturday night, dressing in their Sunday best, and prohibitions against noisy play. Ma read Bible stories and Laura looked at pictures in the large Bible, envying Adam since he could wear fewer clothes. The fictional Laura gets in trouble one day for playing loudly with Jack the dog and saying, "I hate Sunday," when told to sit quietly in a chair. Pa calls her to get a spanking, then changes his mind and tells her "The Story of Grandpa's Sled and the Pig." After she and Mary are in bed, Pa plays the fiddle and sings "Rock of Ages" and "Am I a Soldier of the Cross?" The second verse of the latter song is reproduced. The only other mention of Christian practice is a description of Ma, Laura, and Mary saying their prayers. The prayer from the *New England Primer* is printed in its entirety: "Now I lay me down to sleep, / I pray the Lord my soul to keep. / If I should die before I wake, / I pray the Lord my soul to take."[3]

Some parts of Laura's handwritten manuscript and a typescript of the book are available to researchers. Therefore, it is possible to compare the original manuscript and typescript to what was eventually published. Very little appears to have been changed between the typescript and published book, and there were mainly additions between the manuscript and typescript. The additions were probably made by Rose, possibly in consultation with her mother when they met in May of 1931. Scholars agree that *Little House in the Big Woods* was one of the Little House books that received the lightest editing and reworking from Rose, mainly because she spent less time on it than on subsequent volumes. However, the finished book was the product of a collaboration between the two women. In general, Laura provided

3. Laura Ingalls Wilder, *Little House in the Big Woods*, in *The Little House Books*, ed. Caroline Fraser (New York: Library of America, 2012), 1:47.

the experiences and stories, and Rose provided the structure, details, and editing. In the chapter on Sundays, the only significant difference is that, at the end, the written manuscript also mentions the shortened hymn title "There Is a Fountain." The account of Laura and Mary saying their prayers is only available in the typescript, and it is the same as in the book.

As I address the other Little House books, I will examine the differences between the original manuscripts and the published books, particularly sections that mention faith, God, Christianity, or the church. One can assume that changes were made by Rose, in consultation with Laura. One might wonder if the publisher made additional editorial changes, but there is documentary evidence that this was not the case: Ursula Nordstrom, an editor at Harper's, wrote of the Little House books, "None of the manuscripts ever needed any editing. Not any. They were read and then copy-edited and sent to the printer."[4] This is testimony to Rose's ability as an editor and a collaborator, and it provides confidence that however one construes the changes to Laura's handwritten manuscripts, the books were only substantively changed by Laura and Rose.

In her first published book, Laura described nightly prayers and weekly observance of Sunday as consistent parts of her upbringing. There were few alterations in these descriptions between the handwritten manuscripts and the published books. Christian practices, both weekly and daily, are depicted as occupying an important place in the Ingalls family's life. On the other hand, many more pages are devoted to other aspects of her childhood—food preparation, family dynamics, and extended family relations—than to religious exercises. Faith was important but not central to Laura's first work of children's fiction.

"A Day for Going to Church and Resting": Farmer Boy

Even as *Little House in the Big Woods* was being created from Laura and Rose's manuscript, Laura began work on a second children's book. Instead of returning to *Pioneer Girl* to create another book about her upbringing,

---

4. Nordstrom to Doris K. Stotz, January 11, 1967, in *Dear Genius: The Letters of Ursula Nordstrom*, collected and edited by Leonard S. Marcus (New York: HarperCollins, 1998), 234.

she decided to write about Almanzo's childhood in upstate New York. The book would describe a nineteenth-century boy's life and complement her first book, which described a year in a girl's life. Biographer Pamela Smith Hill notes that this was a shrewd business decision, as publishers have long noted that girls are more likely to read books about boys than boys are to read books about girls. Laura wrote the first draft in late 1931 and early 1932. She asked Rose to begin work on it in March.

Rose had become intensely unhappy with her life. In November 1931, their investment firm had stopped making dividend payments, and Troub Boylston left to get a job in New York. Rose wrote dark comments in her journal, was often unable to write, and got into frequent arguments with her mother and others. She experienced ongoing troubles with tooth and foot pain, her economic difficulties continued, and she may have suffered from clinical depression. In the midst of these challenges, Rose decided to use accounts from *Pioneer Girl* as the core of a story. The narrative was about a couple living on the American frontier, and it was set in the Dakotas during the 1870s. The couple is named Charles and Caroline, they settle in a dugout by "Wild Plum Creek," and Charles walks east to get work when their crops are eaten by grasshoppers. Rose had not asked for her mother's permission to use these accounts. She did not even tell Laura about the story. Rose originally titled it *Courage*, but she later changed the name to *Let the Hurricane Roar*. This title was drawn from a line from the chorus of "The Evergreen Shore," a hymn that Laura had remembered from her childhood.

Rose edited and typed *Farmer Boy*, and she sent both it and *Let the Hurricane Roar* to George Bye in the middle of August 1932. She received word later that month that the *Saturday Evening Post* was going to run *Hurricane* as a serial in October. In September, *Farmer Boy* was rejected by Harper & Brothers. Financial realities were now influencing their publishing decisions, and they asked for significant revisions to the manuscript. The Depression had intensified in 1932, resulting in the landslide election of Franklin Delano Roosevelt in November. A majority of Missouri voters chose him over Herbert Hoover. Even a small majority in Mansfield, usually reliably Republican, voted for Roosevelt. Unemployment, bank failures, economic hardship, and uncertainty spread during the months after the election.

Rose traveled to New York in late 1932 to meet with Bye and to visit friends. A friend from Mansfield, Corrinne Murray, drove. The two took a roundabout route, first driving north to Ottawa, Canada, and stopping in Burr Oak, Iowa, and Spring Valley, Minnesota, on the way. They then stopped in Malone in upstate New York to see where Almanzo had grown up. Rose discovered that the farmhouse of his childhood still stood and got the current owners to show her through it. She sent letters home describing the house, the landscape, the town, and other details of the area. Both she and Laura hoped that this information would help them rework *Farmer Boy*.

Laura learned by accident about Rose's use of the material from *Pioneer Girl*, at a dinner party given by Rose for her parents and several other friends in January 1933. *Let the Hurricane Roar* had appeared as a serial in the *Post* and was set to be published in book form in April. When the book appeared, it sold well. Laura felt betrayed. It shattered their relationship for a while. After her dog Bunting died after being hit by a car in February, Rose began recording in her journal that she had been crying uncontrollably and even desiring to die. She had bought Bunting in Vienna during her second sojourn in Europe, and his death brought Rose to the brink of despair.

Rose's finances and those of Laura and Almanzo were intertwined, and Rose and her mother had completely different ways of responding to economic privation. Laura's approach to financial challenges was shaped by her upbringing and can be described as stoic. She expected hard times, accepted what could not be changed, and worked to change what she could. In the spring of 1933, Laura asked Rose to look at the electric bill for the property, then offered to have the electricity at the rock house disconnected, cutting their expenses significantly. Rose took the offer as a manipulative effort to get her to put more of her funds toward expenses, which she did resentfully, writing in her journal about how her mother made her feel like a miserable failure.

During these months of conflict and distress, however, Laura and Rose somehow found the time, patience, and emotional resources to collaborate on *Farmer Boy*. Rose's diary notes that she worked on the manuscript in January, February, and March. Perhaps the two talked on the phone about it, or one or the other walked over the ridge to discuss the story. They consulted Almanzo about what he remembered, and he provided drawings of the buildings on the farm where he had grown up. They also used material that Rose had collected during her trip to Malone. Rose reworked the first chapters extensively and incorporated a story from *Pioneer Girl* that had occurred when Laura lived in Burr Oak, Iowa. Together they created a manuscript that was accepted by Harper & Brothers in March of 1933, but the contract offered only 5 percent royalties, half the 10 percent that Wilder had received for *Big Woods* and all the subsequent books. Laura accepted the contract, but she resented the reduced royalties for many years.

Farmer Boy was a response to the Depression. Although its author, her collaborator, and their readers may all have been pinched by economic deprivation, the book depicts Almanzo's upbringing as comfortable and prosperous. The Wilder family is hardworking, shrewd, and frugal, but they always have more than they need, especially of food. Almost every chapter includes lavish descriptions of food as the fictional Almanzo eats his way through a formative year of his life. The lessons that he learns have to do with traditionally male activities, including crop raising, bargaining, and the care of large farm animals, especially horses. *Little House in the Big Woods* has a timeless quality; one feels like in the following year, Laura will experience the same round of agricultural labor, food preparation, and family events. *Farmer Boy* features similar detailed descriptions of farm activities, but the story arc moves with more purpose toward a conclusion, driven by vocational choice. Throughout the narrative, Almanzo desires to have a colt of his own to take care of and train. At the end of the book, he must choose whether to become an apprentice to a carriage-maker in town or to become a farmer like his father. Almanzo chooses to pursue farming because of his love for horses.

As in *Big Woods*, *Farmer Boy* contains one reference to nightly prayers and devotes one chapter to the Wilder family's observance of Sunday. The Sunday is in winter, and the family wears their best clothes and rides in the sleigh five miles to town for the worship service. The service is described in between a loving description of stacked pancakes and the abundance of Sunday dinner. Later in the book, the church dining room at the county fairgrounds is the site where Almanzo eats an enormous meal and two and a half pieces of pie. The family also attends church when they take Almanzo's older siblings to boarding school. Finally, God is invoked in relation to the safety of a payment for horses. There are more references to church and Christianity in this volume than in the first Little House book. There are also some intriguing differences between Wilder's original manuscript and the published work.

One complete handwritten manuscript and one typescript of *Farmer Boy* are available. Because the book was reworked and edited multiple times, the differences between what Laura wrote and what was published are significant. The core of Laura's storytelling is present in the manuscript, but the book has much more structure, dialogue, and dramatic tension. Some entire scenes have been added, including vivid descriptions meant to appeal directly to children. The whole is organized to contribute to the themes mentioned above: prosperity, horses, and farming. One imagines that these changes were made by Rose, in collaboration with Laura. For example, here is the end of the description of Sunday in the manuscript: "They never went visiting or had any company on Sunday. That was a day for going to church and resting."[5] The book reads, "Almanzo just sat. He had to. He was not allowed to do anything else, for Sunday was not a day for working or playing. It was a day for going to church and for sitting still."[6] The latter is more direct and the feelings conveyed are more intense. As in *Big Woods*, the narrative's emphasis is on the strictness of Sunday observance in the nineteenth century.

More significant changes are present in the account of Almanzo's father's sale of two horses. He receives a down payment of two hundred dollars, and it is too late in the day to take the bills to the bank. In Wilder's handwritten manuscript:

> Father took the money to Mother. They didn't like to keep $200 in the house overnight, but it was too late to take it to the bank at Malone. Mother put it away in the bureau drawer in her room. She said good Christians ought to feel that the Lord would take care of them, but she'd rather the money were in the bank.[7]

5. Laura Ingalls Wilder, *Farmer Boy* manuscript, folder 10 (unpaginated), Wilder, Laura Ingalls Papers, Microfilm Collection, the State Historical Society of Missouri, Columbia, Missouri.

6. Laura Ingalls Wilder, *Farmer Boy*, in Fraser, *The Little House Books*, 1:141.

7. Wilder, *Farmer Boy* manuscript, folder 11 (unpaginated), Wilder, Laura Ingalls Papers.

This becomes, in the published book, the following exchange:

> "The Lord will take care of us," Father said.
>   "The Lord helps them that help themselves." Mother replied.
> "I wish to goodness that money was safe in the bank."[8]

As it happens, thieves *had* followed the horse buyers into the neighborhood. That evening a stray dog appears on the Wilders' doorstep and the family greets it kindly. The dog then barks several times during the night to warn the family and to scare away the thieves. Here is how the story concludes in the handwritten manuscript: "Father shook his head and said, 'Well! Well! Well!' But Mother said she would always believe the strange dog had been sent by the Lord to watch over them and that he had kept the robbers away."[9] The published book says the following:

> Mother said she would always believe that Providence had sent the strange dog to watch over them. Almanzo thought perhaps he stayed because Alice fed him.
>   "Maybe he was sent to try us," Mother said. "Maybe the Lord was merciful to us because we were merciful to him."[10]

Both exchanges in the published version are more engaging than the original because they are conversation instead of just narrative. These dialogues help to make the account memorable, and they appear to have been supplied by Rose. But the manuscript presents a more conventional Christian understanding of God and his actions in the lives of his people. Mother and Father agree that God is in control, even though they are anxious. Mother believes firmly that it was God who sent the dog to be the means of their protection. In the book, the addition of "The Lord helps them that help themselves"—which many have believed appears in the Bible, even though it does not—and the multiple interpretations given by Mother and Almanzo confuse this more straightforward depiction of God's work in the world.

8. Wilder, *Farmer Boy*, 1:164.
9. Wilder, *Farmer Boy* manuscript, folder 11 (unpaginated).
10. Wilder, *Farmer Boy*, 1:167.

A final difference between the handwritten manuscript and the published book comes in the description of the visit of Nick Brown, the traveling tin peddler. He brought tin pots and pans to trade for Almanzo's mother's rags, and he also brought gossip from the neighborhood, humorous stories, and songs. After dinner, he shares the following joke set in a worship service: "I was at Townly school-house at meeting one Sunday and, announcing the next meetings, Brother Rhodes said, 'The snows are deep on the roads between here an' there, and I don't know as I can get through, but I will preach at the Warner school-house next Sunday, *if the Lord is willing*. And I will preach at the Steel school-house the Sunday after, *whether or no* for the roads will be traveled that way.'"[11] The punchline turns on a phrase used by Christians when speaking about something that is doubtful or something that they hope to do: "if the Lord is willing." The phrase comes from James 4:15, where the author exhorts his readers not to boast or assume that they will be able to do everything that they plan. In the joke, the pastor first follows the admonition, and then he breaks it by saying he will do something whether God is willing or not. This juxtaposition would have been entertaining, especially for Christians. The book omits the joke and other stories told by Brown in the handwritten manuscript. As a result, a particular reference to Christianity and the church was removed along with other details seen as unnecessary.

The typescript must have been a very late draft, because it is almost the same as the published book. There are very few handwritten comments or corrections on it. Because Laura and Rose worked together on the book in person, there was less reason for writing on the typescript itself. Some of the later books, developed when Rose had left Rocky Ridge, have more notes and edits on the typescript pages, because they were mailed from Rose to Laura for her review, and then sent back.

There are more references to Christianity and the church in *Farmer Boy* than in *Little House in the Big Woods*, but the total number is still relatively low. The fact that the family attends church makes it somewhat more important than in *Big Woods*, although the historical Wilder family may not have been able to do that year-round in the way depicted in the novel. Instead, they may have taken advantage of preaching services in

---

11. Wilder, *Farmer Boy* manuscript, folder 11 (unpaginated).

rural schoolhouses like the ones referred to in Nick Brown's joke from the original manuscript. Other changes mean that the more straightforward and traditional understanding of Christianity in the handwritten manuscript is somewhat altered in the published book. One must imagine that Rose's contributions to the collaboration were central to this shift. Since the two women collaborated on the book in person, however, we cannot absolutely assign her all the credit, or all the blame, for the changes.

"There Is a Happy Land": Little House on the Prairie

Even before *Farmer Boy* appeared, Laura was writing again. The next book focused on her family's time in Kansas. *Little House on the Prairie* is a bridge between the first two "one year in the life" stories and the last five books, which cover variable amounts of time, describe the family's progress toward landownership, and narrate the fictional Laura's development into a young woman. While it does address the events of approximately one year's time, *Prairie* does not have either the timeless quality of *Big Woods* or the vocational directionality of *Farmer Boy*. The book presents the story of a family coming face-to-face with wilderness and Indigenous Peoples. It is a narrative where there are no obvious winners and losers, no simple story line leading to the wilderness being tamed by the farmer or American Indians being driven away by whites. At the end of the book, in fact, both the Indians and the Ingallses have left their homes behind.

Laura and Rose's relationship experienced both highs and lows during 1933. Rose continued to struggle with depression, and she often thought about leaving Rocky Ridge. Still, mother and daughter were able to collaborate on *Little House on the Prairie*. While Laura was writing early drafts, she sent letters to librarians and historical societies in Kansas and Oklahoma, hoping to get accurate information about where the family had lived and the Native Americans with whom they had interacted. She apparently believed that her family had settled forty miles south of Independence, Kansas, which would have put their homestead in Oklahoma. In fact, the Ingallses had settled only twelve miles away from the town. Laura also trusted a correspondent in Oklahoma who said that a major Osage leader in 1870 was named Soldat du Chene, which was incorrect. Laura finished working on the manuscript and took it to Rose on February 1, 1934. Rose typed it, the two of them discussed changes, and it was ready to be sent to New York at the end of June.

The book's treatment of American Indians is hard to read for many in the twenty-first century. The Osage are depicted stereotypically, and at times they are called "savages." At different times, their neighbors Mr. and Mrs. Scott both say that "the only good Indian is a dead Indian."[12] Central to the story is the reality that the Ingalls family moved to land assuming that it would be taken from the Osage and given to them. One emotional climax of the book centers around whether the Osage will massacre the Ingalls family and their white neighbors. Nevertheless, I agree with Wilder scholar John Miller that the book's depiction of Indigenous Peoples is more complicated than some have maintained. Certainly, Ma and some of their neighbors have extremely negative views of American Indians. Pa's view of the Osage is more complex. He is friendly toward them, keeps his dog Jack from harming them, and disagrees with Ma when she expresses negative ideas. At the same time, he assumes that Native Americans should be removed when whites moved into an area. Pa's optimistic assumption that he can stay on good terms with his Osage neighbors while waiting for the federal government to give him their land proves incorrect, as they plan to make war on the settlers. The Ingallses endure repeated nights of war cries until the plan to kill them is stopped by one leader, a man Pa calls "one good Indian."[13] The fictional Laura is confronted with these different viewpoints, and as a result her ideas of Indigenous People are conflicted. She is more of Pa's opinion than Ma's, although at times she is afraid of the Osage. She is also drawn to the beautiful feathers they wear, sees them as proud and dignified, and desires to see an Osage baby (a "papoose"). In a secondary climax of the book, the family watches thousands of Osage ride away. At that moment, she sees the papoose and says that she wants it. Like most literature from the early twentieth century, this book (and several of the other Little House books) consistently depicts American Indians as the other, as essentially not like the Ingalls family or Americans in general. At times they are a sympathetic other, sometimes a dangerous other, but at all times they are

---

12. Wilder, *Little House on the Prairie*, in Fraser, *The Little House Books*, 1:356, 386.
13. Wilder, *Little House on the Prairie*, 1:394.

the other. As a result, I understand why those of Indigenous descent—and other twenty-first-century readers—find the book offensive.

Interactions with Indigenous Peoples, the prairie landscape and wildlife, and the security provided by Pa for his family are the major themes of *Little House on the Prairie*. God, Christianity, and faith make very few appearances. The church is not mentioned at all. Concepts from Christianity are only referred to at three different points. The first is when Laura and the family fear that their dear dog Jack has been drowned in a swollen creek that the family had only barely crossed safely in the covered wagon. This dialogue results:

> "Oh, Ma," Laura begged. "Jack has gone to heaven, hasn't he? He was such a good dog, can't he go to heaven?"
>
> Ma did not know what to answer, but Pa said: "Yes, Laura, he can. God that doesn't forget the sparrows won't leave a good dog like Jack out in the cold."[14]

This description of a father reassuring his distraught daughter includes a reference to Matthew 10:29, where Jesus says that a sparrow "shall not fall on the ground without your Father." The second instance comes when Pa and Ma are building their cabin together and a log falls onto Ma's foot. Everyone is relieved that the foot is just sprained and not broken. Then an aside is given: "It was Providential that the foot was not crushed. Only a little hollow in the ground had saved it."[15] This is a way of saying that it was God who had saved Ma's foot. The third and final mention of Christianity comes when Pa has left his wife and children to travel to town. In the middle of the night, Laura awakes to see Ma in the rocking chair by the fire and to hear her singing:

> "There is a happy land,
> Far, far away,
> Where saints in glory stand,
> Bright, bright as day.

14. Wilder, *Little House on the Prairie*, 1:279.
15. Wilder, *Little House on the Prairie*, 1:293.

> "Oh to hear the angels sing,
> Glory to the Lord, our king—"

Laura didn't know that she had gone to sleep. She thought the shining angels began to sing with Ma, and she lay listening to their heavenly singing until suddenly her eyes opened and she saw Pa standing by the fire.[16]

These are brief references to God in the middle of crises that faced the Ingalls family. Unlike the first two Little House books, *Little House on the Prairie* does not include any descriptions of more regular Christian practices, like Sunday observance or nightly prayers.

Three manuscripts for *Little House on the Prairie* in Laura's handwriting exist. Two are partial. One seems like an early draft, as portions of it are written on various types of paper, including the backs of pages of business and personal correspondence. The second is a draft of what became the last eleven chapters of the book. The third is a full manuscript written out on three lined tablets and including page numbers and chapter titles, so it was probably a later draft, perhaps written after she had discussed earlier efforts with Rose. Rose ultimately typed a final version and sent it to Harper's. In general, Rose's collaboration and editing improve everything in the work. The descriptions are more vivid, there is more drama and suspense, and the dialogue is more natural. Overall, the book is more gauged to meet children where they are and appeal to how they feel about the world. The focus on the book's themes is much tighter than in Laura's manuscripts.

The treatment of God and Christianity in the handwritten drafts is surprising. For example, none of the handwritten manuscripts include the story of Jack being lost and thought dead after the crossing of the creek. This was probably added for dramatic effect by Rose. She may have been thinking about the death of her own dog the previous year. It is an effective addition, and when Jack later returns, the reader experiences deep relief. This likely means that Rose contributed the conversation between Laura and Pa about Jack going to heaven. If one compares Laura's and Rose's attitudes toward the church and Christianity in the early 1930s,

---

16. Wilder, *Little House on the Prairie*, 1:359.

one might assume that if a conversation mentioning God, a Scripture reference, and heaven was added, it was Laura's idea. On the other hand, the certainty that a good dog will go to heaven is not necessarily orthodox Christian doctrine. All things considered, it appears that the account was contributed by Rose.

A second difference is that, in all the handwritten drafts, Ma does not help Pa build the house at all; he has assistance from a neighbor from the start. In the book, Ma helps him build the house until the accident; after Ma suffers the sprained ankle, Pa learns that he has a neighbor close enough to assist. This means that it may also have been Rose who added the sentence about God's will and Ma's injury. Just as it seems to have been Rose who used "Providence" to refer to God in the published version of *Farmer Boy*, so it may have been her decision to include "Providential" at this point.

Finally, in the account of Pa's trip to town, the full handwritten manuscript has some additional details about the night before he returns to the cabin:

> After supper Mary and Laura said their prayers and went quietly to bed. The world seemed big and cold with Pa away. Ma sat by the fire, holding baby Carrie's feet to the warmth and singing low,
>
> > "There is a happy land far, far away
> > Where saints in glory stand
> > Bright, bright as day
> > O how those angels sing
> > Glory be to Christ our king
> > Loud let his praises ring
> > Praise! Praise for aye."[17]

There are several important changes made between the draft and the published book. First, Laura's manuscript mentions the children saying their prayers, and that is removed in the book. Second, the book deletes two of the lines of the hymn, and this removes the specific reference to

---

17. Wilder, *Little House on the Prairie* manuscript, folder 17, 143, Wilder, Laura Ingalls Papers.

Christ, leaving only praises to the Lord. The praise is more generic because it does not mention Christ, and it is less emphatic. Finally, Laura's sleepy thought that she can hear the angels singing with Ma were added in the book. This addition is lyrical and dramatic, and it sounds as though it was contributed by Rose.

Little House on the Prairie appeared toward the end of September 1935. Like the earlier two books, this one was reviewed positively. The reviewer in the *New York Times* wrote that the book presents "with humor and with understanding, the picture of a fine and courageous family, who are loyal and imaginative in their relationships to one another."[18] Laura also gave one of her author's copies to the *Mansfield Mirror*, and the paper printed a story about it on the front page. The author of the article noted that the book celebrated "Living simple and happy in Gods [*sic*] great universe."[19]

Faith, the Church, and Authorship

Laura remained active in community activities in Mansfield for much of the 1920s, but her name is less likely to be mentioned in the *Mansfield Mirror* during the early 1930s. She served as a local officer in the Order of the Eastern Star every year between 1924 and 1931. Almanzo also was an Eastern Star officer in 1928. However, in 1931, both Almanzo and Laura demitted, or left the Eastern Star, after almost forty years in the organization. It may be that financial challenges forced them to withdraw so they could save their dues. It may also be that their age and Laura's devotion of more of her time to writing drove the decision to leave. Almanzo remained a member of the Mansfield Lodge and was a master Mason until his death. Laura also remained a member of the Athenian Club, but she attended fewer meetings.

Rose's daily diary entries during the early 1930s provide a look at Laura and Almanzo's ongoing patterns of Sunday observance. They often came to the farmhouse or Rose went to the rock house for their late afternoon meal: it is alternately called "dinner," "high tea," and "supper." Multiple

18. Anne T. Eaton, "The New Books for Boys and Girls," *New York Times Book Review*, November 3, 1935, 10.

19. "Little House on the Prairie," *Mansfield Mirror*, October 3, 1935, 1.

times, Rose records eating at a restaurant in Mansfield or another small town, so Laura and Almanzo had no qualms about that practice. They also visited others in the community, either Laura's friends, Rose's friends, or their neighbors, and had them over to their home. At times Laura went to a movie with Rose and others. It seems clear that Laura and Almanzo did not attend Sunday evening worship services.

Rose's religious beliefs were complicated, though it seems certain that she had rejected traditional Christianity. Her diaries show that she very rarely attended Sunday worship services. She usually worked at writing all day, worked in the morning and socialized in the afternoon, or socialized all day. Her diaries, journals, and letters to multiple correspondents mention her attraction to Islam, nurtured during her time in eastern Europe and the Middle East, especially in Albania. In May of 1932, she wrote in her journal that she had an experience of peace with the world that seemed supernatural. It was a kind of surrender, and she quotes Matthew 11:28, where Christ calls those who are weary to come to him. But she denied the possibility that this experience came from God because it didn't coincide with a religious ceremony: "I only sat on my bed, looking at and listening to the blessedness of rain after drought, and the cool refreshment of earth and grass seemed to spread through me." She concluded that "Religions are perhaps only the psychological mechanisms by which multitudes attain this peace. Allah al illah il allah."[20] After writing that she rejected the idea that a supreme being was behind her spiritual experience, she included a prayer to the god of Islam. Sometimes in her diaries and journals she wrote "Inshallah" (meaning "if Allah wills it") before or after something she hoped to do. She also wrote in her diary after meeting a friend, "Someone thinks it such a pity that I have no Christian faith."[21] Nevertheless, her diary also notes that she had attended an early Mass on a Sunday morning at St. John's in St. Louis. This was probably St. John the Apostle and Evangelist Cathedral. Another entry mentions attending a Pentecostal revival meeting with a female pastor. It appears that she at least had some

20. Rose Wilder Lane, entry for May 28, 1932, in Journal, May 1932–January 1933, box 21, item 45, Rose Wilder Lane Papers, Herbert Hoover Presidential Library, West Branch, Iowa.
21. Rose Wilder Lane, entry for April 17, 1935 in Diary, 1931–1935, box 21, item 37, Rose Wilder Lane Papers.

curiosity about Christian worship services, perhaps in beautiful spaces or with engaging speakers.

At the end of 1935, Laura could have looked back over the previous ten years and considered how much she had to be thankful for. As she approached her sixty-ninth birthday, she had written three published children's books that were selling well and providing income. She and her husband lived in a modern house with running water and electricity. Their daughter had provided their more comfortable living situation and had been an essential contributor to Laura's publishing success.

At the same time, Rose had at times brought grief to her mother. While Rose had worked to get *Pioneer Girl* into print and made it possible for the first Little House books to be published, she had also used stories from Laura's life in a book of her own without asking or even telling Laura. In 1933, a teenage boy, John Turner, had appeared at the door of the farmhouse, willing to work in return for food and lodging. He said he was from Oklahoma and his mother had died. Rose allowed him to stay, even after she found out that these were lies and his home was not far from Mansfield. The next year, Rose invited his younger brother Al to come live at the farmhouse as well. Her approach to parenting was permissive, including allowing them to have friends over for parties that at times lasted late into the night. In early 1935, she was visited by a male writer for the *Saturday Evening Post*. These developments did not escape the notice of neighbors in rural Missouri, and the latter was mentioned in the *Mansfield Mirror*. Rose in turn accused Laura in her journals and correspondence of being proud, judgmental, and ungenerous. Acquaintances later told biographers that Laura and Rose's relationship was close but volatile.

While *Pioneer Girl* provides invaluable information about Wilder's childhood experiences and beliefs, her other writings during the late 1920s and early 1930s tell us little about her adult beliefs. Her patterns of belonging and behavior are somewhat more traceable. Laura and Almanzo's connection to the Mansfield Methodist Episcopal church continued. While her writing career was taking off, there was a pastor at the Methodist church preaching sermons two Sundays out of each month. Methodist pastors in Mansfield brought a variety of life and ministry experiences to their work. A few pastors during the mid-1920s and the mid-1930s had been able to serve the church for more than one year. Both the increased number of preaching services and the longer tenure of pastors allowed members more interaction with the pastor and a greater possibility for ongoing spiritual and identity formation. Maybe regular attenders such as the Wilders also experienced increased pastoral care. Almanzo and Laura attended Sunday school, even when there was not preaching, but they did not attend the evening worship service.

When Laura sat down to write about her life, Christianity occupied an important position in her memoir. *Pioneer Girl* described the Ingalls family's religious practices, particularly in churches in Minnesota and South Dakota, and Laura's own experiences with Christianity, the church, the Bible, and God. The first three Little House books also feature prominent accounts of Sunday observance, prayer, and the family turning to God in time of difficulty. The descriptions of childhood religious beliefs and practices seem to have changed slightly from Laura's initial handwritten manuscripts, especially in the second two books. If Rose was responsible for the changes, some of Laura's descriptions of traditional and orthodox Christian belief and practice were removed in favor of more mixed and generic depictions. In *Little House on the Prairie*, it seems that Rose both added to and subtracted from the book's engagement with spiritual topics. Still, it appears that prayer, religious songs, and a belief in God were important to how Laura remembered her life as a child.

During the spring and summer of 1935, Rose again moved away from Rocky Ridge. She had accepted a contract to write a history of Missouri, and she decided it would be beneficial for her to be close to the library of the State Historical Society of Missouri in Columbia. She took her typewriter and other necessities to a room in the Tiger Hotel at the end of July. Laura and she may not have realized this relocation's significance at the time, but Rose never again lived close to her mother and father. After this, their collaboration on Laura's novels was conducted via correspondence. Surviving letters have enabled scholars to follow their collaboration on the remaining Little House books more closely.

8

The Later Little House Books

1935-1943

During the late 1930s and early 1940s, Mansfield remained a small community. The 1940 census revealed a population of 922, an increase of only 61 persons from ten years earlier. Their automobile enabled Laura and Almanzo to visit friends, frequent businesses, and attend events in nearby small towns, including Hartville, Seymour, Ava, Norwood, and Mountain Grove. Residents also drove fifty miles west on US Route 60 to Springfield to go shopping, visit a doctor, or have a procedure at Burge Hospital (now Cox Medical Center North). The Wilders read important news in the *Mansfield Mirror* about local government, businesses, schools, and community institutions such as churches and clubs. The newspaper also regularly included state and national news. International coverage increased when World War II began in 1939; after the United States joined the war two years later, at least several columns of each issue were dedicated to the war.

By the late 1930s, Mansfield had four churches: Baptist, Cumberland Presbyterian, Methodist Episcopal, and Church of God. During 1941, the *Mirror* reported on a drive to get more people to come to Sunday school. It was the idea of C. W. Foley, pastor of the Baptist church, but the pastors of the three other churches—Ruby Brown of the Church of God, Thomas Shipp of the Methodist church, and Orvie Best of the Presbyterian church—collaborated. The newspaper printed the attendance at each of the Sunday schools for six consecutive weeks, and these figures indicate the relative size of the churches. The average Sunday school attendance figures were: Baptist church, 174; Presbyterian church, 129; Methodist church, 57; and Church of God, 43. Laura and Almanzo were 2 of those 57. Since the 1910s, the *Mirror* had listed regular service times for Mansfield churches, including Sunday school and worship services; the frequency of preaching; and the names of pastors and Sunday school superintendents. In 1936, the Methodist and Baptist churches had preaching services on the first and third Sundays of the month, and the Presbyterian church on the second Sunday. The Church of God's service times are not listed. Unfortunately for researchers, the newspaper underwent a change in ownership in 1936, and the weekly service listing was discontinued by the new publisher.

The Mansfield Methodist Episcopal church was served by five pastors between 1936 and 1943. (Their names are given in the appendix.) Pastors continued to preach in multiple towns: Mansfield and Seymour, Mansfield and Hartville, or in all three churches. One pastor, Thomas Shipp, lived in Springfield and was a ministerial student at Drury College in Springfield. It is not clear if Shipp was in his early twenties when he served in Mansfield, but other pastors had more pastoral experience. Conference records during the 1940s provide individual membership statistics for each church served; between 1942 and 1946, Mansfield's reported membership fluctuated between sixty and seventy-four.

Justamere Club meetings were no longer listed in the newspaper by the middle of the 1930s; it appears that they had been discontinued. The Athenian Club in Hartville continued to meet, although Laura attended less frequently. A new study club was founded in Mansfield during March of 1937, and Laura was present at the organizational meeting. She was assigned to a subcommittee to name the new club, but apparently no creative name was ever chosen. For the next five years, it was alternately called the Study Club, the Book Review Club, the Book Club, the Friday Book Club, and the Friday Afternoon Club in different issues of the *Mirror*. For several years, the club met at Rocky Ridge each February, and Laura briefly served as president of the club in early 1939.

After Rose had moved 150 miles north to Columbia, Laura visited her several times in 1935, arriving on Saturday and then leaving on Sunday. These visits all took place during the second and fourth weekends of the month, not the first or third Sundays when there was preaching at the Methodist church.

As Laura approached her seventieth birthday in February of 1937, she continued to muster the energy necessary to function as an active writer. Laura and Rose exchanged letters frequently for the rest of Laura's life, and the Little House books were shaped by their correspondence. Rose asked questions and made suggestions, Laura answered, and the two women discussed language choices, content decisions, and approaches to problems. Rose also mailed typed drafts to Laura, which Laura wrote comments on and sent back. During the weeks after Laura's death, Rose destroyed many of the letters she sent to her mother, including most letters written after 1940. Those that survive from the 1930s give us a view of the collaboration between the two women on several of the remaining Little House books. These letters, the original and intermediate drafts of the novels, and the published books themselves can be examined to discern the attitude of both women toward Christianity, the church, and faith. My analysis will first consider each published book's treatment of faith, then compare it to earlier manuscripts and correspondence.

"God Is Love": On the Banks of Plum Creek

Laura began drafting the next book about her life in late 1935 and finished early the next year. Rose started editing the work during the summer of 1936. It is clear from their correspondence that they were self-consciously creating a work of fiction. Laura admitted in one letter that she believed that they probably had drunk water straight from the creek, but since that seemed dirty, she had added a spring to the narrative. They also debated how to describe Ma doing chores in their stable during a blizzard while still telling the story from Laura's point of view; they ultimately decided that Laura would imagine what Ma was doing. In addition, the two women discussed what kind of language different characters should use. The final typescript was submitted in September 1936. *On the Banks of Plum Creek* appeared in 1937.

While the first three books cycle through the seasons of just one year, *On the Banks of Plum Creek* covers an indeterminate time of around thirty months. The novel begins when the Ingalls family arrives at their new home, a dugout cabin, during the summer. It ends on Christmas Eve more than two years later. Like the previous books, *Plum Creek* features lavish descriptions of nature and Laura's joy in experiencing it. Like the later books, Laura more consistently engages a larger social world, including the small-town store, school, and church. The story arc centers on Pa's plans to bring in a large wheat crop so that he can pay his debts for building a new house for the family. Tragically, a grasshopper infestation destroys their crops during two consecutive years. Pa walks hundreds of miles east to get wage work to support the family; in his absence, Ma, Mary, Laura, and Carrie face uncertainty, loneliness, and doubt. Near the end of the book, Pa is also lost for four days during a blizzard. The book's descriptions of the feelings of young girls faced with the possible loss of a beloved father are moving for both children and their parents.

Early in the book, one story parallels the account in *Pioneer Girl* of when Laura had eaten an icicle contrary to her mother's instructions. In the novel, Laura attempts to walk to a nearby swimming hole without one of her parents, something she had promised not to do. She does not tell her parents. That night she lies in bed listening to Pa play the fiddle and feels like a liar. She eventually goes to Pa and confesses, and he tells her that because she could not be trusted, she must be watched the entire next day. There is no mention of God or asking for his forgiveness in the novel, as there is in the memoir.

Prayer is described in relation to Christmas. In the days leading to their first Christmas in the dugout, Pa tells the family that he needs horses to plant their wheat crop the following year. Ma then explains to Mary and Laura that Santa Claus is not just one man, but he is present any time that someone is unselfish. Echoes of the emphasis put on Christmas in some of Wilder's *Missouri Ruralist* articles can be seen in this explanation of the identity and significance of Santa Claus. Ma convinces the children to be willing to give up what they want for Christmas so that Pa could get new horses. At the end of the chapter, the girls say the prayer from the *New England Primer* together, and they ask God to bless each member of their family and enable them to be good. Laura then privately asks God to make her glad to only have horses for Christmas.

On the Banks of Plum Creek also introduces the organized church. The family's first experience of Sunday school and a worship service gets extended treatment. Laura and the rest of the family come to love the pastor, Rev. Alden, and he is described sympathetically throughout the rest of the book. The family rides or walks to town every week for Sunday school on days Alden did not come and Sunday school and preaching on the days that he did. The book explicitly mentions when the family does not attend services: when Pa was gone and when winter blizzards threatened. Pa also takes the three dollars he meant to spend on new shoes and donates them to help buy a church bell. Finally, a Christmas party in the church building features an enormous Christmas tree at the front of the sanctuary and dozens of presents sent by Alden's church in the east. All Ingalls family members receive multiple gifts, but Laura is given a fur cape and muff that is nicer than the one that Nellie Oleson has been taunting Laura with all winter. Nellie, a spoiled shopkeeper's daughter who has everything but treats others poorly, first appears in this book; she remains Laura's foil and nemesis for the rest of the series.

The Bible and Christian imagery are also featured in an account rich in symbolism. After the grasshoppers ate every green thing on the prairie, when Pa is gone working for wages in the east, Ma and her daughters face a hot and dry late summer. One Sunday afternoon, Ma reads from the Bible about the locust plague that God brought upon Egypt, likely from Exodus 10. She also reads about the promises of God to bring his people into "a land flowing with milk and honey," probably a reference to Exodus 3:17. Ma tells the children that Pa believes that Minnesota might be just such a land. The heat becomes so unbearable that Laura exclaims that she wishes she were an Indian so she wouldn't have to wear clothes, provoking a shocked reaction from Ma. Then a small cloud appears on the horizon. It grows and brings rain to their farm. The description sounds like the end of 1 Kings 18, where God sends rain to Israel after three years of drought. Grass grows after the rain falls, providing for their cow and horses. The text implies that the rain was God's provision for the Ingalls family, their farm, and their neighborhood.

While these accounts of the church and Christianity are positive, some descriptions in the book are less so. In the chapter about Laura's first trip to Sunday school, her teacher insults her twice by treating her as younger than she really is. In addition, the congregation's singing is depicted as incredibly poor: "They all opened their mouths and tried to sing 'Jerusalem the Golden.' Not many of them knew the words or the tune. Miserable squiggles went up Laura's backbone and the insides of her ears crinkled. She was glad when they all sat down again."[1] Alden's sermon is also described as being too long for the young Laura. These comments do not undermine the positivity of other descriptions of Christianity and the church, but they do provide a bit of an edge to the stories.

Laura's handwritten manuscript shows some differences from the published book. On the day that Laura is watched by her mother, Ma says that Pa should forgive Laura in the manuscript, but the reference to forgiveness is missing from the book. The explanation of Santa Claus is longer in the manuscript, but it does not include the prayer. In the manuscript, during the church service, Pa and Ma go to the front of the building with others and Rev. Alden sprinkles water on this group. It is unclear whether this was referring to baptism or not; the account was left completely out of the book. Sunday school is also described in detail twice in the manuscript, and women from the church come out to help when Ma is dreadfully sick. Ma's sickness is not included in the book. The extended narrative with the references to the biblical locust plague, land of milk and honey, and coming of rain is completely missing from the manuscript.

A significant change between the original manuscript and the published book is the difference of tone in the description of Mrs. Tower, Laura's Sunday school teacher. In Laura's manuscript, the depiction is quite positive:

> The lady told them her name was Mrs. Tower and learned all their names. Then she told a Bible story.
>
> It was one Ma had told Laura and Mary, so they knew it already, but they liked to hear Mrs. Tower tell it. . . .
>
> After the story Mrs. Tower repeated a verse from the Bible to each little girl in turn and told her to remember it and tell it to her next Sunday. That would be her Sunday school lesson.
>
> When Mrs. Tower came to Laura, she said, "My very littlest girl must have a small lesson. It will be just three words, 'God is love.' Can you remember that for a whole week?"

1. Laura Ingalls Wilder, *On the Banks of Plum Creek*, in *The Little House Books*, ed. Caroline Fraser (New York: Library of America, 2012), 1:506.

Laura thought she was not so small as Mrs. Tower imagined. Why! She could remember long verses and whole songs. But she wouldn't hurt Mrs. Tower's feelings by telling her that so she answered, "Yes, Mam!"[2]

This becomes the following exchange in the published book:

When the others were settled on the square of benches, the lady said her name was Mrs. Tower, and she asked their names. Then she said, "Now, I'm going to tell you a story!"

Laura was very pleased. But Mrs. Tower began, "It is all about a little baby, born long ago in Egypt. His name was Moses."

So Laura did not listen any more. She knew all about Moses in the bulrushes. . . .

[Mrs. Tower gives out Bible memory verses:] When it was Laura's turn . . . [Mrs. Tower] said, "My very littlest girl must have a very small lesson. It will be the shortest verse in the Bible!"

Then Laura knew what it was. But Mrs. Tower's eyes smiled and she said, "It is just three words!" She said them, and asked, "Now do you think you can remember that for a whole week?"

Laura was surprised at Mrs. Tower. Why, she remembered long Bible verses and whole songs! But she did not want to hurt Mrs. Tower's feelings. So she said, "Yes, ma'am."

"That's my little girl!" Mrs. Tower said. . . . "I'll tell you again, to help you remember. Just three words," said Mrs. Tower. "Now can you say them after me?"

Laura squirmed.

"Try," Mrs. Tower urged her. Laura's head bowed lower and she whispered the verse.[3]

The changes to this account make it much more direct. One can better feel what a little girl might have felt. However, the tone of the writing and the feelings conveyed to the reader are quite different in the two narratives. In

2. Wilder, *On the Banks of Plum Creek* manuscript, folder 22, 50–51, Wilder, Laura Ingalls Papers, Microfilm Collection, State Historical Society of Missouri, Columbia, Missouri.

3. Wilder, *On the Banks of Plum Creek*, 1:505–6.

the original manuscript, Laura enjoys Mrs. Tower and likes to hear her tell a story, even though she has already heard it. She is surprised at her teacher's notions but does not want to hurt her feelings. In the published book, Laura is offended at being told such a juvenile story and tormented by Mrs. Tower's assumption that she cannot memorize anything longer than a few words. In addition, the shortest verse in the King James Bible is only two words: "Jesus wept" (John 11:35). "God is love" is actually part of 1 John 4:8. It appears that the words "God is love" are deliberately removed from the book.

The depiction of Christianity was not discussed in their correspondence during the summer of 1936. Laura may have approved of the changes; she may not have appreciated them but decided to choose her battles with Rose; or she may have objected to the changes in correspondence that is not extant but ultimately lost the argument. Selections in the published text that do not sound like the handwritten draft were likely made by Rose. These changes might have originated with Rose's memories of her own childhood. Alternatively, they may have been prompted by Rose's idea of what a children's book should be like. Rose's rejection of organized Christianity for Deism and cultural Islam may explain why some of Laura's straightforwardly positive depictions of Christians and the church in the manuscript became the more mixed descriptions found in the published work. At the same time, Rose also added material that is distinctly Christian in nature to the book, including the prayer in the chapter about the Christmas horses and multiple biblical references in the chapter about the coming of rain.

Another explanation is that these changes were part of a broader pattern where straightforward descriptions in the manuscript are endowed with dramatic tension and emotional weight in the final product. Creating that tension often means placing the fictional Laura in opposition to others. In the book, Laura expresses inward resistance to Pa's selling of the horses they brought from Kansas, sleeping inside a dugout, and other parental decisions. Her conflict with Nellie Oleson is referred to more often and is more intense in the book than in the manuscript. This pattern could also help explain the book's description of tension between Laura and Mrs. Tower and between Laura and the church.

Overall, religious observance is described in *On the Banks of Plum Creek* as an important part of the fictional Laura's upbringing. It appears that when Laura thought about the church of her childhood while writing her manuscript, her memories were happy. Rose's contributions made the book's depiction of Christianity more conflicted, but they also make its engagement with faith more extensive and more deeply expressed.

"A Whole Period of American History"

Rose and Laura had created a fourth novel that has gripped readers ever since its publication. Tragically, they were unable to keep from fighting about things they cared about, even at a distance. When Rose moved to Columbia, she left the two teenagers, John and Al Turner, living in the farmhouse on Rocky Ridge, along with her friends Jack and Corinne Murray. During the summer of 1936, Laura wrote to Rose that the Murrays were not taking care of the property, that Jack was taking water from the farm to town to use in his commercial laundry, and that Al had been questioned by the police concerning tires he had taken from an abandoned car. Laura convinced Rose to close the farmhouse. Al Turner moved to Columbia to live with Rose for his senior year of high school, John was sent to a military school in New Mexico, and Rose gave the Murrays her furniture when they moved to town. Rose deeply resented Laura's opposition to her (Rose's) generosity toward her friends. In the late spring of 1937, she left Missouri for New York City. At about the same time, Laura and Almanzo moved back into the farmhouse. Rose did not return to visit Rocky Ridge again until after Almanzo's death in 1949.

When discussing politics in their letters, on the other hand, Laura and Rose agreed with each other completely. Both opposed the major initiatives of Franklin Delano Roosevelt's New Deal. They saw increasing federal authority as unnecessary and dangerous, and they believed New Deal programs made Americans too dependent on the federal government. Laura and Almanzo's previous affiliation with the Democratic Party had been based on its historical commitment to limited government. In the early 1930s, the Wilders switched to supporting Republicans to oppose the expansion of federal government control represented by the New Deal. In addition, parents and daughter cooperated in a deception to decrease their income tax: Laura and Almanzo allowed Rose to claim that she was the head of household at Rocky Ridge. Finally, both parents provided assistance to Rose as she wrote *Free Land.* They sent their daughter multiple letters with answers to questions about Almanzo's early years in Dakota Territory. Rose finished the novel in 1937, and it was published the following year. Based on her father's experiences as a homesteader, it expresses boundless optimism about individual hard work and perseverance.

While she was writing *On the Banks of Plum Creek,* Laura was invited to speak to Sorosis, a women's club in Mountain Grove. Her talk there on March 16, 1936, titled "My Work," presented a new narrative of how the Little House books came to be written. She said that she had planned to write just one book to pass on to children the stories her father told. Letters from children asking for additional books prompted her to write the next three. Following some observations about writing and about memory, Laura listed the values she hoped her books would teach children: "courage, self reliance, independence, integrity, and helpfulness."[4] She asserted that these ideals were needed in contemporary American society. In her parents' generation, she noted, American citizens did not assume that the government should support them; they supported themselves. Laura was communicating a larger purpose for the Little House books, connected to contemporary social and political realities. The speech did not mention the church, faith, or Christianity.

Soon after *On the Banks of Plum Creek* was published in the fall of 1937, Laura was invited to speak on a much larger stage: a book fair in Detroit sponsored by a department store. She and Almanzo were driven there by their young friend Silas Seal, who owned a service station in Mansfield. Rose sent Laura a letter with detailed instructions about how to navigate the hotel and a meeting with her editor from Harper's. Rose also noted that many people were envying Laura and included a charm from sura 99 of the Qur'an: "I flee for refuge to the Lord of the Daybreak, that he may protect me from . . . the mischief of the envious when he envieth."[5] While it is not clear how Rose thought her mother would interpret this quote—or what Laura thought of it when she received the letter—it does indicate that Rose's affinity for ideas from Islam continued.

4. Laura Ingalls Wilder, "My Work," in Fraser, *The Little House Books,* 1:583.
5. Lane to Wilder, October 11, 1937, in Correspondence, 1937, box 13, folder 193, Rose Wilder Lane Papers, Herbert Hoover Presidential Library, West Branch, Iowa.

Laura began her address in Detroit by describing her parents' ancestry and her father's stories. She then placed the books she had written (she did not mention her collaboration with Rose) in the grand story of the American frontier. After writing *Little House in the Big Woods*, she had realized that "in my own life I represented a whole period of American history. That the frontier was gone, and agricultural settlements had taken its place when I married a farmer."[6] She revealed that her plan was to write a seven-volume novel for children about her life, so that children could learn how things used to be. The speech then presented highlights from *Plum Creek*, previews of events in upcoming books, and a promise that Laura and Almanzo would marry at the end of the series. She assured her audience that "Every story in this novel, all the circumstances, each incident are true."[7] But she also said that she had not told the whole truth, because some stories from her childhood were not appropriate for children. She then provided an extensive narrative of the Bender family and placed her father and herself in the middle of their story; multiple details in this account were not true. The speech concludes with some jokes about the West and two songs that her father had sung to her. Like her previous speech, the address did not mention God, the church, or Christianity.

"On the Pilgrim Way": By the Shores of Silver Lake

As Laura navigated relations with her daughter and reenvisioned the creation of the Little House books for a broader audience, she also wrote the next part of the Ingalls family's story: their move from Minnesota to Dakota Territory and settlement on a homestead. Laura completed a draft and sent it to Rose late in 1937. Rose read the work, and the two women corresponded about it during most of 1938. They disagreed, at times vehemently, about significant decisions, including how and where to begin the novel, if the fictional Mary should be blind, and whether to include material that Rose saw as too adult for children's fiction. Laura provided cogent reasons for why Mary's blindness was vital to the story and why they should keep

6. Laura Ingalls Wilder, Detroit Book Fair Speech, in Fraser, *The Little House Books*, 1:586.
7. Wilder, Detroit Book Fair Speech, 1:588.

descriptions of family relatives cheating the railroad company. She argued that as the fictional Laura grows older, the material in the books must become more mature. She ultimately allowed Rose to determine how to start the book. These disagreements and multiple life developments in 1938 delayed the novel's completion. Rose purchased a house and moved to Danbury, Connecticut, in April, and Laura and Almanzo took an automobile trip to the West and De Smet with Silas Seal and his wife, Neta, in May and June. Laura had begun to work on the next manuscript, and to think about subsequent books, before *By the Shores of Silver Lake* was sent to the publisher in May of 1939. The book appeared in October of that year.

When *Silver Lake* begins, two years have passed since the end of *On the Banks of Plum Creek*. Laura is thirteen, Mary is fifteen and has lost her sight, and the family now has a new baby named Grace. The family moves west so that Pa can work for the railroad and find a homestead in Dakota Territory. The book describes time spent in two railroad camps, a winter in the isolated Surveyors' House, and their first days on the homestead. Laura and Rose agreed that obtaining homestead land was the central theme of this novel. Homesteading is mentioned in the first chapter; finding the homestead, filing on the homestead, and moving to the homestead drive much of the action in the book. Laura matures into a teenager during the course of the book. Biographer Pamela Smith Hill observed that this book and the Little House books written after it can be classified as early examples of young adult fiction, a genre that did not become formally recognized as part of American publishing until several decades later.

There are fewer references to Christianity or the church in *Silver Lake* than in *Plum Creek*. The railroad camp is beyond the reach of organized religion, and the Surveyors' House is likewise isolated, so for more than two-thirds of the book there are only brief mentions of religious concepts. In the second chapter, the Ingalls family's beloved dog Jack dies, and Pa tells Laura that he has gone to the "Happy Hunting Grounds."[8] A few chapters later, a railroad worker sings worldly words to the tune of Ma's favorite hymn, "The Happy Land."[9] The man sings, "There is a boarding

8. Laura Ingalls Wilder, *By the Shores of Silver Lake*, in Fraser, *The Little House Books*, 2:2, 12.

9. The first verse of this song appears in *Little House on the Prairie*, and it is discussed in chap. 7.

house / Not far away / Where they have fried ham and eggs / Three times a day. . . ."[10] Ma is scandalized. Later, in commenting on Pa's account of violence at another railroad camp that resulted in the paymaster giving in to rioters' demands, Ma refers to Ecclesiastes 9:4, "a living dog is better than a dead lion." On Christmas Eve, the family reminisces about other Christmases they had enjoyed together, including the one described in *Plum Creek* with the Christmas tree in the church building.

As with *Little House in the Big Woods* and *Farmer Boy*, the treatment of Christianity is contained mostly in one chapter. Instead of describing the spiritual activities of a representative Sunday, this book provides a detailed description of a unique series of events. In chapter 23, "On the Pilgrim Way," the family and their only neighbors are singing the hymn "Lend a Helping Hand" in the Surveyors' House one Sunday evening. They are answered by a voice from outside singing the chorus, which includes the line "Let us lend a hand to those on the pilgrim way."[11] The singer is a young pastor traveling with Rev. Alden from Minnesota; they are accompanied by two homesteaders. The ministers are on their way farther west to investigate the possibilities of planting a church in the new town of Huron. Laura is overjoyed to see Alden, and he speaks kindly of his country girls having grown into young women. In reference to Mary's blindness, Pa notes that while it is hard to accept God's will, he is glad that none of his children had died. Alden responds that Mary's acceptance of her trial is a great example, and that God disciplines those he loves, most likely a reference to Proverbs 3:11–12 or Hebrews 12:6, or both.

More importantly to plot development, Rev. Alden tells the family that there is a college for the blind in Iowa that Mary could attend. Ma, Mary, and Laura are excited about the possibility, although they have no idea how they might be able to pay. Laura knows that Ma and Pa had hoped that one of their daughters would teach school, and since Mary was blind it would have to be Laura, but she often thinks she does not want to be a teacher. Now she is torn between inclination and duty. That evening they have a prayer meeting, and while Rev. Alden is praying, Laura has a religious experience:

10. Wilder, *By the Shores of Silver Lake*, 2:21.
11. Wilder, *By the Shores of Silver Lake*, 2:125.

They all knelt down by their chairs, and Reverend Alden asked God, Who [*sic*] knew their hearts and their secret thoughts, to look down on them there, and to forgive their sins and help them to do right. A quietness was in the room while he spoke. Laura felt as if she were hot, dry, dusty grass parching in a drought, and the quietness was a cool and gentle rain falling on her. It truly was a refreshment. Everything was simple now that she felt so cool and strong, and she would be glad to work hard and go without anything she wanted herself, so that Mary could go to college.[12]

This account is the only time in the Little House books that forgiveness is mentioned as part of the Christian message. The next day, Alden leads a preaching service; all are excited to have celebrated the first church service in the new town of De Smet. He promises to come back to start a church there the next year. God, Christianity, and the church are not mentioned in the rest of the book.

There are two existing manuscripts in Laura's handwriting, one more polished than the other. Both contain much of the same descriptions, stories, and accounts. Significant sections in the manuscripts appear almost unchanged in the published book, especially the descriptions of nature and landscape as the family rides west, the description of birds on Silver Lake, and Laura and Carrie's late-night slide on the frozen lake when they see a large and beautiful wolf. If the alterations in the published work are taken as the result of Rose's efforts, she provided structure, sharpened point of view, and heightened tension and emotions. The book is more gripping, the opening chapter is more effective, and some unnecessary accounts are removed.

In its treatment of faith, Christianity, and the church, there are omissions and additions as well as items that remain the same. The manuscripts include the sections where Pa assures Laura that Jack would have his reward and where the members of the family recount previous Christmases, including the one with gifts handed out in the church. However, in the section where Ecclesiastes is quoted in reference to the riot, Pa is the one who notes that a live dog is better than a dead lion, rather than Ma. The

12. Wilder, *By the Shores of Silver Lake*, 2:127–28.

book also adds the account of the laborer singing the song parodying Ma's favorite hymn, which does not appear in either of the manuscripts.

The manuscripts do provide a description of what the family did on Sundays while living in the Surveyors' House. Everyone dresses in clean clothes, and Ma and the three girls work on their Sunday school lesson, which was mainly Scripture memorization. In the afternoon there is reading aloud, and in the evening the family sings hymns before proceeding to more secular songs. This account sets up the arrival of Alden and the first preaching service in De Smet, as it provides the background for the family's singing hymns when the pastors' company arrives. Missing from both manuscripts is Alden's reference to God disciplining his people. More importantly, neither manuscript includes the prayer meeting and Laura's experience of peace while Rev. Alden prays. The passage appears to have been written by Rose. The handwritten manuscripts contain two additional references to Sunday school and church that do not appear in the published book.

A typed version of *By the Shores of Silver Lake* is also available to researchers. If the typescript of *Farmer Boy* was a late draft, almost the same as the published book, this typescript must have been a very early draft, because it is almost identical to the handwritten manuscript. It retains the original's beginning and the same chapter structure. There are some handwritten editorial comments and passages to be inserted, but the text was significantly revised between this draft and the book.

Differences between the handwritten manuscripts and the published book were most likely the result of Rose's work. In terms of religious ideas, those changes defy easy categorization. The extended and poignant scene of Jack's demise is the only place in the entire series where a character's death is described. It appears to have been written by Rose. Maybe she again drew on her feelings when her beloved dog Bunting died in 1933. It also appears that the description of Laura's experience of God's presence was provided by Rose. Perhaps she considered Laura's description of her religious experience in *Pioneer Girl* as she created the scene. On the other hand, the use of drought and rain as a metaphor for the fictional Laura's feeling of surrender is also quite close to Rose's journal's description of her experience of peace with her life in early 1932. The book removed a chapter on regular Sunday practices, but it added significant material to the remaining chapter about a particular experience with God and his grace. While the church occupies a smaller place in *Silver Lake* than in *Plum Creek*, Christianity is depicted in an overwhelmingly positive light.

"Where No Storms Ever Beat on That Glittering Strand": The Long Winter

The Wilders took a road trip in May 1938 with their friends Silas and Neta Seal. Silas drove, Almanzo navigated, and Neta and Laura visited in the back seat. They headed west on Route 66 through Oklahoma to New Mexico and Arizona, stopping at the Painted Desert, Petrified Forest, and Grand Canyon. They then drove to the ocean, and then north from Santa Monica to Santa Barbara, Oakland, and Redwood country. They continued north to Portland, then turned east to Spokane. They visited Yellowstone National Park before proceeding to Keystone, South Dakota, to see Laura's sister Carrie, whose husband had died the month before. They then headed east to Manchester to visit Grace and her husband, and they stopped at De Smet before driving back to Missouri. The couples had visited a striking number of national parks during the three-week trip. They drove on Sundays and did not stop either to rest or to worship.

It appears that Laura had completed a draft of what she called *The Hard Winter* and sent it to Rose before their travels with the Seals. A lengthy letter in March of 1938 seems to provide Laura's answers to questions from Rose about the narrative. Late that year, Laura began working on what she thought would be the seventh and last novel, which she called "Prairie Girl." At some point, Rose worked on *The Hard Winter* and sent the edited, typewritten pages to Laura. Laura then read through them, answered questions that Rose had included, and suggested changes. The book's title was changed to *The Long Winter* late in the process of publication.

A letter from Laura to Rose in early 1939 indicates that the royalties from the first five Little House books, and rent for the rock house, were providing ongoing economic security for the Wilder household. Laura and Almanzo decided to go to South Dakota in June to attend the Old Settlers Day in De Smet. It was sixty years since Laura and her family had arrived on Silver Lake with the railroad crews in 1879. Laura had finished working with the typewritten pages of *The Hard Winter*, and she mailed them to Rose before they left. Laura and Almanzo drove themselves this trip, and she told Rose that they would not drive on Sunday for safety reasons, not religious ones: "We plan to take our driving easily, stop early and lay over if we are tired. And not drive at all on Sunday when every drunken loon is drunk and on the road."[13] Laura was seventy-two and Almanzo was in his early eighties. This was the last time that they visited De Smet. She later spoke about this trip at a meeting of the Study Club, and she wrote an article about it titled "In the Land of Used-to-Be" for the children's section of the *Christian Science Monitor*. The article does not mention faith, the church, or Christianity.[14]

The Long Winter was released in June of 1940. It covers just nine months, from September to the following May, and has the tightest narrative structure of all the Little House books. During the first chapter, Laura and Pa cut hay and see a muskrat house that is unusually thick, a sign of a hard winter to come. Later in the book, that hay is used to keep the family and their stock alive. The blizzards begin in October and continue until April. Each lasts several days. By January, repeated storms prevent trains from reaching De Smet. Gradually, Laura, her family, and the other townspeople begin to run out of food and fuel. They pursue a variety of substitutes, including killing oxen for meat, twisting hay into sticks to burn, and grinding wheat in coffee mills to make bread. The book depicts the psychological effects of the repeated storms, lack of food, and uncertainty: the children are irritable, Pa curses the blizzards, Ma is short with Pa, and Laura shows signs of giving up. They are only saved by the heroic actions of Almanzo Wilder and Cap Garland, who drive twenty miles from town in subzero weather to buy sixty bushels of a settler's seed wheat. This food keeps everyone in town alive until the trains begin running again in late spring. When the chinook wind blows and melts the snow, the reader shares the characters' deep feelings of relief. The book ends with a Christmas celebration in May.

13. Wilder to Lane, May 23, 1939, in *The Selected Letters of Laura Ingalls Wilder*, ed. William Anderson (New York: HarperCollins, 2016), 199.

14. Laura Ingalls Wilder, "In the Land of Used-to-Be," *Christian Science Monitor*, April 4, 1940; also in Laura Ingalls Wilder and Rose Wilder Lane, *A Little House Sampler: A Collection of Early Stories and Reminiscences*, ed. William Anderson (Lincoln: University of Nebraska Press, 1988), 226–31.

The Long Winter is the only Little House book that includes sections that are not told from Laura's point of view. In all the other books, the narrative depicts only what the fictional Laura would have seen, heard, and experienced. This was insisted upon by Rose and discussed in letters with her mother. In *The Long Winter*, there are two entire chapters and portions of six others that occur away from the Wilder home and Laura's direct observation. In two of these sections, the story is told from Pa's point of view; in the others, it is Almanzo's. They include the decisions leading up to Almanzo's search for the farmer south of town and the dangerous trip to the homestead and back. The extensive attention to Almanzo's affairs makes him a more well-rounded character.

This book has many references to Christianity, God, the Bible, and religious practice. In the first chapter, Pa explains to Laura that God tells muskrats when to build houses with thicker walls. Later, Laura thinks about having wings to flee the coming winter, a reference to Psalm 55:6. On Laura and Carrie's first day of school in town, the teacher opens the day by reading Psalm 23. After a harrowing walk home from school through a blizzard, Laura thinks, "It was so wonderful to be there, safe at home, sheltered from the winds and the cold . . . this must be a little bit like Heaven, where the weary are at rest. She could not imagine that Heaven was better than being where she was, slowly growing warm and comfortable."[15] To pass the time during a blizzard, the girls have a contest to see how many Bible verses they have memorized. The family receives a letter and later a barrel of Christmas gifts from Rev. Alden's church in Minnesota. Carrie gazes at a Sunday school card with a picture of the Good Shepherd. Laura and Mary pray for the safety of Almanzo and Cap on their mission of mercy, and bedtime prayers are mentioned three additional times. A local man is jokingly called "a mighty hunter before the Lord,"[16] the description of Nimrod given in Genesis 10:9. Ma comments on the actions of the train superintendent by saying, "Pride goes before a fall,"[17] a slight misquoting of Proverbs 16:18. Pa reads from the biography of David Livingstone, the nineteenth-century missionary to Africa. Late

15. Laura Ingalls Wilder, *The Long Winter*, in Fraser, *The Little House Books*, 2:227.
16. Wilder, *The Long Winter*, 2:288.
17. Wilder, *The Long Winter*, 2:298.

in the book, Carrie wonders whether they could possibly eat grass, and Pa tells her no and calls her Nebuchadnezzar, a reference to the Babylonian king eating grass in Daniel 4:32–33. The family sings portions of ten different hymns or Christian songs at key points in the narrative. Finally, at the end of the book, the family sits down to a belated Christmas dinner after the arrival of the train, and Pa thanks the Lord for his provision.

One handwritten manuscript and the typescript with comments and corrections by both Rose and Laura are available to researchers. The changes made between the manuscript and the published book are nearly all improvements. Description is changed into dialogue, tension is heightened, emotions are communicated more effectively, and extraneous material is removed. For instance, the manuscript has an account of a birthday party for one of Laura's classmates that is moved to the next book. The manuscript also includes an extended description of Pa's experiences with Mr. Edwards that is completely removed; all that remains in the book is Mr. Edwards's brief meal with the family and his gift of a twenty-dollar bill to Mary. The book adds the sections from Almanzo's point of view that provide the background to his decision to go for the wheat. Overall, the book has a tighter structure, clearer chronology, and more engaging chapter titles.

There are multiple references to Christian practices and the Bible in the published work that do not appear in the handwritten manuscript. The manuscript does not have Pa explaining that God is the one who tells animals what to do, or Laura's comparison of her warm home to heaven. The schoolteacher does not read Psalm 23. The manuscript does not include the brief references to the passages in Psalms, Genesis, Proverbs, or Daniel. There is only one description of Laura and Mary saying their prayers. The Sunday school memory competition is included in the manuscript, although it does not end with Mary and Laura reciting the exact same number of verses as it does in the book. The manuscript also describes an additional Sunday school lesson at home, where Mary recites her favorite psalm, the twenty-third; Laura recites several verses of her favorite psalm, Psalm 19; and Carrie recites Matthew 19:14. The letter from Alden, Carrie's picture of the Good Shepherd, Pa reading about David Livingstone, and his prayer before Christmas dinner are depicted mostly as they appear in the book.

The typescript of the book is much more like the published volume than the handwritten manuscript. However, it also includes significant notes, corrections, suggested changes, and discussions of them by both Rose and Laura, unlike the typescripts of *Farmer Boy* and *Silver Lake*. It includes the sections from Almanzo's point of view where he gives some of his wheat to Pa and comes to the decision that he must go after the wheat south of town. This was an important point for Rose. She believed that Almanzo risking his life to get the wheat could not work as fiction if his only motivation was to save his seed; he had to be saving the town as well. Laura, in a letter from early 1938 and in marginal notes on the typescript, argued that if Almanzo did not plant his seed in April he lost the entire year's crop, and that was reason enough. Rose's interpretation prevailed in what was published. Laura's handwriting provides corrections to language, comments about how the town was laid out, and answers to questions from Rose. At many key points, Laura's changes endure in the book; in other places, they do not.

In relation to Christianity, many of Rose's additions to the handwritten manuscript are present in the typescript, including the reference to God and the muskrats, the teacher reading Psalm 23, the comparison of home to heaven, the Sunday school memory verse contest ending in a tie, and the references to Psalm 55 and Proverbs 16. There are no comments from Laura about any of these additions. There are several exchanges between the women that have to do with faith. In a conversation between Laura and Mary about Mary's going to the college for the blind, the typescript has Mary say, "I am sure that sometime I can go. God cares even when a sparrow falls, so he surely knows how much I want to go to college and he will arrange things somehow, so I can." In the margin, a note in Rose's handwriting asks, "How would she say this?—I can't quite remember the verse—about the sparrows fall."[18] Laura's handwriting provides Matthew 10:29 in the margin, but this reference is completely left out of the published book.

More importantly, the typescript includes two exchanges about Ma and faith. In one scene, the typescript has Ma saying, "It's a lesson to us, not

18. Laura Ingalls Wilder, *The Long Winter* typescript with corrections by Laura, box 15, folder 236, 2, Rose Wilder Lane Papers.

to lose faith." This sentence is crossed out with this explanation in Laura's handwriting: "I cut because it is out of character."[19] It is not clear whether Wilder saw this phrase as inaccurately describing her mother's views of Christianity, or if it was just not the kind of thing that her mother would have said. Later in the typescript, Laura inserted a handwritten note:

Don't cut the hymn Ma sang to Grace while a blizzard raged. I forget where I placed it.

> "I will sing you a song of that beautiful land
> The far away home of the soul
> Where no storms ever beat on that glittering strand
> While the years of eternity roll."

and the rest of it. Shows she was almost hopeless of this world. No one could live through that winter however brave and not come that near to breaking down and [*sic*] as Pa did when he shook his fist at the wind.[20]

Laura must have remembered what she had written incorrectly. This hymn, "The Home of the Soul," is not included in the handwritten manuscript, though it does have a scene were Ma sings a different hymn, "On Jordan's Stormy Banks I Stand," to Grace and to her other daughters. Rose had used this song in the typescript, but in response to Laura's instructions, "The Home of the Soul" appears in its place in the published book. Laura had a clear vision for the characters in the book, and she wanted a particular hymn included so that it showed how close to despair Ma had come.

The Long Winter includes more engagement with the Bible and spiritual things than any of the other Little House books. All the references to Christianity are positive. The characters do not question why God has brought these trials. Scripture and prayer are also presented as framing the family's experience and providing comfort during difficult times. Since

19. Wilder, *The Long Winter* typescript with corrections by Laura, box 15, folder 236, 3.

20. Wilder, *The Long Winter* typescript with corrections by Laura, box 15, folder 237, handwritten paper between pages 89p and 90p, Rose Wilder Lane Papers.

many reach out for the divine when faced by suffering, perhaps it is not surprising that there is more about Christianity, God, and the Bible in this narrative. Many Christian references were introduced between the manuscript and the typescript, and therefore most likely they were added by Rose. It seems that Rose still knew many Scripture passages, and she worked intentionally to use them to contribute to the overall effect of the book. Laura's original manuscript envisioned Christianity as an important part of the fictional Ingalls family's navigation of the hard winter, and the published book confirmed, enhanced, and deepened that vision with additional examples.

"Being Sure of the Goodness of God": Little Town on the Prairie

By the Shores of Silver Lake was published in October of 1939. Because they had already been working on *The Long Winter*, it was published the following June. Both books were named Newbery Honor Books, as *On the Banks of Plum Creek* had been in 1938. Newbery Honor Books were runners-up for the Newbery Medal, awarded by the Children's Library Association, a division of the American Library Association. In January of 1941, *The Long Winter* was reviewed positively in the *New York Times*. The review also gives a summary of the other five Little House books. By this time, Laura had outlined "Prairie Girl," what she believed would be the last volume in the series. She then decided that it would require two books to finish the story.

During the late 1930s, Rose had increasingly been writing about political topics. She had abandoned her book on Missouri history, and her opposition to the New Deal had grown into a philosophical argument that she presented in an article titled "Credo" in the *Saturday Evening Post* in 1936. It praised individualism and condemned socialism, communism, and bureaucracy. The article was quickly published as a pamphlet titled *Give Me Liberty*. In 1938, a federal employee stopped at Rocky Ridge and spoke to Almanzo while he was plowing. The man asked how many acres Almanzo was going to plant, how many he had in pasture, and other questions. Almanzo told him these things were none of his business, ordered him off his property, and went to the house to get his gun. Laura told Rose about the exchange, and Rose was incensed. She was also increasingly disturbed by federal income tax requirements, particularly when she was paid $25,000 in one year for *Free Land*.

Despite her new political interests, Rose still devoted time to improving her mother's fiction. Laura finished a manuscript for *Little Town on the Prairie* during 1940 and sent it to Rose, who typed and edited it during the early months of 1941. The correspondence between the two women about the work has been lost, and there are no existing intermediate typescript drafts. The book was published in November.

Many different types of stories are included in *Little Town on the Prairie*, but the book begins to pull together plot threads that were introduced in the previous two books. The Ingalls family progresses toward proving up on their homestead, Almanzo Wilder shows interest in Laura, and Laura studies to obtain a teaching certificate. The third of these threads serves as the central theme for *Little Town*. One-third of the way into the book, Mary leaves to attend college in Iowa; Laura works to become a teacher so that she can make money to keep Mary there. Nellie Oleson also returns and again serves as Laura's antagonist.

Any reader of *Little Town on the Prairie* must come to terms with its depiction of a blackface minstrel show as the climactic event in the winter season of De Smet's Literary Society. Pa participates in the musical troupe with his whiskers slicked down and blacked so that he is unrecognizable. While such a demeaning depiction of African Americans cannot be defended, it can somewhat be explained. Minstrel shows were popular during the late nineteenth century. Their popularity had faded somewhat when the book was written in 1940, making it possible for them to be viewed as quaint cultural phenomena from the past. There is some evidence that Laura and Rose did not harbor virulent prejudice toward all African Americans. Laura shook hands with a black farmer at a meeting of the Mansfield National Farm Loan Association in 1921, when other white members in attendance were unwilling to. Rose later wrote a regular column for the *Pittsburgh Courier*, an African American newspaper. Perhaps their experiences as women and as outsiders in Florida and the Ozarks enabled them to identify with others who were marginalized. These choices provide context, but they do not constitute an excuse. Laura and Rose's willingness to include the minstrel show in this volume demonstrates that they could not—or at least did not—imagine the negative impact that perpetuating racial stereotypes could have for black (and white) Americans.

Interactions with God, the church, and religious observance are frequent in *Little Town*. The first of three extended passages that engage spiritual topics appears early. During a walk, Laura tells Mary that she (Mary) is truly good. Mary disagrees and says that all humans are sinful and drawn to evil, using words from Jeremiah 17:9 and Job 5:7. They then have this conversation about goodness and God:

> "I don't believe we ought to think so much about ourselves, whether we are bad or good," Mary explained.
>
> "But, my goodness! How can anybody be good without thinking about it?" Laura demanded.
>
> "I don't know, I guess we couldn't," Mary admitted, "I don't know how to say what I mean very well. But—it isn't so much thinking as—as just knowing. Just being sure of the goodness of God." . . .
>
> Everyone knows that God is good. But it seemed to Laura that Mary must be sure of it in some special way.
>
> "You are sure, aren't you?" Laura said.
>
> "Yes, I am sure of it now all the time," Mary answered.[21]

When the fictional Laura initially mentions goodness, she means morality. Mary turns the conversation toward the goodness of God, meaning his mercy toward human beings. What Mary describes as "just knowing" and Laura as Mary's being "sure of it in some special way" could in theological terms be called faith. This gentle meditation on God's goodness appears within the first pages of the book. A harsher view of Christianity is presented close to the end of the book in its depiction of a church revival service.

As was the case in *By the Shores of Silver Lake*, a hymn is used early in the book in a decidedly nonspiritual way. While sewing shirts in a dry-goods shop, Laura sees two drunken men proudly stride down the sidewalk, singing the hymn "Pull for the Shore." As they walk, one puts his foot through the screen door of each business on the main street. This

---

21. Laura Ingalls Wilder, *Little Town on the Prairie*, in Fraser, *The Little House Books*, 2:376–77.

account fits the early chapters' descriptions of the unexpected things that happen in town, as opposed to the serenity of life on the homestead. This account is also mentioned again in the church revival scene.

The second major passage that reflects on God describes an epiphany that Laura has on the Fourth of July. She and Pa and Carrie have gone to town for the celebration. They hear a man read the Declaration of Independence, and then the crowd sings "America" ("My Country 'Tis of Thee"). The last verse of the song mentions freedom and God's kingship. Laura then considers what she had just heard:

> Suddenly she had a completely new thought. The Declaration and the song came together in her mind, and she thought: God is America's King.
>
> She thought: Americans won't obey any king on earth. Americans are free. That means they have to obey their own consciences. No king bosses Pa; he has to boss himself. Why (she thought), when I am a little older, Pa and Ma will stop telling me what to do, and there isn't anyone else who has a right to give me orders. I will have to make myself be good.
>
> Her whole mind seemed to be lighted up by that thought. This is what it means to be free. It means, you have to be good. "Our father's God, author of liberty—" The laws of Nature and of Nature's God endow you with a right to life and liberty. Then you have to keep the laws of God, for God's law is the only thing that gives you a right to be free.[22]

Laura's thoughts are then interrupted by Carrie and Pa calling her to get lemonade. Although the content of these reflections is political, its tone sounds like a religious experience.

The institutional church looms large in this book. Ma and Pa participate in the organizational meeting for the church, a foundation is laid, and the building is erected. At school, Laura befriends Ida Brown, the adopted daughter of the new pastor, Rev. Brown. Ma and Pa are disappointed that he was the pastor of the local church rather than Rev. Alden. Later in the book, we learn that Brown dresses untidily, and Laura's engagement with

22. Wilder, *Little Town on the Prairie*, 2:412.

his sermons was not based on what she could learn, but because he looked like a picture of John Brown, the antislavery activist. She also enjoys reworking his sentences in her mind, improving their grammar. Laura does not take care to remember anything from his sermons, for Pa only required her to remember the morning's Scripture passage. These accounts present an unenthusiastic portrait of Brown, and by association the church does not appear in a very positive light. The church appears in an even less positive light in the third significant description of Laura's engagement with Christianity: the church's revival service. This account can be best considered in comparison with the work's original manuscript.

There are substantial changes made between Laura's handwritten manuscript and the book. The book reworks the overall structure of the manuscript to provide additional suspense at the beginning about Laura's first job in town, and to make the book's treatment of events more chronological and less topical. The focus of the book is more consistently on Laura's efforts to get a teaching certificate. There are also additional descriptions, especially of the town, in early chapters. A chapter about the children keeping house while Pa and Ma go with Mary to Iowa does not appear in the manuscript. The manuscript does mention that Mary's college tuition was being paid by the Dakota territorial government; the family just had to pay for clothing, railroad fare, and incidentals. The published book removes these details, and the result is to make the family look more self-reliant than the historical Ingallses were. Still, some accounts from the manuscript appear in the published book with only light editing. Developments in the schoolhouse between Laura, Nellie Oleson, and their teacher, Miss Eliza Jane Wilder, are pretty much the same in the manuscript and the book.

There are also significant changes to the treatment of Christianity between the handwritten manuscript and the published book. Nothing like the discussion between Laura and Mary about goodness and God appears in the manuscript. Its expression of teenage questioning sounds more like Rose's writing than Laura's. The chapter on the Fourth of July celebration is also quite different. The manuscript has the entire family preparing for the day and going to town to celebrate with a picnic dinner, short speeches, and races. The book has just Pa, Laura, and Carrie going to town, which matches what Laura originally wrote in *Pioneer Girl*. The book also includes much more of the Declaration of Independence, primarily from the section on the examples of the king's tyranny. No part of the meditation on God as America's king is present in the manuscript. Laura's manuscripts never include passages using stream-of-consciousness narration. This passage was most likely created by Rose. It fits with her embrace of a Deist conception of God and her increasing preoccupation with the abstract underpinnings of individual freedom and government authority.

At other key points, references to God or the Bible appear in the book but not in the manuscript. In response to Laura's questioning whether they must move to town for the winter, Ma replies that they must not tempt Providence. During the troubles between Laura and her teacher, Laura's attitude is described in this way: "She did not think then of the Bible verse that speaks of the cup and platter that were clean only on the outside, but the truth is that she was like that cup and platter. She hated Miss Wilder. . . . Outside she was shining clean with good behavior, but she made not the least effort to be truly good inside."[23] The reference is to Matthew 23, where Jesus condemned Jewish leaders for their hypocrisy. It appears that Rose added these accounts to the book to better depict the personalities of the characters involved. Since they remain in what was published, we can assume that Laura at least tacitly approved them.

There are subtractions from the original manuscript as well. The manuscript notes that Laura's good friend Mary Power did not attend Sunday school and church because her family was Roman Catholic, but this information is not included in the book. Furthermore, the manuscript consistently says that "the Congregational Church" or "the Ladies Aid of the Congregational Church" sponsored events, including a sociable, a New England supper, and revival services. In each case, the book just has "the church." This makes the church seem like a more universal institution. Finally, the manuscript includes a lengthy account about Sunday school superintendent Barnes, who did not get back from Chicago one Saturday night. His wife is certain that his convictions about traveling on the Sabbath will prevent him from coming home on the train on Sunday, but he does just that. A similar account was included in *Pioneer Girl*, but it does not appear in the published edition of *Little Town on the Prairie*.

23. Wilder, *Little Town on the Prairie*, 2:464.

This brings us to the differences between the manuscript and the book in the depiction of the revival service at the church. Both the book and the manuscript describe the family's arrival at the church and the singing of the hymn "The Ninety and Nine." Then both describe the long prayer. In the manuscript, "Laura bent her head and closed her eyes, as others did; but as Rev. Brown prayed on and on, she couldn't keep from thinking it was a waste of time for him to tell the Lord so many things that He must know already."[24] This becomes more simply in the book, "Laura bent her head and closed her eyes, while Reverend Brown's harsh voice singsonged on and on."[25] Brown then delivers the sermon. In the manuscript, the end of the service is described in this way:

"We will sing once more and this is the last call," he said finally. "If there are any here who repent and want to be saved, let them come forward and give me their hands while we sing." And his loud voice led all the other voices, "Pull for the shore sailor . . ." [Five more lines from the song are reproduced here.]

A nervous chill crept up Laura's back and she could feel the excitement in the church as a man and a woman, she did not know, walked up the aisle and shook hands with Reverend Brown.

No one else could be persuaded to go forward, so after a short prayer and another hymn, Rev. Brown pronounced the benediction and the meeting was over.

People in the front seats gathered, in a group, around Rev. Brown and the converts, but Pa said in a low voice, "Come Caroline! Let's go. There are enough people with the Amen corner, to welcome the two."[26]

This becomes in the published book:

Chills ran up Laura's spine and over her scalp. She seemed to feel something rising from all those people, something dark and fright-

24. Wilder, *Little Town on the Prairie* manuscript, tablet 3, 158, Pomona Public Library, Pomona, California.
25. Wilder, *Little Town on the Prairie*, 2:527.
26. Wilder, *Little Town on the Prairie* manuscript, tablet 3, 160–61, Pomona Public Library.

ening that grew and grew under that thrashing voice. The words no longer made sense, they were not sentences, they were only dreadful words. For one horrible instant Laura imagined that Reverend Brown was the Devil. His eyes had fire in them.

"Come forward, come forward and be saved! Come to salvation! Repent, ye sinners! Stand up, stand up and sing! Oh, lost lambs! Flee from the wrath! Pull, pull for the shore!" His hands lifted them all to their feet, his loud voice sang, "Pull for the shore . . ." [Three more lines from the song are included here, and a young man comes up to the front.]

The first words of that hymn had made Laura want to laugh. She remembered the tall thin man and the pudgy little one, so solemnly singing it, and all the storekeepers popping from the torn screen doors. Now she felt that all the noise and excitement was not touching her. . . .

Another young man, and then an older woman, went forward and knelt. Then church was over, yet somehow not over. People were pressing forward to crowd around those three and wrestle for their souls.[27]

The manuscript's description of the revival is at the core of the published book's account, but the descriptions in the book are much more vivid and emotional. The tone is also less positive. In the manuscript, Laura experiences the tension in the room as the pastor calls people to repent and come forward, but the book adds that Laura feared briefly that the pastor was the devil. The reference to the drunk men neatly connects this account to the book's early scenes, but the idea that Laura would have drawn comfort from the humorous juxtaposition of the two uses of the hymn is nowhere in the manuscript. Those who go forward are welcomed in the manuscript, while the implication is that they are rather exhorted—and perhaps harassed—in the book.

These accounts can be seen as describing Christian preaching and worship with a distinctly negative edge, or they can be seen as portraying Brown and the phenomenon of revival services negatively, not the church or Christianity. It seems clear that Wilder's dislike of the historical

27. Wilder, *Little Town on the Prairie*, 2:528.

Rev. Brown and her discomfort with open expressions of Christian devotion impacted how she depicted the church and Christianity in her original manuscript. It also appears that Rose took the disagreeable view of Brown and revivals in the manuscript and strengthened it into a more straightforwardly negative view of these Christian practices in the book.

In both the manuscript and the book, the revival service is a key moment in plot development, because Almanzo Wilder first asks Laura if he can walk her home from church that night. In the book, a second revival meeting is described, Almanzo walks her home again, and their conversation is less awkward because she has thought of things to say. This second night does not appear in the manuscript.

In *Little Town on the Prairie*, several significant meditations on God and the good life and some minor but important references to Providence and Scripture do not appear in the handwritten manuscript. They appear to have been supplied by Rose. At the same time, Laura's story about the Sunday school superintendent is not included in the book, along with some other descriptions of denominational differences. It appears that Rose influenced both the extent to which Christian ideas are present in this volume and the nature of their treatment. In both the manuscript and the book, Rev. Brown and his actions during the revival service are depicted negatively. Otherwise, the church and Christian ideas are presented as important to individual characters and to the community.

"Reverend Brown Was Preaching Earnestly": These Happy Golden Years

Little Town on the Prairie was named a Newbery Honor book for 1942. Laura had continued to write and had finished a draft of the last volume of the series by the middle of that year. As with the previous books, Rose edited and typed the book. She then sent the typescript to Laura with questions to be answered. It may be that Laura then sent the typescript with her corrections and answers directly to the publisher. *These Happy Golden Years* was published in March 1943.

This book brings the narrative of Laura's coming of age to a conclusion. Becoming an adult means two things: working outside of home for money and dating Almanzo Wilder. The first chapters are dominated by the story of Laura's first teaching experience. The Brewster school is located twelve miles from town, and she must stay with a homesteader and his angry wife during the week. The pupils don't always obey her, and one night the homesteader's wife threatens her husband with a knife. Laura is mainly able to handle the situation because Almanzo comes every Friday with a bobsled to take her back to her family for the weekend. After these trips, Laura continues to go riding with him in the bobsled, and later in his buggy, on Sundays. Eventually he proposes. Laura teaches two additional terms at other schools, sews in town for two different employers, and helps a homesteader's wife live on their claim during one summer. The book ends with Laura and Almanzo's marriage and move to the little house that he has built her.

Sundays loom larger in this book than in any of the others, because Laura and Almanzo's courtship takes place almost exclusively on Sunday afternoons. The weekly pattern is that Laura attends Sunday school and the morning worship service with her family, returns home for Sunday dinner, then goes out riding with Almanzo. The church held a Sunday evening worship service (Laura's friend Ida mentions it at one point), but Laura and her family never attend. At times only certain members of the family go to morning services. In one instance, Laura and her younger sisters attend while her parents stay home to visit with Ma's brother. Later, it is too warm for Ma, so only Pa and Mary and Laura go to church. That service is interrupted by the entry of a kitten chased by a dog, and the kitten takes refuge under Laura's hoop skirts. Sunday observance is also mentioned at many other points. When Laura is holding down the claim with Mrs. McKee, the presence of Mr. McKee means that they can't laugh or smile on Sundays. As a strict Presbyterian, he believed Sunday was a day for reading the Bible and the catechism and talking about Christianity. Later, Pa buys Ma a sewing machine, but they can't use it on Sunday. After they are engaged, Almanzo spends winter Sunday afternoons with Laura and her family. When they decide to move up their wedding near the conclusion of the book, Almanzo stops by on a Sunday afternoon wearing work clothes to say that he is working on the house and therefore breaking the Sabbath.

There are several non-Sunday-related engagements with Christianity described. When Mary comes home from college, she muses on how many

Bible verses she had memorized and explains how they helped her learn Braille. A party with a Christmas tree is held in the new church building; Laura gets a brush and comb, and Pa tells her he saw Almanzo buying them at the drug store. There is also a singing school for De Smet's young people held in the church building. Most of the songs were not religious, but there is an anthem near the end of the book based on the first three verses of Psalm 19. It is one of the songs that Laura sings to Almanzo and to the empty prairie on the evening when he asks her if she would like an engagement ring.

While Sunday is described fondly, that can't be said of the pastor of the church. Rev. Brown and his preaching again come in for some abuse in this book. In different places across the work, Brown's sermons are described as long, stupid, dull, and uninteresting. Brown does please Laura and Almanzo at the end of the book, however, because he does not require her to vow to obey her husband during their wedding ceremony.

There are fewer major changes made between Laura's handwritten manuscript and the published book than any volume since *Little House in the Big Woods*. The overall structure of the narrative is the same in both, though some accounts are moved slightly between chapters. It appears that Rose's changes improve dialogue, increase emotional tension at key points, and add a few memorable lines and scenes. The ages of several children in the first school are increased so that they are older than Laura, the narrative of one sleigh ride in subzero temperatures is extended, and the description of the new married couple's house is expanded. Perhaps most significantly, Laura does not insist on removing "obey" from her wedding vows in the manuscript. This conviction was described in *Pioneer Girl*, and the conversation with Almanzo is expanded in the published novel. Some accounts in the manuscript do not appear in the book, including an overnight stay in a hotel with Mrs. McKee, a description of the Ingalls family's neighbors, and Laura helping to put out a fire that threatens the schoolhouse during her third teaching contract. Still, most of the descriptions and some of the conversations are changed very little between the manuscript and the book, including the descriptions of teaching, clothing, and interactions with classmates and Laura's family.

There are some changes to the depiction of Christianity and the church between the manuscript and the book. A couple of the descriptions of

Brown's preaching are more negative in the book than in the manuscript. The first time that Sunday school and worship are mentioned in the manuscript, we are told that "Laura knew the sermon would be long but after she made sure she would remember the text when Pa asked her to repeat it, she let her thoughts wander to other things."[28] This becomes in the published book: "Reverend Brown preached one of his long, stupid sermons. . . . Laura made sure that she remembered the text, to repeat at home when Pa asked her; then she need not listen any more."[29] In a later account, the manuscript reads: "Reverend Brown was preaching earnestly and everyone was quiet and attentive when Laura saw a stray kitten walking up the aisle."[30] The book has: "Reverend Brown was preaching earnestly and Laura was wishing that with so much sincerity he could say something interesting, when she saw a small plump kitten straying up the aisle."[31] These changes can be seen as an intensification of the emotions that was often accomplished by Rose's editing. In this case the intensification is of a negative view of Brown.

There are also two references to Bible verses in the manuscript that do not appear in the book. During the trials at her first school, Laura remembers Proverbs 16:32, "He that ruleth his spirit [is greater] than he that taketh a city." Perhaps it was removed in favor of the narrative showing that this is what Laura was attempting to do instead of telling about it. Later, when reflecting on her success in securing a higher-paying school, the manuscript has Pa tell Laura, "'Whatsoever a man soweth, that shall he also reap.' You sowed the seeds of knowledge with a lot of hard study and cultivated them with kindness. Looks to me like you're going to reap a good crop."[32] The quote is from Galatians 6:7. This entire speech was removed; perhaps Rose saw it as unnecessary commentary. There are no biblical passages or references to God that appear in the published book and

28. Laura Ingalls Wilder, *These Happy Golden Years* manuscript, tablet 1, 39, Burton Historical Collection, Detroit Public Library, Detroit, Michigan.

29. Laura Ingalls Wilder, *These Happy Golden Years*, in Fraser, *The Little House Books*, 2:575.

30. Wilder, *These Happy Golden Years* manuscript, tablet 5, 279, Burton Historical Collection.

31. Wilder, *These Happy Golden Years*, 2:712–13.

32. Wilder, *These Happy Golden Years* manuscript, tablet 4, 251, Burton Historical Collection.

not in the manuscript, but the account of Almanzo working to build their future home on Sunday is a wholesale addition in the published book.

There is an additional typescript draft available to researchers. It could be that this was the only intermediate draft, sent to Laura for her additions and corrections. Laura did make some handwritten edits. Almost all of what is typed and most of the handwritten edits are reproduced exactly in the published book. At times there are typed questions from Rose to Laura, and Laura provides handwritten answers that were then incorporated into the text. Rose's notes request direction about plot matters, for descriptions of minor characters, and for guidance concerning the names of materials for sheets and clothes. None of the questions or edits have to do with depictions of Rev. Brown, the church, or subjects relating to faith.

In *These Happy Golden Years*, with the marriage of Laura and Almanzo, the Little House books draw to a close. The book presents a mixed view of Christianity and faith. Christian themes do not receive as sympathetic a depiction as in *By the Shores of Silver Lake* or *The Long Winter*. Some depictions of the church are positive, others have a negative feel like those in *On the Banks of Plum Creek* and *Little Town on the Prairie*. Sundays are especially significant because they are the occasion for Laura and Almanzo to be together, often in a sleigh or buggy in motion across the prairie. Worship is shown as important to the Ingalls family, though they only go to one of the services on Sunday and at times members of the family stay home. Considering the differences between the handwritten manuscript and the published book, and thereby the contributions of Rose to the story, in general more descriptions are unchanged than in most of the other Little House books. Still, it appears that Rose took the time and effort to remove two references to the Bible, to intensify negative descriptions of Rev. Brown's preaching, and to add an instance of Almanzo working on Sunday.

Faith, Life, and the Little House Books

At the end of September 1942, Laura wrote a letter to George Bye that accompanied the signed contract for *These Happy Golden Years*; she stated that her story was now complete. In her review of the book published in April 1943, the *New York Times* reviewer concluded that the Little House books were "an invaluable addition to our list of genuinely American stories, and as such they have a special significance for us today."[33] Laura and Rose had finished what Laura had set out to do. She was seventy-six years old.

By the early 1940s, Laura and Almanzo's life on the farm was quite different than it had been twenty years earlier. They no longer owned horses, but Almanzo had a donkey to pull loads too large to carry and several goats for milk. Laura no longer raised chickens. Both worked in their garden growing vegetables and flowers. They drove a Chrysler. They also had a hired man to help with work on the property. Ongoing income from rent on the rock house and royalties from the Little House books had made them economically independent.

Despite their debates about the novels, Laura felt free to share gossip with Rose about local events in her letters. Several letters in early 1939 mentioned church matters. In January, after describing events surrounding Mansfield's Study Club, Laura observed that she had increasing difficulty fitting in with the group, and she might have to "go with the old church crowd"[34] instead. She continued to attend Study Club meetings into the early 1940s, but by the end of 1942 reports of their meetings in the *Mansfield Mirror* did not include her name. In February 1939, she shared gossip about a mutual friend, Ruth Freeman, who had become a Roman Catholic and was driving both her children and a neighbor's children to Mass in Mountain Grove. The next month, she told Rose that members of the Methodist ladies' aid society had informed another friend, Mrs. Hoover, that they did not need her help with their dinners. Laura commented that she was glad that she had quit the group. Despite this comment, late in 1942, at about the same time that she stopped attending Study Club meetings, she began occasionally attending meetings of the Women's Society for Christian Service, the rebranded Methodist ladies' aid society. On Wednesday, August 25, 1943, a dinner was held at the Methodist church to celebrate Laura and Almanzo's fifty-eighth wedding anniversary. As they entered their late seventies and late eighties respectively, their ties to the Mansfield Methodist church appear to have been strong.

33. Anne T. Eaton, review of *These Happy Golden Years*, by Laura Ingalls Wilder, *New York Times Book Review*, April 4, 1943.

34. Wilder to Lane, January 27, 1939, in *The Selected Letters of Laura Ingalls Wilder*, 191.

The Little House books' depiction of topics related to Christianity and the church suggests several things about Laura's faith. In all the books, Christianity is presented as an important feature in the lives of the Ingalls family and Laura herself. Furthermore, the depiction of Christianity and the church is complex. There is much more material that engages faith in the last five books than in the first three. The first three engage faith mainly through Sunday observance, nightly prayers, and sporadic references to God or Scripture. The church is introduced in *On the Banks of Plum Creek*, makes a brief appearance in *By the Shores of Silver Lake* and *The Long Winter*, and then occupies a more significant place in the last two volumes. Some Christian characters are depicted in a consistently positive light, particularly Rev. Alden, Ma and Pa, and Mary. The depiction of Rev. Brown is much less favorable. Brown's presence in the final two volumes makes their presentation of the church and Christian practices quite negative. It's somewhat clear that the unfavorable comments in those works should be applied to Brown in particular rather than to Christian worship in general, but that distinction is not always easy to maintain. By contrast, depictions of Christian faith and action are consistently positive in *By the Shores of Silver Lake* and *The Long Winter*. *The Long Winter* contains the most interactions with God and Christianity, and it is the book where faith is most central to the characters' lives. In the other books, faith is important but not central.

Rose's contributions to what the Little House books say about Christianity and faith are complex. If we can credit the additions, exclusions, and alterations between the handwritten manuscripts and the published books to Rose, then Rose introduced many Christian and biblical themes to the books, especially *Little House on the Prairie*, *By the Shores of Silver Lake*, *The Long Winter*, and *Little Town on the Prairie*. It appears that Rose knew Scripture, and she understood what Christianity meant to the lives of others, even if she had rejected traditional Christian beliefs. Many accounts in the Little House books are richer in their engagement of Christianity and faith because of her collaboration. On the other hand, alterations to some depictions of Christians and their practices do change the understanding of Christianity communicated. This is the case for the understanding of God's providence in *Farmer Boy*, the picture of Mrs. Tower in *On the Banks of Plum Creek*, and the actions of Brown in the final two books. Finally, in every single book, there are references to God, faith, and the Bible that appear in a manuscript but do not appear in the published book. Some of these removals may be explained by animus against Christianity on Rose's part. Others were likely for the sake of streamlining the narrative.

Taken together, the Little House books describe the many ways that the church, belief in God, and Christian practices influenced young people's lives in the upper Midwest during the late nineteenth century. Both Laura and Rose knew the Bible, and passages are used to illumine characters' motivation and worldview. Christian hymns play an important role in the series, and especially in *The Long Winter*. The Little House books don't provide direct information about the nature of Wilder's adult Christian beliefs beyond the basics: God's existence and care and children's responsibility to obey his law. The name of Jesus is never mentioned in any of the Little House books. There is only one reference to forgiveness.

During these years of Laura's life, many characteristics of her faith remain evident. She believed the basic doctrines of mainstream, Protestant Christianity. She identified with the Methodist church, went to Sunday school and morning worship services regularly, and at times engaged the Women's Society of Christian Service. On the other hand, she did not attend evening services, she did not become a member of the church, she did not worship while she was away from home, and she did not mention faith in either of the speeches that reflected on her past and what contemporaries should learn from it. These patterns suggest that perhaps the best way to describe Laura's understanding of Christianity and the church is that they were important but not central to her life and her worldview.

After the series was complete, Laura did not again write for publication. Instead, she dedicated her time to correspondence, spending time with Almanzo on the farm, and some neighborhood and community engagement. There is more evidence that Christian worship and practices were part of her weekly routine after the writing of the Little House books.

9

Aging, Together and Apart

1943-1957

A s early as 1933, when only *Little House in the Big Woods* was published, Laura began receiving letters from children, librarians, schoolteachers, and other adults who had enjoyed reading it. They arrived from all parts of the country. The volume of mail increased as additional Little House books were written, and it continued to grow during the 1940s. She also received cards, especially around Christmas, Valentine's Day, and her birthday. Some children sent photographs of themselves. Laura attempted to answer as many of these cards and letters as possible. Once she was no longer writing books, she had more time to return this correspondence. By the end of the decade, keeping up with the flood of letters had become a significant task: in 1948 she wrote her editor at Harper's that she had just finished answering 210 Christmas cards. In addition, those who had read and loved the books sometimes stopped by Rocky Ridge in hopes of meeting Laura and Almanzo. Laura often spoke with them outside the farmhouse; at times she invited them in.

During the early 1940s, Laura and Almanzo's names rarely appeared in the *Mansfield Mirror*, but when they did, it was because they had visited Silas and Neta Seal, because the Seals had spent time in their home, or because the Seals and the Wilders had together visited Springfield, Ava, or another nearby town. Silas and Neta were the Wilders' closest friends. The Seals owned a building in Mansfield and rented out rooms, and at some point Almanzo suggested to his wife that they sell the farm and move to one of these apartments. Laura did not want to leave their home, so after her husband had mentioned it several times, she told him that if they were going to move, they could not keep all his tools, and he should decide which ones to sell. He did not bring up the idea again. In 1948, the Wilders did sell their property to neighbors in an arrangement like a reverse mortgage; the price was $8,000, and the Wilders received $2,000 down and monthly payments with the stipulation that they could live in the farmhouse for the rest of their lives. Royalty income from the Little House books provided complete financial security.

Laura's letters to those who had read her books followed a pattern, probably to enable her to answer as many questions from readers as possible. She thanked them for writing, commented briefly on what they had told her about their lives, and answered their questions. Questions often concerned what happened to characters from the books. From the letters that have been collected and made available, it does not appear that readers asked questions about her religious beliefs; she did not often give answers that describe her faith directly. Once the series was complete, many correspondents asked if she was going to write any more books, but she always declined.

In multiple letters, she repeated to her readers what she had said in her speech in Detroit: that everything in the books was true. For example, a letter she wrote in 1938 to a third-grade class includes: "The books are true, you know. All those things happened to me and my parents and sisters, just as I have written them."[1] Five years later, she wrote to another correspondent, "My series of stories, as you know, are literally true, names, dates, places, every anecdote and much of the conversation are historically and actually true."[2] However, she had also acknowledged to Aubrey Sherwood, longtime resident of De Smet and editor of the local newspaper, that some parts of the books were not completely true. He had inquired about the account in *By the Shores of Silver Lake* about Pa's visit to the land office in Brookings, South Dakota, to file on their homestead. She admitted in

1. Wilder to third-graders at Washington School (location unidentified), n.d., in *The Selected Letters of Laura Ingalls Wilder*, ed. William Anderson (New York: HarperCollins, 2016), 145–46.
2. Wilder to Mrs. Phraner, May 10, 1943, in *The Selected Letters of Laura Ingalls Wilder*, 247.

her reply "that chapter is fiction. Such things did happen in those days and I placed it there to emphasize the rush for land. You understand how those things are done in writing."[3] Her misrepresentation of the books as factually true was probably repeated to many other correspondents.

After *Free Land*, Rose stopped writing fiction. She pursued new avenues for publication during the 1940s. In 1943, she published *The Discovery of Freedom*, a work of imaginative political theory that presented a passionate defense of individual liberties and a celebration of individualism. It sold poorly, and Rose came to believe that leaders of New York publishing houses were colluding with federal officials to suppress it. From 1942 to 1945, Rose wrote a column titled Rose Lane Says for the *Pittsburgh Courier*, an African American newspaper with a circulation of at least 250,000 nationwide. She was told about the paper by a woman who worked for her as domestic help. Rose enjoyed the paper's passionate prose and reached out to one of the columnists to ask if she could write for them. In the *Courier*, she used her individualist convictions to argue for equality for black Americans. In 1945, the paper canceled her column, and she became the book review editor for the monthly *National Economic Council Review of Books*. The National Economic Council was a conservative political and educational organization. This publication was an even more congenial medium for Rose's opinions about politics, economics, and individual freedom. She wrote for the review until 1950.

In 1949, Laura sent instructions to George Bye to assign 10 percent of the royalties from the Little House books to Rose. Her letter says that she wanted Rose to receive the money for her assistance selling and publicizing the books. Neither the formal assignment letter nor the informal letter to Bye that accompanied it mentioned Rose's extensive work editing and preparing the books for publication. For the rest of their lives, both Laura and Rose worked to keep secret the collaboration that had produced the Little House books.

During the late 1940s, libraries and businesses, particularly in the Midwest, began to recognize the influence of the Little House books and the love that thousands of readers had for them. In 1947, a poll was taken of

3. Wilder to Sherwood, November 18, 1939, in *The Selected Letters of Laura Ingalls Wilder*, 211.

Chicago schoolchildren and Wilder was declared their favorite children's author. She was honored by an eightieth birthday party at Chicago's Merchandise Mart, sponsored by department store Carson Pirie Scott. She sent a letter to the "Children of Chicago" that was read at the event. It contained these words: "But the real things haven't changed. It is still best to be honest and truthful; to make the most of what we have; and to be happy with simple pleasures and to be cheerful and have courage when things go wrong."[4] During the late twentieth century, this quote became famous as a summary of her approach to life. In December of 1948, the Detroit Public Library notified Laura that they were naming a branch library after her. She was invited to the dedication in early 1949, but she declined, citing her age and Almanzo's health. Instead of attending, she sent a short message and her handwritten manuscripts of *The Long Winter* and *These Happy Golden Years*.

Mansfield's Religious Landscape in the 1940s

Mansfield's citizens had expanded options for religious identification during the 1940s. In late 1943, a group of local Roman Catholics bought a gas station in town and renovated it into a chapel, which they named Immaculate Heart of Mary Church. The group included several individuals mentioned by Laura in her 1939 letter to Rose. The priest from Mountain Grove, Father Robert Ready, celebrated Mass in both towns. In 1947, a church building was built and dedicated. By the end of the decade, Father Claud Barton was celebrating Mass at the church every weekday at 8 a.m. and every Sunday at either 6:30 or 10 a.m. In addition, a Church of Christ was again founded in town in 1944. By 1948, it had 25 members who met in a private residence that had been purchased and remodeled.

In 1947, the *Mansfield Mirror* reported on another community effort to motivate residents to come to Mansfield's Christian services. The paper reported the attendance at Sunday school, Sunday morning worship, and Sunday evening worship for five churches during the month of April. The size of the churches was about what it had been six years earlier. The Baptist

---

4. Wilder to Children of Chicago, n.d., in *The Selected Letters of Laura Ingalls Wilder*, 284.

and Presbyterian churches had services all four weeks. The Baptist church averaged 165 in Sunday school, 180 at Sunday morning worship, and 107 at Sunday evening worship, while the numbers for the Presbyterian church were 87, 112, and 45, respectively. The Methodist church did not have a morning worship service the first and third week of the month or an evening service for the first three weeks of the month. It averaged 50 for Sunday school and the morning worship service and 32 for the lone evening service. The Church of Christ had Sunday school all four weeks and an average of 28 attendees; it only had worship services the last week of the month and reported 30 at each service. Finally, the Assembly of God church reported services every week and an average of 24 at Sunday school and Sunday morning worship and 37 at Sunday evening worship. The newspaper does not report statistics for Mass at the Roman Catholic church. The editor may have excluded it for prejudicial reasons; he may have just neglected it; or the priest may have declined to participate. These possible explanations may also apply to the Church of God; it was mentioned in the newspaper during the 1930s and the 1950s, but it did not appear in these reports.

It appears that the Methodist church, like all the other Protestant churches in Mansfield, held Sunday school every Sunday. In 1945, an article about the church in the *Mirror* stated that morning worship service with preaching was only available on the third Sunday of the month. In 1947, the church had a morning worship service on the second and fourth Sundays. Later that year, the *Mirror* announced that "There will be preaching services at the Methodist Church each Sunday beginning in September. The pastor will be present three Sundays for the month, and a committee of laymen are providing for services the first Sunday of each month."[5] It is not clear for how long this arrangement lasted.

In 1946, thirty-year-old Carlton Knight was assigned to the churches in Mansfield, Seymour, and Hartville. Born in the Ozarks, he felt a call to the ministry while attending Southwest Missouri State Teacher's College (now Missouri State University) and attended Southern Methodist University in Dallas, Texas. Later in life, Knight was asked for his memories of Laura and Almanzo. He said that Laura was a gracious host, serving tea and graham crackers with a spread made of powdered sugar whenever he

5. "Methodist Church Notes," *Mansfield Mirror*, September 4, 1947, 3.

and his family visited Rocky Ridge. Almanzo's health was failing during the late 1940s, and Knight did not recall his attending worship with Laura, who attended regularly and was always very well dressed, often in a dark red velvet dress, even in the summer. Knight did not remember that she was active in other church activities. According to the *Mirror*, her most regular attendance at the Women's Society for Christian Service meetings was during the early 1940s, before Knight became pastor. He also recalled that while the church had about one hundred members on their rolls, only about forty or fifty attended services.

The relatively low percentage of members who attended led the Methodist church to introduce an unusual way of increasing attendance in September 1949: giving members tickets to services. Pink tickets were handed out to each resident member for each Sunday in the month with the request that it be brought to the service either by that member or given to someone else. The tickets were then collected and displayed on a wall in the church building. If a pink ticket was not brought in, a white ticket was placed on the wall in its place. As a result, it was obvious how many tickets had been used. According to the *Mirror*, "One would hardly let a ticket to a Cardinal-Dodgers ball game coming up soon go unused. If he couldn't use it he would give or sell it to someone who could. The church insists that just because a ticket to church doesn't cost $2.10 plus tax, it is no less valuable, and therefore should be used."[6] On the first two Sundays of the month, 71 percent and 67 percent of the tickets were used. It is not reported whether Pastor Knight or a lay leader of the congregation initiated this idea, and it is unclear whether it was used elsewhere. Since Laura and Almanzo had never become members, this initiative would not have been aimed at them, although Laura's attendance did become less regular as Almanzo's health failed.

Life without Almanzo

Laura's sister Carrie Swanzey visited Rocky Ridge in October 1944. Grace Dow had died of heart disease and diabetes in 1941, and her husband, Nate, had followed several years later. Laura and Carrie were the last two remain-

6. "Unique 'Admittance' Ticket Plan Used by Methodists to Increase Attendance," *Mansfield Mirror*, September 15, 1949, 1.

ing members of their family. Carrie took the train back to Keystone, South
Dakota; she died two years later in June 1946. Almanzo turned ninety-
two—or perhaps just ninety, depending on which historical documents
one trusts for his birth year—in February 1949, then in July he had a heart
attack. Neta Seal spent several nights at Rocky Ridge in August because
he was sick. After this he appeared to improve, but he became ill again
in October. On Sunday morning, October 23, Laura called Neta to come
to the house. She saw immediately that Almanzo had died. His obituary
was carried in the next issue of the *Mansfield Mirror*; it said that he had
died of a sudden heart attack. Rose arrived on Wednesday, and the funeral
was held in the Methodist church on Friday, October 28. Carlton Knight
officiated. Laura and Almanzo had been married for sixty-four years.

Laura missed him intensely. In multiple letters she wrote how lonely
she was. Despite her loneliness and the impact of aging, she was able to
stay at Rocky Ridge. The children of her neighbors, Sheldon and Roscoe
Jones, often came to the farmhouse to help. They brought the mail, did
chores, and spent time with Laura. She could have groceries delivered to
the door. Her neighbor Iola Jones drove her to church services. Neta Seal
often came to stay when Laura was sick. The *Mirror* noted that when Neta
hosted the Baptist Women's Missionary Union meeting in her home in
January 1950, Laura attended. The newspaper also reported that Neta and
Laura drove to Mountain Grove multiple times that year.

Additional honors came from libraries both far and near. In May of
1950, the Pomona Public Library in Pomona, California, renamed their
children's reading room after Laura. She declined an invitation to attend
the dedication but sent a statement to be read at the event and gave
them the original, handwritten manuscript of *Little Town on the Prairie*.
In August of that year, 135 people from across southwest Missouri and
neighboring states attended the Athenian Club's "Laura Ingalls Wilder
Day" at the Wright County Library in Hartville. In May of 1951, the
Wright County Library announced that it was renaming its Mansfield
Branch the Laura Ingalls Wilder Library. On September 28, a ceremony
was held in the Mansfield High School auditorium to honor Laura and
celebrate the new library name. She read a brief message of thanks. The
speech of dedication was given by Missouri state librarian Paxton P. Price.
A reception at the library building followed. In November of 1952, Brown

Brothers bookstore in Springfield held an event where Laura signed more than two hundred books.

When the Little House books were first published, Harper & Brothers had changed the format of the later books, starting with *By the Shores of Silver Lake*, to look more like adult novels. Laura opposed this change because she saw her books as a set, but the decision was made over her objections. Several years after the last Little House book appeared, editor Ursula Nordstrom decided to bring out a new edition of all eight books with a uniform format. She hired artist Garth Williams, who had previously illustrated E. B. White's *Stuart Little*, to draw new illustrations. Williams visited Rocky Ridge in late 1947 to make drawings of Laura's family pictures. He also visited the small towns where the Ingalls family had lived in Wisconsin, Minnesota, and South Dakota to get ideas and inspiration for his drawings. He was finished by the early 1950s. The uniform edition of the Little House books appeared in 1953. The new edition also allowed Laura and Harper's to address some concerns about the content in the books. Chapter 1 of *Little House on the Prairie* had said that Pa had wanted to go to a place where "there were no people. Only Indians lived there."[7] At least one reader had written to the publisher to argue that this implied that American Indians were not people. The new edition changed the end of the first sentence to "there were no settlers."[8] In addition, the account of the minstrel show in *Little Town on the Prairie* was changed to remove one verse of a song that included a particularly offensive term. The new set was immediately embraced by readers, both children and adults, and sold well for decades.

Christianity in Mansfield during the 1950s

In 1950, the *Mansfield Mirror* reported that a new congregation of the Reorganized Church of Jesus Christ of Latter Day Saints (RLDS) held a revival at their building west of Mansfield. This church was descended from a group that had split from the Church of Jesus Christ of Latter-day Saints to follow the descendants of Joseph Smith, rather than the

7. Laura Ingalls Wilder, *Little House on the Prairie* (New York: Harper & Brothers, 1935), 1.

8. Laura Ingalls Wilder, *Little House on the Prairie* (New York: Harper & Brothers, 1953), 2.

leadership of Brigham Young, during the mid-1800s. The denomination is headquartered in Independence, Missouri, outside of Kansas City. Also in 1950, Highway Church of the Nazarene began meeting in a building west of Mansfield on Route 60. This congregation completed a church building and manse in town in March of 1953.

In 1954 the *Mirror* was sold to a new group of publishers, and Ralph O. Watters, who had edited the newspaper for eighteen years, stepped down. As a result, weekly church listings were again included in the newspaper, which makes possible a fuller reconstruction of the religious world of Mansfield. By the end of the year, eight denominations were represented in the regular listing: Assembly of God, Baptist, Church of God of Prophecy, Catholic, Nazarene, Methodist, Presbyterian, and RLDS. By May of 1955, the listing also included a Church of Christ and the Mansfield Seventh-day Adventist Church, which met in the Mansfield Hotel.

In the listing, the Mansfield Methodist church had the following Sunday services: church school at 10:00 a.m., worship service at 11:00 a.m., Methodist Youth Fellowship at 6:30 p.m., and worship service at 7:45 p.m. Most of the other churches had similar weekly schedules with morning and evening services. By this time, pastors who served multiple churches in multiple locations, as Methodist pastors in southwest Missouri did, often preached the same sermon in multiple places. Services were held at different times of the day, and the minister drove an automobile from one church building to the other.

The founding of additional congregations after World War II can be explained by the desire of local Christians to worship in a church of their choosing. It was also made possible by the relative health of the national and local economy during the 1950s, which made it more feasible for congregations to pay for a church building and for rural residents to own a car. Automobile ownership meant that Christians could go farther from home to find a church that reflected their beliefs. This meant that rural congregations often closed when members decided to drive to church in Mansfield or other small towns; it was, in effect, a process of consolidation. The Wilders lived only a short distance from Mansfield, but car ownership made the trip to town for worship services easier.

In 1939, the Methodist Episcopal Church (MEC), the Methodist Episcopal Church, South (MECS), and Methodist Protestant Church (MPC) all united to become the Methodist Church. During the next twenty years, the pastor of a circuit of churches often encouraged members of smaller churches to transfer to churches in the larger towns; then the smaller churches closed. During the 1930s, there were around forty churches, including Mansfield, in the Springfield District of the Missouri Conference of the MEC. Several years after the merger, in 1947, there were ninety-six churches in the Springfield District of the Southwest Missouri Conference of the Methodist Church. That year, Carlton Knight was assigned to the Mansfield Circuit, which comprised six churches. The church in Mansfield had 91 active members, Norwood had 28, and the remaining four churches had 12 or fewer. It appears that the members of several of the smaller churches were gradually added to the Mansfield church, so that by 1952, Knight was serving only the churches in Mansfield and Hartville, and Mansfield had 154 members. There were only eighty-three churches in the Springfield District that year.

Frank Nelson served as pastor of the Methodist churches in Mansfield and Hartville in 1953 and 1954. The church held a "Church Attendance Crusade" during the first few months of 1954. Nelson was allowed by the *Mirror* to place weekly updates in the paper on progress of the crusade and the topics of his weekly sermons. The crusade was proclaimed a success because attendance increased 13 percent, but no actual attendance numbers were ever provided. At the fall 1954 conference meeting there was not a pastor assigned to Mansfield and Hartville; preaching during the month of October was done by Nell Mitchell. Mitchell was the first female pastor to serve the Methodist church in Mansfield. The MEC and MECS had not ordained women as pastors, but the MPC had ordained women since the late 1800s. Mitchell had been ordained before coming into the Methodist church in 1947. Her name is given in historical documents from the church and in the *History of Wright County*, even though she only served for a month. Kenneth Bunting was appointed by the conference, took up his duties in November, and pastored the church for a year. Walter Brunner was appointed to the Mansfield and Hartville Methodist churches in fall of 1955, where he served during the last years of Laura's life.

"It Is Wonderful That You Will Pray for Me": Laura's Final Years

After Almanzo's death, Laura could again attend worship services regularly. In a letter to the librarian at the Pomona Public Library, Laura noted, "I call a taxi once a week for shopping and visiting and to church Sunday."[9] Neta Seal, who was active in multiple ministries at the Baptist church in Mansfield, later recalled in an interview that she and Laura did not talk often about Christianity, though they did sometimes exchange stories about their experiences in their respective churches.

Neta also noted that Laura knew the Bible very well. In a letter to a reader of the books, Laura said that her favorite verse was Psalm 19:1; she went on, "The whole book of Psalms is a favorite of mine and I can repeat all. Can you?"[10] This sounds like Laura was asserting that she had memorized all 150 psalms. This would have been an incredible accomplishment, for the Psalms contains more than two thousand verses. She may have meant that she had memorized parts of all the psalms and could identify them, or something else. Her neighbor Iola Jones later said in an interview that Laura had told her that she had memorized a book of the Bible, but she (Jones) could not remember which book. Wilder biographer William Anderson recalled that he had heard that at one point late in life, Laura attempted to memorize the book of John. Laura kept a small Bible on the table next to her rocking chair. She had written a guide for important Bible references on a piece of lined paper that she kept inside of it:

> In facing a crisis read 46 Psalm
> When discouraged read 23 & 24 Psalm
> Lonely or fearful read 27 Psalm
> Planning budget read St. Luke chapter 19
> To live successfully with others read Romans chapter 12
> Sick or in pain read 91 Psalm
> When you travel carry with you 121 Psalm
> When very weary read Matthew 11_28&30 and Romans 8_31
>   to 39
> When things are going from bad to worse 2 Timothy 3d
> When friends go back on you hold to 1 Corinthians 13th
> For inward peace the 14th chapter of St. John Gospel

9. Wilder to Clara Webber, April 19, 1950, in *The Selected Letters of Laura Ingalls Wilder*, 320.

10. Wilder to Suzanna, September 29, 1952, in *The Selected Letters of Laura Ingalls Wilder*, 342.

To avoid misfortune Matthew 7_24 to 27
For record of what trust in God can do Hebrews 11
If you have to put up a fight—the end of Ephesians
When you have sinned read 1 John 3_1 to 21
And make Psalm 51 your prayer[11]

Laura copied the list from an issue of the *Saturday Evening Post* in October 1943. Next to an article on the Gideons, the *Post* included a box with the list titled "Where to Look."[12] The Wilders had subscribed to the magazine for many years. She had taken the time to copy the entries from the magazine onto a separate sheet of paper, which she kept until her death. Her Bible and the guide are now at the Laura Ingalls Wilder Historic Home and Museum. The handwritten list has been reproduced for sale in the gift shops of several historical sites, and it is available on the Internet.

Letters also provide evidence that Laura prayed. In 1955, she wrote to a woman who lived near Mansfield and assured her that she prayed every evening: "It is wonderful that you will pray for me. I need it. I will remember you in my prayers every night."[13] A later letter to the same correspondent is similar: "I thank you for your sweet note and shall remember you when I say my prayers. I hope you will do the same for me. One needs the prayers of their friends."[14] When Laura died, she had only several religious books in her collection other than the Bible. One was *The Soul's Sincere Desire* by Glenn Clark, a book on prayer. The others were J. G. Pike's *Persuasives to Early Piety*, inherited from her parents, and *Mother, Home and Heaven*, the courting gift from Almanzo.[15]

The publication of the new edition of the Little House books led to additional honors for the books and their author. In December 1953, the *Horn Book*, a magazine devoted to children's literature, published an entire issue on Laura and the Little House books. The issue featured articles

11. Laura Ingalls Wilder, *A Little House Reader: A Collection of Writings by Laura Ingalls Wilder*, ed. William Anderson (New York: HarperCollins, 1998), 194.
12. "Where to Look," *Saturday Evening Post*, October 2, 1943, 22.
13. Wilder to Dorothy, July 21, 1955, in *The Selected Letters of Laura Ingalls Wilder*, 372.
14. Wilder to Dorothy, n.d., in *The Selected Letters of Laura Ingalls Wilder*, 372.
15. Pike's book is described in chap. 1; *Mother, Home, and Heaven* is discussed in chap. 3.

about the content, publication, and illustration of the books. The next year, the Children's Library Association established the Laura Ingalls Wilder Award, a new honor to be given periodically to an author who had made significant contributions to children's literature. Laura was named the first recipient at ceremonies in Minneapolis, which she was unable to attend because of her age and health. In 1955, the Missouri State Highway Association installed a metal historical marker for Wright County on State Route 5 north of Mansfield that mentions that Mansfield was "the early home of novelist Rose Wilder Lane and the home of Laura Ingalls Wilder, the writer of children's stories."[16]

By the middle of the 1950s, the volume of fan mail had become so great that she could not keep up. In a letter to Nordstrom, Laura mentioned that she had six hundred or seven hundred letters that she was not able to answer. She was also less likely to invite out-of-town visitors into the house at Rocky Ridge. Instead, visitors could go to the Laura Ingalls Wilder Library in Mansfield, which had a bookshelf dedicated to Laura and the Little House books. It featured dolls of the characters in the series sent to her by the Pomona Public Library in California and a trowel and sickle that had belonged to Almanzo's father. The *Mirror* mentioned visitors to the library from Arkansas, Georgia, Kansas, Iowa, South Dakota, and locations throughout southern Missouri. In correspondence, Laura increasingly mentioned having to rest because of her heart. She also often referred to missing Almanzo.

Laura took one more trip in 1954. Rose had been periodically coming to spend time with her at Rocky Ridge after Almanzo's death, and she prevailed upon her mother to fly to visit her at her home in Danbury, Connecticut. Laura had traveled throughout the Midwest in covered wagons during the late nineteenth century; by the end of her life, she had also flown. Rose enjoyed showing her mother the house that she had remodeled and her extensive gardens. We don't know if she spent a Sunday in Connecticut. Laura stayed a short time, met Rose's neighbors, and flew back to Missouri.

In April 1955, Laura fell and injured her head. Neta Seal stayed with her for a week while she healed. Early the next month, Fred Kiewit, a reporter

---

16. "Historical Marker Set in Roadside Park North of Town," *Mansfield Mirror*, May 3, 1956, 1.

from the *Kansas City Star*, visited Rocky Ridge and interviewed Laura. He subsequently published an article whose title and subtitle almost seem to say it all: "Stories That Had to Be Told: Laura Ingalls Wilder Wrote Eight Books after She Was 65, but Now, at 88 and in Poor Health, She's Quitting." Laura told him about the support network she had with friends and about the handgun and shotgun she kept in the house. It was the last interview that she gave to a member of the news media.[17]

Rose traveled to Rocky Ridge shortly before Thanksgiving in 1956 and found that Laura was in particularly poor health. An ambulance took Laura to the hospital in Springfield, and she stayed there until just after Christmas. She was diagnosed with diabetes, and Rose was kept busy managing her diet. In January 1957, friends began taking turns staying overnight at the farmhouse to assist Rose. Laura Ingalls Wilder died on February 10, 1957, three days after her ninetieth birthday. Her funeral was held on February 13 at 2:00 in the afternoon in the Mansfield Methodist church. Rev. Brunner officiated. She was buried in Mansfield's cemetery, next to Almanzo.

"The Pearly Gates Would Surely Open"

Laura spent the last years of her life in ways that many might envy. She was able to stay in her own home, the house that she and Almanzo had built together and where she had lived for fifty years. She corresponded with friends, distant relatives, and readers of the Little House books. She visited with neighbors and kept in touch with Rose via letters, phone calls, and visits. The honors showered on the books she and Rose had written must have been gratifying. As she encountered more health challenges, maybe she thought more about her spiritual home or about her hopes of joining Almanzo there. Perhaps even more than Almanzo, she might have thought of her father. Caroline Fraser points us to Laura's words, written sometime after her father's death: "Whatever religion, romance and patriotism I have I owe largely to the violin and my Father playing in

17. Fred Kiewit, "Stories That Had to Be Told: Laura Ingalls Wilder Wrote Eight Books after She Was 65, but Now, at 88 and in Poor Health, She's Quitting," *Kansas City Star*, May 22, 1955.

the twilight. I am sure that when I come to die, if Father might only be playing for me I should be wafted straight to heaven on the strains of 'The Sweet By And By,' for the pearly gates would surely open."[18]

What the last two decades of Laura's life tell us about her Christianity is very much like what we learn from studying earlier periods. It appears that she possessed Christian faith, but she gave little information in her writings—or to those around her—about the doctrinal content of her beliefs. In terms of behavior, we again have documentary evidence that Laura continued the Christian practices that she probably had done throughout her life: Sunday school and morning worship, daily Bible reading, and nightly prayers. Although there were new possibilities for religious worship in Mansfield, Laura remained faithful to the Mansfield Methodist church, even though she had never formally become a member. She attended meetings of the Women's Society for Christian Service when she was able. She did not attend evening worship, and it is unclear how much she took advantage of other opportunities for Christian fellowship. Christianity and the church were important for Laura, but they were not central to her life.

In her correspondence and interactions with others, Laura steadfastly concealed the role that Rose had played in bringing the Little House books to life. It is true that authors do not always mention their editors, but the collaboration that had created the novels went beyond mere editing. She also repeated to multiple correspondents the myth that everything in the books was factually true. That she maintained these untruths points to the Christian idea that all human beings are fallen and sinful, including those who trust in Christ for their salvation.

Laura's obituary appeared in the *Mansfield Mirror* on February 14, 1957. It called her "Mansfield's own internationally known authoress"[19] and gave a brief history of her life and the writing of the Little House books. It carried an estimate that more than half a million children had read them. An obituary in the *New York Times* provided a more complete account of Laura's accomplishments, noting her contributions to the *Missouri Ruralist*, giving the names of seven of the Little House books, and mentioning

18. Wilder, *A Little House Reader*, 161–63.
19. "Mrs. Wilder's Pen Stilled at Age of 90," *Mansfield Mirror*, February 14, 1957, 1.

the Laura Ingalls Wilder Award. The books' popularity was the only reason that a national newspaper reported her death; without them she would have remained an obscure farmer's wife, born in Wisconsin, unsuccessful at homesteading in South Dakota, living in the hills of southwestern Missouri. Both papers included a photograph. Only the local newspaper mentioned the Methodist church.

10

Remembering Laura

Since 1957

I t is unlikely that Laura, members of the Methodist church she attended, or any of the residents of Mansfield in 1957 imagined the fame
that the Little House books would come to enjoy. However, some local
citizens understood their popularity at the time and thought about
the possibility of revenue for the local economy if Rocky Ridge were to
become a tourist attraction. The week after her death, the *Mansfield Mirror*
reported that the newspaper had sold an additional two hundred copies
of the issue with her obituary in it. Requests for it had been received from
across Missouri and from seven other states. The newspaper supported
the efforts of a committee of citizens to pursue a charter to preserve the
Rocky Ridge farmhouse as a historic home. In the May 2 issue, it printed a
special section with seven articles about Wilder's life, writings, and home,
accompanied by seven photographs. Later in May, women's groups in
Mansfield hosted an open house at the farmhouse that was attended by
more than five hundred people, some from as far away as Omaha, Nebraska; Concordia, Kansas; and Joliet, Illinois.

After Laura's death, Rose was exhausted, troubled, and grieved. She
was seventy years old, and she had been working hard caring for her
mother, probably with limited sleep, for nearly two months. During her
days at the Rocky Ridge farmhouse, she burned some of her letters to
Laura and other papers. At some point after returning to her home in
Danbury, she also burned many of Laura's letters to her. When repre-

sentatives of the local group reached out to her and offered to manage affairs at the farmhouse, it was a relief. The Laura Ingalls Wilder Home Association of Mansfield was incorporated in late 1957. The major obstacle to establishing the Rocky Ridge farmhouse as a historic home was the fact that Laura and Almanzo had already sold it. The Association's leaders initially thought they would have to pursue a major fund-raising campaign to purchase the property, but Rose repurchased the farmhouse from its new owners and deeded it and several acres of surrounding land to the Association. Visitors almost immediately began to arrive; they were escorted through the house by local volunteers.

"The Truth and Only the Truth": Rose's Shaping of Laura's Legacy

Rose acted to shape how readers remembered Laura when she decided to publish Laura's diary of the family's trip from De Smet to Mansfield in 1894. Harper & Row released the diary in 1962 as *On the Way Home: The Diary of a Trip from South Dakota to Mansfield, Missouri, in 1894*. Rose wrote a prologue and an epilogue for the book and edited the entries of the diary itself. Harper's included eighteen photographs, including portraits of Almanzo, Laura, and Rose. A map of the journey also accompanied the text. Five years after Laura's death, and almost twenty years after the publication of the last Little House book, the public received a quite different view of Laura and Almanzo. Ever since, readers have experienced a shock when they encounter this volume. In the material Rose added, Laura is portrayed as intelligent and beautiful, but also selfish, easily angered, and abrupt toward her husband and daughter. Almanzo is depicted as resourceful and hardworking, but also as foolish for returning to work too quickly when he had diphtheria, and as allowing his love for his wife to lessen his love for his daughter. Rose's first major contribution to Little House readers' understanding of Laura and Almanzo was not complimentary.

On the other hand, Rose continued to assert that the Little House books were completely true and based only on Laura's memories of her childhood experiences. In December 1963, Louise Mortensen, a columnist for *Elementary English*, a journal for elementary school teachers, reported that census records revealed that Laura was only three years old when the

Ingalls family had moved to Kansas, not five as she is depicted in *Little House on the Prairie*. Rose wrote to Mortensen, and she published the letter in the journal in early 1964. Rose first argued untruthfully that Harper's had required them to change Laura's age in *Little House in the Big Woods*. She then asserted that the books

> are the truth, and only the truth; every detail in them is written as my mother remembered it . . . she added nothing and "fictionalized" nothing that she wrote. The books are entirely the "true stories" that they claim to be. . . .
>
> A fiction writer myself, I agree that my mother could have added to artistic effects by altering facts, but she did not write fiction. She did not want to. She wanted to set down the facts of her childhood as she knew them when she was a child.[1]

It appears that in addition to defending the historicity of the Little House books, Rose was working to distinguish herself from her mother. She (Rose) was the artist and the writer of fiction; her mother was just writing down what she remembered from her childhood.

Two years later, William Anderson wrote a pamphlet about the historical Ingalls family to be used by the Wilder Home Association in Mansfield and the Laura Ingalls Wilder Memorial Society in De Smet. He sent it to Rose for her approval, and she wrote back to vehemently object to his description of the Ingalls family having some neighbors during their first winter in De Smet. The letter accused him of calling Laura a liar and ordered him to make his work match the description in *By the Shores of Silver Lake*. Rose later explained to him, "If my mother's books are not absolutely accurate, she will be discredited as a person and as a writer, since a great part of the value of her books is that they are '*true* stories.'"[2] As with her correspondence with Mortensen, Rose had her own reasons for insisting that everything in the Little House books was historically accurate, but insist on it she did.

1. Lane to Mortensen, in "Idea Inventory," *Elementary English* 41, no. 4 (April 1964): 428–29.

2. Lane to Anderson, July 13, 1966, quoted in William Holtz, *The Ghost in the Little House: A Life of Rose Wilder Lane* (Columbia: University of Missouri Press, 1993), 353.

Rose's last book was the *Woman's Day Book of American Needlework*, published in 1963. Lavishly illustrated, it combines history with how-to-do-it instructions for embroidery, cross-stitch, quilting, knitting, and other forms of needlework. It also provided Rose with opportunities to include observations from her individualist philosophy. She asserted that American women had taken European needlework and transformed it in the same way that American statesmen had taken European ideas about liberty and transformed them. Two years later, she went to Vietnam as a war correspondent for *Woman's Day*. Her article, "August in Viet Nam," appeared in December 1965. It was evocative, anticommunist, and pro-freedom. It appeared the same month that she turned seventy-nine years old. Three years later, she planned to travel around the world. She died in her sleep on October 30, 1968, just days before she was to set out.

Laura's Memory over Five Decades

Rose left everything that she had to Roger Lea MacBride, a young man that she had informally adopted as a grandson during the 1950s. He had also become her personal lawyer. While looking through Rose's papers after her death, he discovered the adult novel that Laura had written during the 1930s. Rose had seen it and decided not to do anything with it, but MacBride took it to Ursula Nordstrom at Harper & Row, who was jubilant. Harper's published it with minimal editing as *The First Four Years* in 1971. MacBride wrote a brief introduction, and there are several illustrations by Garth Williams. This work presented another new portrait of Laura and Almanzo. It tells what happened to the newlywed couple, but its content and tone are strikingly different from the Little House books. While *The First Four Years* has been marketed ever since as the ninth Little House book, readers are often left disappointed by it.

Additional writing by Laura was published during the late twentieth century. In 1974, Harper's published Laura's letters to Almanzo from San Francisco in 1915 as *West from Home*. MacBride edited the volume and wrote an introduction to it, and the publisher included many photographs from the Panama-Pacific International Exposition. When compared to the actual letters available at the Herbert Hoover Presidential Library, sections of some letters appear to have been removed, but no ellipses were supplied. MacBride treated the letters in the same way that Rose treated Laura's diary twelve years earlier. Laura's ability to describe a scene and her love for Almanzo are on full display in the letters, along with the fascinating juxtaposition of Laura and a world's fair.

The popularity of the Little House books received an additional boost when the television series *Little House on the Prairie* appeared in 1974. MacBride had licensed the stories to Ed Friendly Productions, Inc. Before starting his own production company, Friendly held management positions at both ABC and NBC. He realized the power of the Little House books to connect with readers when his daughter told him that she reread the books every year. Friendly signed Michael Landon to direct and play the role of Pa. The series aired on NBC from 1974 to 1983. Landon's vision of the frontier was not Laura's. Like many historical broadcast productions, the series takes a setting from the past—in this case the 1870s—and uses it to engage issues, conflicts, and realities of the present—in this case the 1970s. The Ingalls family never leaves Walnut Grove, and many other events never described in the Little House books occur, including Mary getting married, Nellie Oleson running a restaurant, and the major buildings of the town being blown up. The church also occupies a more central place in the series than it does in the novels, and the Christianity depicted presents Landon's vision of spirituality. *Little House on the Prairie* went into syndication immediately, and it has never been off the air. There are multiple ways to view the show today.

The television series also boosted the popularity of historic sites in the different locations where the Ingalls and Wilder families had lived. The Home Association in Mansfield and the Memorial Society in De Smet were the first to be organized. The De Smet site included the Surveyors' House where the Ingalls family had lived. By the twenty-first century, lovers of the books could visit Almanzo's childhood home outside of Malone, New York; a reconstructed log cabin on the site where Laura was born outside of Pepin, Wisconsin; the hand-dug well on the homestead outside of Independence, Kansas; the site of the dugout near Walnut Grove, Minnesota; the hotel the Ingalls family lived in in Burr Oak, Iowa; and the Ingalls Homestead, an entire historical complex outside of De Smet on the site of the homestead itself, including a church building moved from a town ten miles away. Museums had also been created in Walnut

Grove—with portions dedicated to the historical Ingalls family, *On the Banks of Plum Creek*, and the *Little House on the Prairie* TV series—and Spring Valley, Minnesota, where Almanzo's family had lived. Readers can now visit a variety of landscapes that Laura experienced. Each summer, the towns of Walnut Grove and De Smet also feature pageants that interpret various events from the books.

Historians began researching the historical Ingalls and Wilder families shortly after Laura's death. William Anderson was perhaps the most indefatigable. During his junior high, high school, and college years, he did research, volunteered at the historical site in De Smet, and wrote booklets about the Ingalls and Wilder families. He became a high school history and English teacher, and in 1982 he wrote his master's thesis at South Dakota State University about the collaboration between Laura and Rose. Portions of his research were published in *South Dakota History*; his biography of Laura for young people appeared in 1992; and he continued to publish into the 2010s.

Since the 1980s, more of Laura's writings, additional biographies, and a variety of interpretations of her life and works have appeared. Many are engaged in the introduction and the note on sources of this book.

"On the Pilgrim Way": The Faith of Laura Ingalls Wilder

Laura Ingalls Wilder was a Christian. This conclusion is supported by her lifelong Christian practices and her patterns of church attendance. Once her family began attending Sunday school and Sunday morning worship services in Walnut Grove, Minnesota, she attended for the rest of her life. While she lived in the upper Midwest, she attended Congregational churches with her family. When she and Almanzo moved to the Ozarks, she attended Sunday school and Sunday morning worship at the Mansfield Methodist church. She also occasionally attended services at other churches of a variety of denominations, at times when invited by friends, at times out of curiosity. Evidence from her childhood and old age suggests that she prayed every day before she went to bed and read the Bible, probably daily. She had memorized large numbers of Scripture verses when she was a child, and she knew the Bible well as an adult. Thousands of visitors to one of the historic sites have taken home a reproduction of the handwritten guide to Bible verses for specific occasions that she kept in her personal Bible.

In addition, Laura included Christianity, Christian ideas, and the church in her writing. Her columns in the *Missouri Ruralist* did not mention these topics often, but when they did, Laura presented traditional Protestant views of God, his laws, and his goodness. Prayer, Bible reading and memorization, and Sunday school and Sunday worship appear in *Pioneer Girl* and later in the Little House books. In general, the view of Christianity presented in her writing is oriented toward God's rules for behavior and right living, not the gospel of God's free offer of salvation in Jesus Christ. It seems clear that she understood the biblical message from a moderate Protestant point of view, and that she focused more on obedience than forgiveness. This set her apart from the more conservative fundamentalists and evangelicals of the early twentieth century, including the Pentecostals of the Ozarks. She was also not a liberal or a modernist.

Laura did describe a personal experience with God's presence and grace in *Pioneer Girl*. It came while she was praying before bed, when she was experiencing difficult circumstances as a preteen. She remembered it more than fifty years later when she sat down to write the first draft of the memoir. It was significant enough that she included the account, even though the memoir also described her reluctance to talk about her religious beliefs and the awkwardness she felt around those who discussed their faith publicly.

Wilder's unwillingness to write openly about her beliefs makes it difficult to describe them in detail, but some contours can be given. She believed in the existence of God, the importance of the Bible, and the enduring applicability of God's law. She believed that everyone is responsible for his or her actions, and that the most important rule of life is to love others. All these ideas would have been preached in the Congregational churches of her upbringing and in the Methodist church of her adulthood. She rejected the doctrine of predestination. The Methodist church in Mansfield would not have preached this or other specific denominational beliefs emphasized in the Baptist, Church of Christ, Church of God, or Presbyterian churches during the late nineteenth and early twentieth centuries. Churches founded in Mansfield after World War II, including the Roman Catholic, Reorganized Latter Day Saints, and Assemblies of God congregations, would have required even more particular beliefs. Laura and Almanzo remained committed to worshiping at the Methodist church.

One other important influence on Laura's belief system was stoicism. In letters to Rose, Laura describes the stoicism of her parents, of her family, and of midwestern rural people during the late nineteenth century, as a way of explaining their actions. The people Laura wrote about expected that hard times would come, and they endured them because they were things that must be. This is a stoic approach to life more than it is a Reformed or evangelical Protestant approach, since individuals in these groups more consistently invoke God's sovereignty or providence in their engagement with life's challenges. It appears that this stoic attitude was important to how the historical Charles and Caroline Ingalls approached the financial difficulties they encountered throughout their lives. Stoicism also influenced the way that Laura approached Almanzo's health challenges and the necessity for her to work to provide income for the family, whether that be by working to increase their farm's production, raising hens and selling eggs, or writing for publication. Rose did not deal with difficulty and disappointment in this spirit; life challenges caused her psychological anguish, which she shared with her friends, diaries, and correspondents. This difference in temperament contributed to some of the conflicts between the two women.

While Wilder's faith informed her worldview and her life choices, there were limits to the commitment she showed to the church and Christian beliefs and practices. First, she attended Sunday school and morning worship services in Mansfield but not evening worship services. This also appears to be her family's pattern in Walnut Grove and De Smet. Second, there is no evidence in any of her writings about her cross-country travels that she ever attended worship services on Sunday while away from home. On their 1894 journey from South Dakota to Missouri, the family rested on Sunday but did not worship. On other trips, there is ample evidence that travel, sightseeing, and other activities were pursued on Sundays. Third, she never officially became a member of the Methodist church in Mansfield, and it is possible that she never became a member of any church. Church records don't exist to confirm or disprove this possibility, but it may be that she never received Christian baptism and never formally became a member of a Christian body of believers. Finally, although she read books, magazines, and the Bible, it appears that she did not often read books about the Bible, theology, or the Christian life, for her library contained only several explicitly Christian books.

If I am correct that Laura's faith was important but not central to her life, her friend Neta Seal provides an illustrative contrast. The Baptist church, both locally and in its broader regional and national contexts, was central to Neta's life. While Laura attended meetings of the Methodist ladies' aid society, and later the Women's Society for Christian Service, only occasionally, Neta attended meetings of the Baptist ladies' aid society and the Women's Missionary Union on a regular basis, usually every month. She frequently hosted meetings of one of the two groups. For many years she taught a children's Sunday school class at the Baptist church and held parties for them at her home. She also attended ordination services at Baptist churches elsewhere in Wright County. During the late spring of 1953, she accompanied her pastor and his wife to the Southern Baptist Convention in Houston, Texas. In August of 1956, she both took young people to a local Baptist camp and hosted the Business Circle of the First Baptist Church in her home. Neta Seal's Christianity and her Baptist affiliation were absolutely central to her life. This was not the case for Laura Ingalls Wilder.

The idea that Christianity was important but not central to Wilder also provides a way of describing the treatment of the church and Christian ideas in the Little House books. It appears that Christianity was important but not central to the fictional Ingalls family. In only one book can faith be seen as close to the center of the narrative and the characters' lives: *The Long Winter*, with its enormous environmental challenges driving the characters to prayer, to Scripture, and to Christian hymns. Otherwise, Christianity is mainly addressed in one chapter each in the first two books, and it is almost completely absent from *Little House on the Prairie*. The church appears more in *On the Banks of Plum Creek*, but not until its twenty-fourth chapter. *By the Shores of Silver Lake* again confines consideration of Christian ideas to one chapter. In the last two books, the church is a consistent feature of the Ingalls family's life as it provides the setting for Almanzo's first asking to see Laura home, and it is one of the two institutions (the other is the school) that shapes Laura's character development.

While Christian songs are important to the family's experience of life, more secular songs are mentioned in the books than Christian songs, and they appear more often.

The view of Christian ideas presented in the books is also rule-centered, not gospel-centered. Ma and Pa work to inculcate morality in their children, and the church and Christianity are important parts of that. There is no direct mention of Jesus Christ and his sacrifice for sin, and just one reference to forgiveness. Furthermore, Christian ideas compete with stoic views in the books. When the Ingalls family faces difficulties, their approach is not usually to think about God, either his role in bringing the hardship or his ability to deliver them out of it. At some of the most dire moments, members of the family do turn to God in prayer. However, more often the approach is to turn to their own resources and make do with what they have. When confronting loss, the fictional family's response is never something like, "The LORD gave, and the LORD hath taken away; blessed be the name of the LORD" (Job 1:21). Rather, it is "There's no great loss without some small gain."[3] This is a stoic attitude, not a Christian one.

Overall, the view of the church presented in the Little House books is mixed, mainly depending on the pastor involved. Rev. Alden is an entirely good character in the books in which he appears. He loves his parishioners and serves them faithfully. As a result, the descriptions of the church drawn in *On the Banks of Plum Creek* and *By the Shores of Silver Lake* are primarily positive. On the other hand, Rev. Brown is described unfavorably, and as a result the depiction of the church in *Little Town on the Prairie* and *These Happy Golden Years* has a negative edge. Brown is willing to allow Laura to remove "obey" from her wedding vows, but he is also compared to the devil during a revival, and Laura does not appreciate his preaching and is not required by Pa to pay attention to it.

Laura's collaboration with Rose impacted the Little House books in multiple ways. It appears that Rose changed some of the straightforward treatments of Christianity in Laura's handwritten drafts, particularly in *Farmer Boy* and *On the Banks of Plum Creek*, into more mixed and more

---

3. Laura Ingalls Wilder, *Little Town on the Prairie*, in *The Little House Books*, ed. Caroline Fraser (New York: Library of America, 2012), 2:426.

negative accounts. There are similar changes made in the final two books. However, Rose added many references to God, Christianity, and Bible passages that did not appear in Laura's original manuscripts, giving faith greater importance and the books' characters greater spiritual depth. It does not appear that the description of Christian ideas was ever a subject of conflict — or even much in the way of conversation — in the existing correspondence between Laura and Rose, with the exception of two exchanges in the typescript of *The Long Winter*. It seems that Laura saw descriptions of the church and Christian ideas as important to include in the books, but they were not central enough to cause debate between the collaborators about how faith was depicted.

Final considerations about Laura's life that impact our understanding of her faith involve personal morality. Stereotypical and negative descriptions of American Indians and African Americans in the Little House books show that Laura did not understand the Bible's injunctions to love one's neighbor in the same way that we do today. Her many arguments with Rose might also call into question her judgment of how best to love her daughter. She also asserted in her correspondence and in her Detroit Book Fair address that the books communicated only what had happened in her life, when this was clearly not true. Laura and Rose combined historical characters, left out people who had lived with the family, and created some stories out of whole cloth. It was also unlikely that her family or she had any direct connection with the Bender family. Misrepresenting the fact that the Little House books were fiction, not simply descriptions of what had happened, was a violation of the ninth commandment. The same is the case for their collusion to deceive the Internal Revenue Service and cut their tax burden. Some of Laura's letters express pride and less than Christian love toward neighbors, politicians, and others. That Laura was a flawed individual should not surprise Christians, who believe that "all have sinned, and come short of the glory of God" (Rom. 3:23). While one should not excuse her failings, one should also be humble about our own. By God's grace, her writings encourage right behavior and love for family, for others, and for nature. The misrepresentations she perpetuated, her lack of love for Rose and others, and the shortcomings in the Little House books' depictions of people of other cultures all display the brokenness caused by sin in the world.

Laura Ingalls Wilder was not a perfect human being; she was a sinner. She was also a Christian. Her faith was important to her life, and she nurtured that faith by what Reformed Christians call the ordinary means of grace: reading God's Word, praying, and attending worship. She cannot be classified as an evangelical Christian, for, unlike others in Mansfield like Neta Seal, Christianity, while important to her, was not central to her life. This distinction can be seen in the major writings that we have from her hand: her articles in the *Missouri Ruralist*; her memoir, *Pioneer Girl*; and in the Little House books, both her handwritten manuscripts and the published books.

In chapter 23 of *By the Shores of Silver Lake*, the Ingalls family sings the first verse of Fanny Crosby's hymn "Lend a Helping Hand," and the chorus is finished by Rev. Stuart. The words given match those in musicologist Dale Cockrell's 2011 *Ingalls Wilder Family Songbook*, which reproduces all the songs mentioned in the published Little House books:

> When cheerful we meet in our pleasant home
> And the song of joy is swelling,
> Do we pause to think of the tears that flow
> In sorrow's lonely dwelling?
>
> (Chorus:) Let us lend a hand,
> To those who are faint and weary;
> Let us lend a hand,
> To those on the pilgrim way.[4]

These words may be applied to the life and works of Laura Ingalls Wilder in multiple ways. She wanted her writing, both in the *Missouri Ruralist* and in her books, to help others to live a better and happier life. She desired to "lend a hand" to those attempting to live the good life in this world. At times this meant giving advice drawn from the Bible, Christianity, and her own beliefs. At the same time, since Christianity was im-

---

4. *The Ingalls Wilder Family Songbook*, ed. Dale Cockrell (Middleton, WI: A-R Editions, 2011), 199, and Laura Ingalls Wilder, *By the Shores of Silver Lake*, in Fraser, *The Little House Books*, 2:125.

portant but not central to her own life, faith is depicted as important but not central in her writing. The Little House books often addressed what is referred to in the first line of the song: the Ingalls family's "cheerful" life in their "pleasant" little houses. The books do not shy away from hardship and difficulty—from "sorrow's lonely dwelling"—but their main thrust is toward success and happiness. Their enduring popularity, however, suggests that millions of readers have in fact found them to be a helping hand to those on the pilgrim way.

Personal Afterword

Faith and the Popularity
of the Little House Books

T hose who write about Laura Ingalls Wilder often discuss their personal relationship to the Little House books. Many authors had read the books as children. My story is different. I grew up on a one-hundred-acre farm in western Pennsylvania, but I did not read the books until my early twenties. My wife, Paula, who had read them several times during her childhood, and I read the books together during our first years of marriage in the early 1990s. I was impressed by their direct prose and detailed descriptions, and I was deeply moved by their intimate portrait of family life. When I began graduate study in history at Duquesne University in downtown Pittsburgh in 1995, I had to choose a subject for primary research projects. Most other students were writing about urban history or labor history, but topics in those areas did not interest me. Paula suggested that I do research on Wilder. I had just read *Little House in the Ozarks*, the first compilation of articles and columns from the *Missouri Ruralist*. I wrote about those articles and Wilder's relationship to early twentieth-century women's movements. I went on to write a dissertation at the University of Iowa on farm newspapers in the Midwest at the turn of the twentieth century that featured the *Ruralist* and three other papers. It later became my first book.

As I researched Wilder's life, I learned what everyone who enjoys the Little House books must learn when they first read a biography of Wilder: not everything in the books happened exactly as described. This can be a hard truth to encounter. The way that the books are written, with their details and plain prose, invites one to believe that this was just how things were. It was a significant mental transition to realize that Laura (and her collaborator, Rose) changed things that happened, left characters and events out of the books, and shaped the narrative for literary purposes. I initially tried to integrate new information—from the early pamphlets and biographies of Wilder by William Anderson and John Miller—with the narrative presented in the Little House books. I eventually had to admit that there were actually two different worlds: the literary world of the Little House books and the world that the historical Wilder lived in. The life of Laura in the books is in many ways different than the life of Laura Ingalls Wilder, the author of the books.[1]

I believe that this unsettling experience is a reality for many people who have read and loved the Little House books, especially those who read and loved them as they were growing up. I attempt to be kind when I answer questions about the historical Wilder, because at times I am the first one to tell someone that Laura's life was not exactly as it is presented in the books. I understand why many are saddened and disappointed when they learn that depictions in the Little House books are not the realities of all rural, late nineteenth-century, Midwestern families. History would be much simpler if they were.

On the other hand, some authors seem angry at Wilder for creating the Little House books, because they give people false ideas, both about the past and about the possibility of families living as the fictional Ingalls family did. I do not share that anger. I attempt to tell the truth about Wilder's life and faith, but not because I want to debunk the books or Wilder's vision of the good life. I believe that there is a place for books of fiction that inspire us to live better lives, even if they are not historically accurate. But it is important to understand and remember that the Little House books are fiction. They do not accurately describe the life that the historical Laura lived.

In addition, it is common for Americans today to view their lives in comparison with the lives of others, both those they know and those they learn about from books or from the Internet. For example, we are tempted

1. This is complicated further by a third world, the world of the *Little House on the Prairie* television series.

to make assumptions about other people's spirituality and to compare it with our own. We often initially consider those we are just getting to know as being as committed (or not committed) to the church or Christianity as we are. If we learn otherwise, we may see those who are more devout in their religious practices as going overboard or even being fanatical. We may view those who are less devout as slackers or freeloaders. It may be that many readers of the Little House books have imposed their own understanding of Christianity onto them, and onto the life of the historical Laura Ingalls Wilder. If Christianity is central to their lives, they may see it as central to Laura's life. If it is peripheral to their own lives, they may see it as similarly peripheral to Laura's. Because of this, before writing this book, I think that I believed that the historical Wilder was more devout than she actually was. My mind was changed as the result of my research. I have attempted to be fair to Laura and Rose in my description of their relationship to Christianity, the church, and faith. It is my conclusion that Christianity was important but not central to Laura's life. I believe that this best explains how she lived and what she wrote. I don't say this to condemn her or her experience of Christianity, only to attempt to describe it accurately. It is my hope that having a greater understanding of Wilder's actual life and beliefs will enable us to love her and others of our neighbors who lived in the past better.

I think the books are loved and enjoyed by both children and adults because of several characteristics. The first is their straightforward prose. The writing in the Little House books is direct and simple, it provides meticulous descriptions, and it includes age-appropriate dialogue. The story is told from the perspective of a young girl, and it accurately depicts her development into a young woman from inside that point of view. It effectively communicates what the fictional Laura felt, thought, and did. The second characteristic is the books' beautiful vision of family flourishing. They successfully describe Ma and Pa's love for each other, their love for their children, and the security their children feel. Some scholars and critics have given this as a reason that the books appeal to Americans on the political right, but I think that the desire for a tight-knit, loving family is shared by individuals from across the political spectrum. The third characteristic is their passionate engagement with nature and wilderness. The books provide detailed descriptions of landscape, the plants and animals that inhabit it, and the ways that nature can engage the heart and soul. Some have seen this as a reason for the books' appeal to those on the political left, but I believe that a love for nature and the outdoors is enjoyed by those of all political persuasions. Some readers are drawn more to the books' descriptions of family togetherness than their depictions of nature and wilderness, and vice versa. These three characteristics have enduring attraction, even when readers are disturbed by other aspects of the books.

The characterization I have presented of the Little House books' depiction of Christianity and church—that faith is important to the books, but it is not central—may also have contributed to the immense popularity of the books over time. Christians who read the books encounter families who are committed to God, faith, and the church. Those who are not Christians can embrace them for other characteristics. Because the depiction of Christianity is important but not central, either interpretation is possible.[2]

Even though the Little House books are not historically accurate, I think they present many important truths about life, family, growing up, and the natural world. As a result, I understand why many see the Little House books as continuing to lend a helping hand to those on the pilgrim way.

2. The world of the television series complicates engagement with the books' and the historical Wilder's view of faith, because the church and Christianity are much more central to the show's vision of the Ingalls family.

A Note on Sources

Harper & Brothers published the Little House books as Laura and Rose completed them between 1932 and 1943: *Little House in the Big Woods* (1932), *Farmer Boy* (1934), *Little House on the Prairie* (1935), *On the Banks of Plum Creek* (1937), *By the Shores of Silver Lake* (1939), *The Long Winter* (1940), *Little Town on the Prairie* (1941), and *These Happy Golden Years* (1943). Harper's published a uniform edition of all eight books in 1953. *The First Four Years* appeared in 1971; it subsequently joined the other eight Little House books in future boxed sets of the series. The Library of America published a two-volume edition of the eight books, two speeches, and *The First Four Years* in 2012.

Handwritten manuscripts of *Little House in the Big Woods*, *Farmer Boy*, *Little House on the Prairie*, *On the Banks of Plum Creek*, and *By the Shores of Silver Lake* are held by the Laura Ingalls Wilder Home Association in Mansfield, Missouri. They have been microfilmed by the State Historical Society of Missouri and may be viewed at one of its research centers. Manuscripts of *The Long Winter* and *These Happy Golden Years* are at the Burton Historical Collection at the Detroit Public Library in Detroit, Michigan. The manuscript of *Little Town on the Prairie* is owned by the Pomona Public Library in Pomona, California. Typescripts of *Farmer Boy*, *On the Banks of Plum Creek*, *By the Shores of Silver Lake*, and *The Long Winter* are held by the Herbert Hoover Presidential Library in West Branch, Iowa. They are part of the Rose Wilder Lane Papers, which includes Rose's extensive correspondence, diaries, journals, and other materials. It also is the home of the manuscript for *The First Four Years* and several of the typescripts of *Pioneer Girl*.

Additional books of Laura's writings include *On the Way Home: The Diary of a Trip from South Dakota to Mansfield, Missouri, in 1894*, with a setting by Rose Wilder Lane (New York: Harper & Row, 1962); *West from Home: Letters of Laura Ingalls Wilder, San Francisco, 1915* (New York: Harper & Row, 1974); and *A Little House Traveler: Writings from Laura Ingalls Wilder's Journeys across America* (New York: HarperCollins, 2006), which reproduces *On the Way Home* and *West from Home*, packaged with the diary Laura kept during her trip to De Smet in 1931. William Anderson edited *A Little House Sampler: A Collection of Early Stories and Reminiscences* (Lincoln: University of Nebraska Press, 1988, now published by HarperCollins), which contains writings from both Laura and Rose, and *A Little House Reader* (New York: HarperCollins, 1998), which contains some writings by Laura's parents and sisters in addition to material by Laura. *The Selected Letters of Laura Ingalls Wilder*, also edited by Anderson (New York: HarperCollins, 2016), reproduces Laura's existing letters to Rose and to a variety of correspondents, selected from the Hoover Presidential Library, other collections, and private sources.

Stephen W. Hines edited and published Laura's articles and columns from the *Missouri Ruralist* in multiple books, including *Little House in the Ozarks: The Rediscovered Writings* (Nashville: Nelson, 1991) and *Saving Graces: The Inspirational Faith of Laura Ingalls Wilder* (Nashville: Broadman & Holman, 1997). *Writings to Young Women from Laura Ingalls Wilder* (Nashville: Tommy Nelson, 2006) is a set of three, small, topical books. A one-volume collection of all of Laura's *Ruralist* material is *Laura Ingalls Wilder, Farm Journalist: Writings from the Ozarks* (Columbia: University of Missouri Press, 2007).

Laura's memoir was published as *Pioneer Girl: The Annotated Autobiography*, edited by Pamela Smith Hill (Pierre: South Dakota Historical Society Press, 2014). This was followed by *Pioneer Girl Perspectives*, edited by Nancy Tystad Koupal (Pierre: South Dakota Historical Society Press, 2017), a collection of essays issued the year of Laura's 150th birthday, and *Pioneer Girl: The Revised Texts*, edited by Nancy Tystad Koupal (Pierre: South Dakota Historical Society Press, 2021), which compares the handwritten manuscript to Rose's three typed editions. It also contains helpful background about each place (Kansas, Wisconsin, Minnesota, Iowa, Dakota Territory) mentioned in the memoir. Koupal also edited *Pioneer Girl: The Path into Fiction* (Pierre: South Dakota Historical Society Press, 2023), which reproduced the intermediate manuscripts between the memoir and *Little House in the Big Woods.*

The first full biography of Wilder was Donald Zochert's *Laura: The Life of Laura Ingalls Wilder* (Chicago: Regnery, 1976). Anderson wrote a series of booklets about the Ingalls and Wilder families, and then *Laura Ingalls Wilder: A Biography* (New York: HarperCollins, 1992). William Holtz's *The Ghost in the Little House: A Life of Rose Wilder Lane* (Columbia: University of Missouri Press, 1993) mainly presented Rose's life, but some passages argued that Laura was an amateurish writer and Rose was the source of what readers loved in the Little House books. John E. Miller wrote *Becoming Laura Ingalls Wilder: The Woman behind the Legend* (Columbia: University of Missouri Press, 1998) partially as a response to Holtz's work. Miller argued that the contributions of Laura and Rose to the Little House books should be seen as a collaboration. Miller had previously published *Laura Ingalls Wilder's Little Town* (Lawrence: University Press of Kansas, 1994), a collection of essays about De Smet, and he later wrote *Laura Ingalls Wilder and Rose Wilder Lane: Authorship, Place, Time, and Culture* (Columbia: University of Missouri Press, 2008), a collection of essays about their collaboration. Pamela Smith Hill's *Laura Ingalls Wilder: A Writer's Life* (Pierre: South Dakota State Historical Society, 2007) highlighted Laura's identity and practice as a writer; she asserted that Rose should be seen as mainly an editor of Laura's writing. Caroline Fraser wrote the most encyclopedic biography, *Prairie Fires: The American Dreams of Laura Ingalls Wilder* (New York: Picador, 2018), which won the Pulitzer Prize for biography in 2018. Fraser emphasizes the hardships of Laura's life and the ways that the Little House books transformed the narrative of her upbringing. John Miller provided an extended response to Fraser's book in "Midwestern Dreams or Nightmares: An Appreciation and Critique of Caroline Fraser's *Prairie Fires: The American Dreams of Laura Ingalls Wilder,*" *Middle West Review* 6, nos. 1–2 (Fall 2019–Spring 2020): 1–36.

Books that focus on Wilder and Lane's politics include Anita Claire Fellman's *Little House, Long Shadow* (Columbia: University of Missouri Press, 2008), which argues that the books were key to the revitalization of the Republican Party during the mid-to-late twentieth century, and Christine Woodside's *Libertarians on the Prairie: Laura Ingalls Wilder, Rose Wilder Lane, and the Making of the Little House Books* (New York: Arcade, 2016), which emphasizes Rose's contributions and her connections to libertarian politics. Remembrances of Wilder's neighbors in Missouri are available in Helen Burkhiser's *Neta, Laura's Friend* (self-published, 1989) and *"I Remember Laura,"* edited by Stephen W. Hines (Nashville: Nelson, 1994). Teresa Lynn traced the Ingalls and Wilder families' connections to the Masons and the Order of the Eastern Star in *Little Lodges on the Prairie: Freemasonry and Laura Ingalls Wilder* (Austin, TX: Tranquility, 2014). Selections from Rose's journalism are available in *The Rediscovered Writings of Rose Wilder Lane, Literary Journalist*, edited by Amy Mattson Lauters (Columbia: University of Missouri Press, 2007). The most recent collection of literary criticism of the books is *Reconsidering Laura Ingalls Wilder: Little House and Beyond*, edited by Miranda A. Green-Barteet and Anne K. Phillips (Jackson: University Press of Mississippi, 2019).

The Ingalls Wilder Family Songbook, edited by Dale Cockrell (Middleton, WI: A-R Editions, for the American Musicological Society, 2011), provides music and lyrics for all songs mentioned in the Little House books. For farm newspapers at the turn of the twentieth century, see John J. Fry, *The Farm Press, Reform, and Rural Change: 1895–1920* (New York: Routledge, 2005). The history of Methodism in Missouri is given in Frank C. Tucker, *The Methodist Church in Missouri, 1798–1939: A Brief History* (Nashville: Parthenon, 1966), and John O. Gooch, *Circuit Riders to Crusades: Essays in Missouri Methodist History* (Franklin, TN: Providence House, 2000). An excellent history of the Ozarks is Brooks Blevins, *A History of the Ozarks*, vol. 1, *The Old Ozarks* (Urbana: University of Illinois Press, 2018), vol. 2, *The Conflicted Ozarks* (Urbana: University of Illinois Press, 2019), and vol. 3, *The Ozarkers* (Urbana: University of Illinois Press, 2021).

Multiple websites and groups on Facebook discuss the Little House books, the historical Ingalls and Wilder families, and readers' ongoing engagement with both. These include PioneerGirlProject.org, founded in 2010 by the South Dakota Historical Society Press to accompany their work publishing *Pioneer Girl*, and LittleHouseonthePrairie.com, created by Friendly Family Productions in 2015 to provide information about the television series as well as the books and Laura's life. In its own category is the Laura Ingalls Wilder Legacy and Research Association (LIWLRA), which maintains a website, publishes a regular newsletter, and sponsors biennial LauraPalooza conferences. These conferences feature both academic presentations and fan activities; some of the best amateur and professional research is first presented at LauraPalooza.

Appendix

Pastors of the Mansfield Methodist Episcopal Church, 1895-1939, and the Mansfield Methodist Church, 1939-1958

E. G. Cattermol, pastor in Seymour and Rogersville,
  helps to establish the church, 1895
J. S. Meracle, 1896–1897
Francis P. Leckliter, 1898
Charles Frank Tippin, 1898–1900
William H. Yount, 1901–1904
John J. (perhaps H.) Frazier, 1904
John W. Slusher, 1905–1906
Burrel Douglas Jones 1907–1909
A. R. Wassell, 1910–1911
Newton Hockensmith, 1911–1912
B. E. Niblack, 1912–1913
John J. Wolfe, 1913–1914
John W. Needham, 1914–1916
Guy Willis Holmes, 1916–1919
Thomas E. Prall, 1919–1920
A. J. Graves, 1920–1921
Clyde Edward Little, 1921–1922
J. W. Paterson, assistant pastor, 1922
W. A. Gray, 1922–1923
M. O. Morris, 1923–1924
George Andrew Wells, 1924–1927

Christopher C. VanZant, 1927–1929

William A. Dahlem, 1929–1930

J. E. Owen, 1930–1931

Andrew C. Runge, 1931–1932

David S. Frazier, 1932–1933

R. Holley Day, 1933–1937

Carl A. Stevenson, 1938–1939

Thomas Shipp, 1939–1941

William Wilbur Garrett, 1941–1942

Wilbur A. Wilson, 1942–1946

W. Carlton Knight, 1946–1953

Frank Raymond Nelson, 1953–1954

Nell Mitchell, October 1954

Kenneth H. Bunting, 1954–1955

Walter Brunner, 1955–1958

Index

122–23, 135, 145; "Credo" or *Give Me Liberty,* 158–59; death of son, 84; depression, 122–23, 128; *The Discovery of Freedom,* 176; end-of-life care for Laura, 186–87; European travels, 106, 112, 113, 114; *Free Land,* 145–46, 159; influence on Little House books, 6, 120–21, 125–28, 131–33, 136, 142–45, 150–52, 155–58, 162–66, 168–70, 172–73, 176, 188, 193–94; knowledge of Bible, 126, 130–32, 144, 154–56, 158, 163, 172–73; *Let the Hurricane Roar,* 122–23; *National Economic Council Review of Books,* 176; *On the Way Home,* 72, 74–75, 191; *Pioneer Girl,* 1–2, 116–18; *Pittsburgh Courier,* 159, 176; religious beliefs, 6, 133–35; Sunday observance, 74, 114, 134–35; *Woman's Day Book of American Needlework,* 193

Laura Ingalls Wilder Award, 3, 186

Laura Ingalls Wilder Historic Home and Museum, Mansfield, Missouri, 10, 35, 56, 185

Laura Ingalls Wilder Home Association, Mansfield, Missouri, 190–91

Laura Ingalls Wilder Library, Mansfield, Missouri, 180–81, 186

Laura Ingalls Wilder Memorial Society, De Smet, South Dakota, 194–95

Little House books: Christianity, 120–21, 124–28, 130–33, 136, 140–45, 148–52, 154–58, 160–66, 167–70, 172–73, 198–200, 206; controversy, 3, 129–30, 159–60, 181; popularity,

2, 146–47, 174–77, 180–81, 185–86, 194–95, 205–6. *See also titles of individual works*

Little House in the Big Woods, 119–21

Little House on the Prairie (book), 3, 16, 128–33, 181, 198

Little House on the Prairie (television series), 2, 194

Little Town on the Prairie, 3, 159–66, 181, 199

Long Winter, The, 152–58, 198, 200

"Love Your Enemies" (poem), 48–49

Lynn, Teresa, 86

MacBride, Roger Lea, 92–93, 193–94

Mansfield, Missouri, 69, 75–76, 100–101, 105–6, 137–38, 181–83, 190–91

Mansfield Farm Loan Association, 105, 112–13, 159

Mansfield Mirror, 77, 101–6, 111–12, 114–15, 133–35, 137–38, 171, 174, 177–83, 186, 188–89, 190

Masters, Genevieve (or Geneive), 31–32, 48

Methodist church, Mansfield, Missouri, 171, 177–79, 182–83, 188, 196–97

Methodist Episcopal church, Mansfield, Missouri, 77–80, 85–86, 100–103, 107–8, 114–15, 135–38

Methodist ladies' aid society, Mansfield, Missouri, 78, 103, 171. *See also* Women's Society for Christian Service

Methodist Sunday school, Walnut Grove, Minnesota, 34–35

Titles published in the

LIBRARY OF RELIGIOUS BIOGRAPHY SERIES